NON SANZ DROICT.

William Shakespeare

The Tragedy of
ANTONY
and
CLEOPATRA

Edited by Barbara Everett

The Signet Classic Shakespeare
GENERAL EDITOR: SYLVAN BARNET

A SIGNET CLASSIC from
NEW AMERICAN LIBRARY
TIMES MIRROR
New York and Scarborough, Ontario
The New English Library Limited, London

SIGNET CLASSIC TRADEMARK REG. U.S. PAT. OFF. AND FOREIGN COUNTRIES
REGISTERED TRADEMARK—MARCA REGISTRADA
HECHO EN CHICAGO, U.S.A.

SIGNET, SIGNET CLASSICS, MENTOR, PLUME AND MERIDIAN BOOKS
are published *in the United States* by
The New American Library, Inc.,
1301 Avenue of the Americas, New York, New York 10019,
in Canada by The New American Library of Canada Limited,
81 Mack Avenue, Scarborough, 704, Ontario,
in the United Kingdom by The New English Library Limited,
Barnard's Inn, Holborn, London, E.C. 1, England

10 11 12 13 14 15 16 17 18

PRINTED IN THE UNITED STATES OF AMERICA

Contents

Shakespeare: Prefatory Remarks

Between the record of his baptism in Stratford on 26 April 1564 and the record of his burial in Stratford on 25 April 1616, some forty documents name Shakespeare, and many others name his parents, his children, and his grandchildren. More facts are known about William Shakespeare than about any other playwright of the period except Ben Jonson. The facts should, however, be distinguished from the legends. The latter, inevitably more engaging and better known, tell us that the Stratford boy killed a calf in high style, poached deer and rabbits, and was forced to flee to London, where he held horses outside a playhouse. These traditions are only traditions; they may be true, but no evidence supports them, and it is well to stick to the facts.

Mary Arden, the dramatist's mother, was the daughter of a substantial landowner; about 1557 she married John Shakespeare, who was a glove-maker and trader in various farm commodities. In 1557 John Shakespeare was a member of the Council (the governing body of Stratford), in 1558 a constable of the borough, in 1561 one of the two town chamberlains, in 1565 an alderman (entitling him to the appellation "Mr."), in 1568 high bailiff—the town's highest political office, equivalent to mayor. After 1577, for an unknown reason he drops out of local politics. The birthday of William Shakespeare, the eldest son of this locally prominent man, is unrecorded; but the Stratford parish register records that the infant was baptized on 26 April 1564. (It is quite possible that he was born on 23 April, but this date has probably been assigned by tradition because it is the date on which, fifty-two years later, he died.) The attendance records of the Stratford grammar school of the period are not extant, but it is reasonable to assume that the son of a local official attended the school and received substantial training in Latin. The masters of the school from Shakespeare's seventh to fifteenth years held Oxford degrees; the Elizabethan curriculum excluded mathematics and the natural sciences but taught a good deal of Latin rhetoric, logic, and literature. On 27 November 1582 a marriage license was issued to Shakespeare and Anne Hathaway, eight years his senior. The couple had a child in May, 1583. Perhaps the marriage was necessary, but perhaps the couple had earlier engaged in a formal "troth plight" which would render their children legitimate even if no further ceremony were performed. In 1585 Anne Hathaway bore Shakespeare twins.

That Shakespeare was born is excellent; that he married and had children is pleasant; but that we know nothing about his departure from Stratford to London, or about the beginning of his theatrical career, is lamentable and must be admitted. We would gladly sacrifice details about his children's baptism for details about his earliest days on the stage. Perhaps the poaching episode is true (but it is first reported almost a century after Shakespeare's death), or perhaps he first left Stratford to be a schoolteacher, as another tradition holds; perhaps he was moved by

> Such wind as scatters young men through the world,
> To seek their fortunes further than at home
> Where small experience grows.

In 1592, thanks to the cantankerousness of Robert Greene, a rival playwright and a pamphleteer, we have our first reference, a snarling one, to Shakespeare as an actor and playwright. Greene warns those of his own educated friends who wrote for the theater against an actor who has presumed to turn playwright:

> There is an upstart crow, beautified with our feathers, that with his *tiger's heart wrapped in a player's hide*

supposes he is as well able to bombast out a blank verse as the best of you, and being an absolute Johannes-factotum is in his own conceit the only Shake-scene in a country.

The reference to the player, as well as the allusion to Aesop's crow (who strutted in borrowed plumage, as an actor struts in fine words not his own), makes it clear that by this date Shakespeare had both acted and written. That Shakespeare is meant is indicated not only by "Shake-scene" but by the parody of a line from one of Shakespeare's plays, *3 Henry VI*: "O, tiger's heart wrapped in a woman's hide." If Shakespeare in 1592 was prominent enough to be attacked by an envious dramatist, he probably had served an apprenticeship in the theater for at least a few years.

In any case, by 1592 Shakespeare had acted and written, and there are a number of subsequent references to him as an actor: documents indicate that in 1598 he is a "principal comedian," in 1603 a "principal tragedian," in 1608 he is one of the "men players." The profession of actor was not for a gentleman, and it occasionally drew the scorn of university men who resented writing speeches for persons less educated than themselves, but it was respectable enough: players, if prosperous, were in effect members of the bourgeoisie, and there is nothing to suggest that Stratford considered William Shakespeare less than a solid citizen. When, in 1596, the Shakespeares were granted a coat of arms, the grant was made to Shakespeare's father, but probably William Shakespeare (who the next year bought the second-largest house in town) had arranged the matter on his own behalf. In subsequent transactions he is occasionally styled a gentleman.

Although in 1593 and 1594 Shakespeare published two narrative poems dedicated to the Earl of Southampton, *Venus and Adonis* and *The Rape of Lucrece,* and may well have written most or all of his sonnets in the middle nineties, Shakespeare's literary activity seems to have been almost entirely devoted to the theater. (It may be significant that the two narrative poems were written in years when the plague closed the theaters for several months.) In 1594 he was a charter member of a theatrical company called the

Chamberlain's Men (which in 1603 changed its name to the King's Men); until he retired to Stratford (about 1611, apparently), he was with this remarkably stable company. From 1599 the company acted primarily at the Globe Theatre, in which Shakespeare held a one-tenth interest. Other Elizabethan dramatists are known to have acted, but no other is known also to have been entitled to a share in the profits of the playhouse.

Shakespeare's first eight published plays did not have his name on them, but this is not remarkable; the most popular play of the sixteenth century, Thomas Kyd's *The Spanish Tragedy,* went through many editions without naming Kyd, and Kyd's authorship is known only because a book on the profession of acting happens to quote (and attribute to Kyd) some lines on the interest of Roman emperors in the drama. What is remarkable is that after 1598 Shakespeare's name commonly appears on printed plays—some of which are not his. Another indication of his popularity comes from Francis Meres, author of *Palladis Tamia: Wit's Treasury* (1598): in this anthology of snippets accompanied by an essay on literature, many playwrights are mentioned, but Shakespeare's name occurs more often than any other, and Shakespeare is the only playwright whose plays are listed.

From his acting, playwriting, and share in a theater, Shakespeare seems to have made considerable money. He put it to work, making substantial investments in Stratford real estate. When he made his will (less than a month before he died), he sought to leave his property intact to his descendants. Of small bequests to relatives and to friends (including three actors, Richard Burbage, John Heminges, and Henry Condell), that to his wife of the second-best bed has provoked the most comment; perhaps it was the bed the couple had slept in, the best being reserved for visitors. In any case, had Shakespeare not excepted it, the bed would have gone (with the rest of his household possessions) to his daughter and her husband. On 25 April 1616 he was buried within the chancel of the church at Stratford. An unattractive monument to his memory, placed on a wall near the grave, says he died on 23 April. Over the grave itself are the lines, perhaps by Shakespeare, that (more than his literary fame) have kept his bones undisturbed in the crowded burial ground where old bones were often dislodgèd to make way for new:

> Good friend, for Jesus' sake forbear
> To dig the dust enclosèd here.
> Blessed be the man that spares these stones
> And cursed be he that moves my bones.

Thirty-seven plays, as well as some nondramatic poems, are held to constitute the Shakespeare canon. The dates of composition of most of the works are highly uncertain, but there is often evidence of a *terminus a quo* (starting point) and/or a *terminus ad quem* (terminal point) that provides a framework for intelligent guessing. For example, *Richard II* cannot be earlier than 1595, the publication date of some material to which it is indebted; *The Merchant of Venice* cannot be later than 1598, the year Francis Meres mentioned it. Sometimes arguments for a date hang on an alleged topical allusion, such as the lines about the unseasonable weather in *A Midsummer Night's Dream,* II.i.81–117, but such an allusion (if indeed it is an allusion) can be variously interpreted, and in any case there is always the possibility that a topical allusion was inserted during a revision, years after the composition of a play. Dates are often attributed on the basis of style, and although conjectures about style usually rest on other conjectures, sooner or later one must rely on one's literary sense. There is no real proof, for example, that *Othello* is not as early as *Romeo and Juliet,* but one feels *Othello* is later, and because the first record of its performance is 1604, one is glad enough to set its composition at that date and not push it back into Shakespeare's early years. The following chronology, then, is as much indebted to informed guesswork and sensitivity as it is to fact. The dates, necessarily imprecise, indicate something like a scholarly consensus.

PLAYS

1588–93	*The Comedy of Errors*
1588–94	*Love's Labor's Lost*

1590–91	*2 Henry VI*
1590–91	*3 Henry VI*
1591–92	*1 Henry VI*
1592–93	*Richard III*
1592–94	*Titus Andronicus*
1593–94	*The Taming of the Shrew*
1593–95	*The Two Gentlemen of Verona*
1594–96	*Romeo and Juliet*
1595	*Richard II*
1594–96	*A Midsummer Night's Dream*
1596–97	*King John*
1596–97	*The Merchant of Venice*
1597	*1 Henry IV*
1597–98	*2 Henry IV*
1598–1600	*Much Ado About Nothing*
1598–99	*Henry V*
1599	*Julius Caesar*
1599–1600	*As You Like It*
1599–1600	*Twelfth Night*
1600–01	*Hamlet*
1597–1601	*The Merry Wives of Windsor*
1601–02	*Troilus and Cressida*
1602–04	*All's Well That Ends Well*
1603–04	*Othello*
1604	*Measure for Measure*
1605–06	*King Lear*
1605–06	*Macbeth*
1606–07	*Antony and Cleopatra*
1605–08	*Timon of Athens*
1607–09	*Coriolanus*
1608–09	*Pericles*
1609–10	*Cymbeline*
1610–11	*The Winter's Tale*
1611	*The Tempest*
1612–13	*Henry VIII*

POEMS

| 1592 | *Venus and Adonis* |
| 1593–94 | *The Rape of Lucrece* |

Shakespeare's Theater

In Shakespeare's infancy, Elizabethan actors performed wherever they could—in great halls, at court, in the courtyards of inns. The innyards must have made rather unsatisfactory theaters: on some days they were unavailable because carters bringing goods to London used them as depots; when available, they had to be rented from the innkeeper; perhaps most important, London inns were subject to the Common Council of London, which was not well disposed toward theatricals. In 1574 the Common Council required that plays and playing places in London be licensed. It asserted that

> sundry great disorders and inconveniences have been found to ensue to this city by the inordinate haunting of great multitudes of people, specially youth, to plays, interludes, and shows, namely occasion of frays and quarrels, evil practices of incontinency in great inns having chambers and secret places adjoining to their open stages and galleries,

and ordered that innkeepers who wished licenses to hold performances put up a bond and make contributions to the poor.

The requirement that plays and innyard theaters be licensed, along with the other drawbacks of playing at inns, probably drove James Burbage (a carpenter-turned-actor) to rent in 1576 a plot of land northeast of the city walls and to build here—on property outside the jurisdiction of the city—England's first permanent construction designed for plays. He called it simply the Theatre. About all that is known of its construction is that it was wood. It soon had imitators, the most famous being the Globe (1599), built across the Thames (again outside the city's jurisdiction), out of timbers of the Theatre, which had been dismantled when Burbage's lease ran out.

There are three important sources of information about the structure of Elizabethan playhouses—drawings, a contract, and stage directions in plays. Of drawings, only the so-called De Witt drawing (c. 1596) of the Swan—really a friend's copy of De Witt's drawing—is of much significance. It shows a building of three tiers, with a stage jutting from a wall into the yard or center of the building. The tiers are roofed, and part of the stage is covered by a roof that projects from the rear and is supported at its front on two posts, but the groundlings, who paid a penny to stand in front of the stage, were exposed to the sky. (Performances in such a playhouse were held only in the daytime; artificial illumination was not used.) At the rear of the stage are two doors; above the stage is a gallery. The second major source of information, the contract for the Fortune, specifies that although the Globe is to be the model, the Fortune is to be square, eighty feet outside and fifty-five inside. The stage is to be forty-three feet broad, and is to extend into the middle of the yard (i.e., it is twenty-seven and a half feet deep). For patrons willing to pay more than the general admission charged of the groundlings, there were to be three galleries provided with seats. From the third chief source, stage directions, one learns that entrance to the stage was by doors, presumably spaced widely apart at the rear ("Enter one citizen at one door, and another at the other"), and that in addition to the platform stage there was occasionally some sort of curtained booth or alcove allowing for "discovery" scenes, and some sort of playing space "aloft" or "above" to represent (for example) the top of a city's walls or a room above the street. Doubtless each theater had its own peculiarities, but perhaps we can talk about a "typical" Elizabethan theater if we realize that no theater need exactly have fit the description, just as no father is the typical father with 3.7 children. This hypothetical theater is wooden, round or polygonal (in *Henry V* Shakespeare calls it a "wooden *O*"), capable of holding some eight hundred spectators standing in the yard around the projecting elevated stage and some fifteen hundred additional spectators seated in the three roofed galleries. The stage, protected by a "shadow" or "heavens" or roof, is entered by two doors; behind the doors is the "tiring house" (attiring house, i.e., dressing room), and above the doors is some sort of gallery that may sometimes hold spectators but that can be used (for example) as the bedroom from which Romeo—according to a stage direction in one text—"goeth down." Some evidence suggests that a throne can be lowered onto the platform stage, perhaps from the "shadow"; certainly characters can descend from the stage through a trap or traps into the cellar or "hell." Sometimes this space beneath the platform accommodates a sound-effects man or musician (in *Antony and Cleopatra* "music of the hautboys is under the stage") or an actor (in *Hamlet* the "Ghost cries under the stage"). Most characters simply walk on and off, but because there is no curtain in front of the platform, corpses will have to be carried off (Hamlet must lug Polonius' guts into the neighbor room), or will have to fall at the rear, where the curtain on the alcove or booth can be drawn to conceal them.

Such may have been the so-called "public theater." Another kind of theater, called the "private theater" because its much greater admission charge limited its audience to the wealthy or the prodigal, must be briefly mentioned. The private theater was basically a large room, entirely roofed and therefore artificially illuminated, with a stage at one end. In 1576 one such theater was established in Blackfriars, a Dominican priory in London that had been suppressed in 1538 and confiscated by the Crown and thus was not under the city's jurisdiction. All the actors in the Blackfriars theater were boys about eight to thirteen years old (in the public theaters similar boys played female parts; a boy Lady Macbeth played to a man Macbeth). This private theater had a precarious existence, and ceased operations in 1584. In 1596 James Burbage, who had already made theatrical history by building the Theatre, began to construct a second Blackfriars theater. He died in 1597, and for several years this second Blackfriars theater was used by a troupe of boys, but in 1608 two of Burbage's sons and five other actors (including Shakespeare) became joint operators of the theater, using it in the winter when the open-air Globe was unsuitable. Perhaps such a smaller theater, roofed, artificially illuminated, and with a tradition of a courtly audience, exerted an influence on Shakespeare's late plays.

Performances in the private theaters may well have had intermissions during which music was played, but in the public theaters the action was probably uninterrupted, flowing from scene to scene almost without a break. Actors would enter, speak, exit, and others would immediately enter and establish (if necessary) the new locale by a few properties and by words and gestures. Here are some samples of Shakespeare's scene painting:

> This is Illyria, lady.

> Well, this is the Forest of Arden.

> This castle hath a pleasant seat; the air
> Nimbly and sweetly recommends itself
> Unto our gentle senses.

On the other hand, it is a mistake to conceive of the Elizabethan stage as bare. Although Shakespeare's Chorus in *Henry V* calls the stage an "unworthy scaffold" and urges the spectators to "eke out our performance with your mind," there was considerable spectacle. The last act of *Macbeth*, for example, has five stage directions calling for "drum and colors," and another sort of appeal to the eye is indicated by the stage direction "Enter Macduff, with Macbeth's head." Some scenery and properties may have been substantial; doubtless a throne was used, and in one play of the period we encounter this direction: "Hector takes up a great piece of rock and casts at Ajax, who tears up a young tree by the roots and assails Hector." The matter is of some importance, and will be glanced at again in the next section.

The Texts of Shakespeare

Though eighteen of his plays were published during his lifetime, Shakespeare seems never to have supervised their publication. There is nothing unusual here; when a playwright sold a play to a theatrical company he surrendered his ownership of it. Normally a company would not publish the play, because to publish it meant to allow competitors to acquire the piece. Some plays, however, did get published: apparently treacherous actors sometimes pieced together a play for a publisher, sometimes a company in need of money sold a play, and sometimes a company allowed a play to be published that no longer drew audiences. That Shakespeare did not concern himself with publication, then, is scarcely remarkable; of his contemporaries only Ben Jonson carefully supervised the publication of his own plays. In 1623, seven years after Shakespeare's death, John Heminges and Henry Condell (two senior members of Shakespeare's company, who had performed with him for about twenty years) collected his plays—published and unpublished—into a large volume, commonly called the First Folio. (A folio is a volume consisting of sheets that have been folded once, each sheet thus making two leaves, or four pages. The eighteen plays published during Shakespeare's lifetime had been issued one play per volume in small books called quartos. Each sheet in a quarto has been folded twice, making four leaves, or eight pages.) The First Folio contains thirty-six plays; a thirty-seventh, *Pericles,* though not in the Folio, is regarded as canonical. Heminges and Condell suggest in an address "To the great variety of readers" that the republished plays are presented in better form than in the quartos: "Before you were abused with diverse stolen and surreptitious copies, maimed and deformed by the frauds and stealths of injurious impostors that exposed them; even those, are now offered to your view cured and perfect of their limbs, and all the rest absolute in their numbers, as he [i.e., Shakespeare] conceived them."

Whoever was assigned to prepare the texts for publication in the First Folio seems to have taken his job seriously and yet not to have performed it with uniform care. The sources of the texts seem to have been, in general, good unpublished copies or the best published copies. The first play in the collection, *The Tempest,* is divided into acts and scenes, has unusually full stage directions and descriptions of spectacle, and concludes with a list of the characters, but the editor was not able (or willing) to present all of the succeeding texts so fully dressed. Later texts occasionally show signs of carelessness: in one scene of *Much Ado About Nothing* the names of actors, instead of characters, appear as speech prefixes, as they had in the quarto, which the Folio reprints; proofreading throughout the Folio is spotty and apparently was done without reference to the printer's copy; the pagination of *Hamlet* jumps from 156 to 257.

A modern editor of Shakespeare must first select his copy; no problem if the play exists only in the Folio, but a considerable problem if the relationship between a quarto and the Folio—or an early quarto and a later one—is unclear. When an editor has chosen what seems to him to be the most authoritative text or texts for his copy, he has not done with making decisions. First of all, he must reckon with Elizabethan spelling. If he is not producing a facsimile, he probably modernizes it, but ought he to preserve the old form of words that apparently were pronounced quite unlike their modern forms—"lanthorn," "alablaster"? If he preserves these forms, is he really preserving Shakespeare's forms or perhaps those of a compositor in the printing house? What is one to do when one finds "lanthorn" and "lantern" in adjacent lines? (The editors of this series in general, but not invariably, assume that words should be spelled in their modern form.) Elizabethan punctuation, too, presents problems. For example in the First Folio, the only text for the play, Macbeth rejects his wife's idea that he can wash the blood from his hand:

> no: this my Hand will rather
> The multitudinous Seas incarnardine,
> Making the Greene one, Red.

Obviously an editor will remove the superfluous capitals, and he will probably alter the spelling to "incarnadine," but will he leave the comma before "red," letting Macbeth speak of the sea as "the green one," or will he (like most modern editors) remove the comma and thus have Macbeth say that his hand will make the ocean *uniformly* red?

An editor will sometimes have to change more than spelling or punctuation. Macbeth says to his wife:

> I dare do all that may become a man,
> Who dares no more, is none.

For two centuries editors have agreed that the second line is unsatisfactory, and have emended "no" to "do": "Who dares do more is none." But when in the same play Ross says that fearful persons

> floate vpon a wilde and violent Sea
> Each way, and moue,

need "move" be emended to "none," as it often is, on the hunch that the compositor misread the manuscript? The editors of the Signet Classic Shakespeare have restrained themselves from making abundant emendations. In their minds they hear Dr. Johnson on the dangers of emending: "I have adopted the Roman sentiment, that it is more honorable to save a citizen than to kill an enemy." Some departures (in addition to spelling, punctuation, and lineation) from the copy text have of course been made, but the original readings are listed in a note following the play, so that the reader can evaluate them for himself.

The editors of the Signet Classic Shakespeare, following tradition, have added line numbers and in many cases act and scene divisions as well as indications of locale at the beginning of scenes. The Folio divided most of the plays into acts and some into scenes. Early eighteenth-century editors increased the divisions. These divisions, which provide a convenient way of referring to passages in the plays, have been retained, but when not in the text chosen as the basis for the Signet Classic text they are enclosed in square brackets [ ] to indicate that they are editorial additions. Similarly, although no play of Shakespeare's published during his lifetime was equipped with indications of locale at the heads of scene divisions, locales have here been added in square brackets for the convenience of the reader, who lacks the information afforded to spectators by costumes, properties, and gestures. The spectator can tell at a glance he is in the throne room, but without an editorial indication the reader may be puzzled for a while. It should be mentioned, incidentally, that there are a few authentic stage directions—perhaps Shakespeare's, perhaps a prompter's—that suggest locales: for example, "Enter Brutus in his orchard," and "They go up into the Senate house." It is hoped that the bracketed additions provide the reader with the sort of help provided in these two authentic directions, but it is equally hoped that the reader will remember that the stage was not loaded with scenery.

No editor during the course of his work can fail to recollect some words Heminges and Condell prefixed to the Folio:

> It had been a thing, we confess, worthy to have been wished, that the author himself had lived to have set forth and overseen his own writings. But since it hath been ordained otherwise, and he by death departed from that right, we pray you do not envy his friends the office of their care and pain to have collected and published them.

Nor can an editor, after he has done his best, forget Heminges and Condell's final words: "And so we leave you to other of his friends, whom if you need can be your guides. If you need them not, you can lead yourselves, and others. And such readers we wish him."

SYLVAN BARNET
Tufts University

Introduction

Antony and Cleopatra was written in 1607, or a little earlier. That is, it probably followed immediately after the four great tragedies, *Hamlet, Othello, King Lear,* and *Macbeth,* all of which were written in the half-dozen years after the turn of the century—the period at which Shakespeare's genius was at its most assured, mature, and profound. And *Antony and Cleopatra* itself witnesses to this authoritative mastery of an artistic maturity: Coleridge, in a fine phrase, spoke of the play as being "in all exhibitions of a giant power in its strength and vigor of maturity, a formidable rival of the *Macbeth, Lear, Othello,* and *Hamlet.*" But whether the play is, in reality, a tragedy, is a more open question: its uniqueness of form and mood is a part of its power, and unique things are not easy to classify. When the Folio editors came to collect the plays together after Shakespeare's death, they named this *The Tragedie of Anthonie, and Cleopatra* (unless the title was Shakespeare's own) and placed it in the "Tragedies" section that closed the Folio. But the play is, in its total effect, so unlike the tragedies that preceded it, that for long now critics have hesitated to group it with them. The words with which Coleridge praises the play are in themselves suggestive of a distinction; Bradley, later, did not include it in his *Shakespearean Tragedy,* and G. Wilson Knight similarly excludes it from his study of the tragedies, *The Wheel of Fire*—though both discuss it elsewhere. New classifications of the play have been made in the attempt to specify its highly individual quality. It is most usually referred to, now, as a "Roman Play" and grouped as such with *Julius Caesar* and *Coriolanus:* on the grounds that all three, in taking their materials from North's Plutarch, take also from these "Lives of the Noble Grecians and Romans" an interest that is at least as historical and political as it is tragical, and an ethos that is at least as classical as it is Christian. A recent study has classified it anew, as a "Problem Play," and grouped it as such with *Julius Caesar* and *Measure for Measure,* arguing that all three are alike, and unusual, in presenting a specifically moral problem in such a way as to leave radical indecision as to the rights and wrongs of the case. And lastly, though no critic has ever gone so far as to group the play with the Comedies, several have pointed out—and with good reason—how comic its effect sometimes is.

Obviously, categorizing a play is not vital to understanding it. Moreover, the exercise of classifying a thing can only aim at the comparative, and hope to create some limited definition within which unlike things may be compared and contrasted, and so throw light on one another. However, the attempts to classify *Antony and Cleopatra*—and the difficulties met with in the process—do have an unusual interest. For it is "uncategorizable" in a new and special way. There are one or two plays of Shakespeare—*Troilus and Cressida* and *Measure for Measure* are probably the best examples—which are similarly hard to classify, but which remain much simpler propositions. Though brilliant and full of interest, they are far from perfect or coherent works of art; and it is therefore easier to see in them (or to imagine one sees) the marks of changing purpose, or of discordances within the given materials, that make the act of classification so difficult. It is possible to suggest that *Measure for Measure* was intended to be a comedy on a not unfamiliar pattern, though in an unfamiliar milieu, but that the development in Shakespeare's artistic vision broke apart the preconceived notion on which the play began. Similarly, it is possible to suggest that *Troilus and Cressida* may have begun as a love tragedy on the same design as *Romeo and Juliet,* but that a greatly changed mood and insight destroyed that simpler romantic formula. Both plays at least offer materials for such hesitant suggestions with their sudden changes of mood, their strange discordances in characterization, their awkward or seemingly patched-up endings. *Antony and Cleopatra,* by contrast, suggests no such change of purpose or uncertainty in handling materials. It is, in final poetic and dramatic effect, one of the most triumphantly harmonious, coherent, and "finished" plays that Shakespeare ever wrote, from first to last line bearing the impress of a unified purpose powerfully carried out. Coleridge, again, seizes on this dominant effect of the play when he points out the degree to which Shakespeare "impresses the notion of giant strength. . . . This [is] owing to the manner in which it is sustained throughout—that he *lives* in and through the play." And yet, though the impression of a unified purpose is so strong, it is far from easy to decide what that unified purpose is.

One of the reasons for this is that the play "works" at many different levels and in many different ways. In it, many different—and even contradictory—kinds of experience are fused together; with the result that the play is continually suggestive of different kinds and categories of drama. Diversity and complexity of experience are of course a part of the strength and power of the preceding tragedies: but in them all diversities are subsumed under a dominating tragic discipline, by which the play moves steadily to its catastrophic climax. Hamlet's Gravedigger, Lear's Fool, Macbeth's Porter do not provide "comic relief," though this phrase is sometimes used of them: rather, they substantiate the tragic experience from a point of view at a large distance from the heroic—and therefore substantiate it the more impressively. In *Antony and Cleopatra,* the tragic and the comic experience coexist, among others. It is tragic not only in the sense of containing the "sad" and the "serious" (for many of Shakespeare's best and truest comedies also do that) but also in the expression of an irremediable loss, incurred consciously and borne responsibly: Antony reaches "the very heart of loss," and knows it. And yet it is also comic, not only in the sense of containing the satirical or the farcical (for

Shakespeare's tragedies also do that) but also in the expression of an ineffaceable lightheartedness: as when Cleopatra, preparing for death, says:

>   go fetch
> My best attires. I am again for Cydnus,
> To meet Mark Antony. . . .   (V.ii.227–29)

and, to the asp that kills her:

>   O, couldst thou speak,
> That I might hear thee call great Caesar ass
> Unpolicied!   (V.ii.306–08)

"Lighthearted" is not, admittedly, a complete enough word for this: the somewhat old-fashioned word "highhearted" is perhaps closer to it. But however it is named, the mood evoked here, and elsewhere in the play, is nearer to the experience evoked in the mature comedies than it is to the gravely responsible tone of Hamlet at his death, Othello's solemn bravura, Lear's agonized questioning, or Macbeth's desperate obduracy. The tone and presentation throughout the play is thus so compounded of strangely blended elements as to be elusive of a final classification. The play can be described from several different points of view, and in the terms of several different categories, and each would point to elements really present in it: but none would describe it quite completely enough.

There is, for instance, good reason to call *Antony and Cleopatra* a "Roman Play," and to point out the historical and political interest that distinguishes it from the earlier tragedies. As in *Julius Caesar,* which had been written some eight years earlier (that is, just before *Hamlet,* the first of the mature tragedies), Shakespeare has taken his materials from well-known history—so well-known, in fact, as in part to circumscribe his treatment of it. The basis of *Hamlet, King Lear,* and *Macbeth* is also of course historical, but presented Shakespeare with nothing as radically unalterable as the murder of Julius Caesar, the fate of Antony, or the coming to power of Octavius Caesar.

Shakespeare's Octavius—Caesar, as he is always called in *Antony and Cleopatra*—was to become Augustus, perhaps greatest of Roman emperors, creator of the Pax Romana that closed the long period of unrest, revolution, and war, with the time of peace in which Christ was to be born. Thus, in the war with Antony, when Antony's allies have deserted and sympathy for him is at its strongest, Caesar redresses the balance by a brief but significant reminder of his future role in history:

> The time of universal peace is near.
> Prove this a prosp'rous day, the three-nooked world
> Shall bear the olive freely.   (IV.vi.5–7)

Antony's course is as much a "given factor" as Caesar's. Plutarch's life of Antony (perhaps somewhat romanticizing the case) had established the cause of Antony's downfall: he had lost the world because of his love for Cleopatra. Whether that love were treated with some severity (as Plutarch treated it) or with tender admiration (as Chaucer and many others had treated it) its fatality had become an historical fact.

The political battle, then, is between two men sharply distinguished in their roles: Caesar, the young, sober, peace-loving imperial administrator, and Antony, the middle-aged soldier, orator, and lover, a hardened campaigner in war, politics, and love. And the battle is fought for a large enough issue: the rule of the whole civilized world some forty years before the birth of Christ. For Antony and Caesar are two of the triumvirs who rule the Empire between them, and early in the play it becomes clear that the third, Lepidus, is an insignificant go-between. The scale of the prize that the two men are fighting for is also established at once in the play. Philo bitterly sees Antony as

> The triple pillar of the world transformed
> Into a strumpet's fool.   (I.i.12–13)

And Antony himself turns an exhilarated affirmation of his love into a rejection of the whole Empire:

Let Rome in Tiber melt, and the wide arch
Of the ranged empire fall! Here is my space. . . .
(I.i.33–34)

On Antony's second appearance in the play, he is presented in a scene all the more sharply effective for its contrast with the immediately preceding scene of the fortune-
telling, which is slow, sleepy, and casual: he appears as a
man facing a rapid and cumulatively urgent succession of
news from all over the Empire—the wars of his wife Fulvia
and his brother Lucius, their conjunct war against Caesar,
the swift and victorious invasions of the Parthian Labienus,
Fulvia's death, the threats of Pompey, and the dangerously
shifting sympathies of the Roman people. Caesar, in his
turn, is presented on his first appearance in an exactly com-
parable way, as a man habituated to an enormous and
urgent sphere of action. Both these scenes are brilliantly
effective in their conversion of necessary exposition to
purely dramatic purposes: they move with an almost
breathless speed and energy, and establish Antony and
Caesar as men of affairs at a very high level indeed. This
effect is maintained, though by less concentrated means,
throughout the play. The action moves rapidly from place
to place in the great Empire, from Alexandria to Rome,
from Misenum to "a plain in Syria," from Athens to Rome
again. The characters think and plan—sometimes rhetor-
ically, sometimes merely with an easy and businesslike pre-
cision—in terms of the whole world:

[his] quality, going on,
The sides o' th' world may danger. . . . (I.ii.193–94)

. . . thou, the greatest soldier of the world . . . (I.iii.38)

The demi-Atlas of this earth . . . (I.v.23)

The third o' th' world is yours . . . (II.ii.67)

To you all three,
The senators alone of this great world . . . (II.vi.8–9)

Wilt thou be lord of all the world? (II.vii.63)

These three world-sharers . . . (II.vii.72)

                              Wars 'twixt you twain would be
As if the world should cleave . . . (III.iv.30–31)

The greater cantle of the world is lost
With very ignorance . . . (III.x.6–7)

Such language (of which this is only a selection) is the
medium of the play, and it establishes the size of the battlefield—real and metaphorical—on which the contest for
power is being fought.

The course of this battle for power is simple in outline.
The first appearance of Antony and Caesar—Antony in
his "Egyptian fetters," though still able to throw them off:
Caesar revealing in clear, precise terms his cool disgust at
Antony's way of life and aware also of the dangers of such
a political associate—presents them as personally incompatible and potentially rivals. As Caesar says:

                              [it] cannot be
We shall remain in friendship, our conditions
So diff'ring in their acts.   (II.ii.117–19)

The two are reconciled under the pressure of Pompey's
threat to the triumvirate and seal their peace by Antony's
marriage to Octavia, Caesar's sister. The desertion of Octavia by Antony gives Caesar the pretext for war, once
he has himself gained some advantage in power. After the
ruinous defeat at Actium, Antony's fall is rapid: his allies
and his armies desert to the more powerful man, and he is
lost. Through an apparently leisurely and circuitous stream
of events that keeps closely to the historical sequence, there
emerges into prominence the political theme: the maneuvers and manipulations, the honors and dishonors, of a
battle between incompatible standards for the government
of the whole Roman world.

To describe the play in these terms is to give it something of the discipline, and something of the limitation, of
any game of power—say, a game of chess played out on

the board of the world. And such an image would not be entirely alien to the mood of the play: Antony, for instance, accuses Cleopatra in similar terms, in a moment of despairing anger:

> she, Eros, has
> Packed cards with Caesar, and false-played my glory
> Unto an enemy's triumph. (IV.xiv.18–20)

And yet to use this image of the game is to realize how much in the play it does not comprehend: indeed, even as Antony uses this image, there is a sudden and significant sense that he has lost even his imaginative command of the full weight of the situation. If the play presents a game of history and politics, it presents also something deeper and more important: a tragedy of human experience. When Antony finds himself at "the very heart of loss," he is maddened at both the loss of the world and the loss of all trust in Cleopatra: but in losing both, he is also crying out at the loss of himself.

It is not enough to say, simply, that Shakespeare is far more interested in the loser, Antony, than he is in the winner, Caesar; or even to say that his interest is with that relation between Antony and Cleopatra that caused the loss of the world. It is rather that the whole situation is presented so that the historical and political interest—the gain or loss of world power—becomes a part or facet of another and greater subject: the ruin of two people, and with them, of a whole sphere of human experience. Any political history may have its "human interest"; Plutarch's "Life of Antony" is vivid, shrewd, and alive in its portraiture, and Shakespeare is largely and unusually indebted to Plutarch's characterization of Antony. What differentiates *Antony and Cleopatra* is not merely a livelier, or even a deeper characterization, but a transformation of all action and event into a process of tragic and individual experience.

This touches several characters besides the hero and heroine. The mere opportunist, Pompey, soon to disappear from the play, has a moment of sudden importance, seriousness, and dignity in the galley scene, when he rejects the chance of world power on a point of honor. The tough, cynical, common-sense soldier, Enobarbus (who in Plutarch dies of an ague) dies of a broken heart at his desertion of Antony, and the scene has, again, a weight of dignity and solemnity. Caesar himself, on hearing of the death of Antony, is moved—for the first time in the play— by a sudden access of personal feeling, in the awareness of what of himself he has lost by that death. None of these incidents could have any historical or political importance, though they might, perhaps, be shown as having historical and political effects; their significance and their weight lie in a different sphere of value. It is significant that each of these small incidents has the effect of isolating the person concerned, so that he appears for a moment as detached from, or even alien to, the world around him; for tragedy deals with the experience of a man, or of Man, rather than of men.

The greatest individuals in the play are, of course, Antony and Cleopatra: it is on their absolute selfhood that they base their glory. "We stand up peerless." And it is this arrogant and obdurate sense of themselves that distinguishes them from Caesar—though all three are, in fact, engaged on a quite similar quest for power that makes them, on a detached view, remarkably alike. Caesar can speak as nobly, as authoritatively, and as impressively as the other two; but he speaks a different language. His words have, at their best, the stature of judgment: of a rational social wisdom that takes its force from its generality. To him, Antony is

> A man who is th' abstract of all faults
> That all men follow.   (I.iv.9–10)

He surveys Antony with a level detachment that reduces his actions to caricature, and gives the final condemnation a rigorous justice:

> to confound such time
> That drums him from his sport and speaks as loud

As his own state and ours, 'tis to be chid
As we rate boys who, being mature in knowledge,
Pawn their experience to their present pleasure
And so rebel to judgment.   (I.iv.28–33)

This is powerfully spoken, and its effect is largely that of
the judicial and weighty summary of a situation from outside; it is the voice of common judgment and social wisdom. This voice interposes its realities throughout the play,
and is not confined to Caesar alone: Antony too can speak
with the voice of "Rome." But the language that Antony
and Cleopatra make their own is something very different,
and challenges the sober judgment of Rome. It is a language expressive of a whole radically different way of
living and feeling: a language of immediate individual
experience, sensory in its apprehension, exalted or intense
in its tone, and arrogant in its claims. Love or desolation,
exhilaration or rage become their own argument, and the
intense experience of an exceptional individual becomes
its own rationale. So Antony, proclaiming his love for
Cleopatra, converts his profession into a challenge of Rome
and all that Rome stands for:

Let Rome in Tiber melt, and the wide arch
Of the ranged empire fall! Here is my space,
Kingdoms are clay: our dungy earth alike
Feeds beast as man. The nobleness of life
Is to do thus; when such a mutual pair
And such a twain can do't, in which I bind,
On pain of punishment, the world to weet
We stand up peerless.   (I.i.33–40)

So also Cleopatra, exquisitely lamenting the death of
Antony, transforms her desolation into a vision of an
empty world:

O, see, my women,
The crown o' th' earth doth melt. My lord!
O, withered is the garland of the war,
The soldier's pole is fall'n: young boys and girls
Are level now with men. The odds is gone,

And there is nothing left remarkable
Beneath the visiting moon. (IV.xv.62–68)

Both these speeches reveal an element vital to the characterization of Antony and Cleopatra. The first is more than a profession of love—whether we choose to regard that love as the glorification of sensual excitement or as the affirmation of a noble passion; the second is more than a woman's lament for a dead man—whether we choose to regard that lament as profound insight or as delusion. Each is an affirmation of selfhood, and a proclamation that this self is "peerless," "remarkable," incomparable, in its love and in its loss and in its very existence. Antony and Cleopatra are—to put the matter at its simplest—proud: proud of being themselves, and proud of being greater than anyone else in the world. Nor are they monstrous in this, for the whole world of the play is governed by the ideal of pride, and in it "honor" and "nobility," "greatness" and "reputation" are the very fabric of existence. Antony's fame, eminence, and power; Cleopatra's royalty; their love for each other; the admiration of their followers—all these things feed their pride and are fed by it. And all their great and good qualities serve it: Antony's courage and generosity and largeness of spirit, Cleopatra's wit and charm and enormous abundance of life. When their "greatness" is destroyed, the world is empty to them, for the loss of pride is a death:

The soul and body rive not more in parting
Than greatness going off. (IV.xiii.5–6)

The tragedy of Antony and Cleopatra, then, is not simply their loss of the world, nor even their death, but the destruction of pride that accompanies both. All that makes them admirable is inextricably confused with its own corruptions: their energy, vitality, and power are self-defeating. Antony is caught between the dual and mutually destructive sources of his pride, power in Rome and pleasure in Egypt; Cleopatra discovers or proves at Actium her full power over Antony, and in doing so loses both him and the world. Cleopatra fights to hold Antony, and Antony fights to hold the world, and in the process all Antony's courage reveals itself as inextricable from blind and irrational violence, and his generosity from sensual obsession; all Cleopatra's vitality and self-possession reveals itself as wayward, demanding, and treacherous. Caesar sees clearly when he calls Antony "the old ruffian," and Antony knows Cleopatra for a "boggler ever." In defeat—a defeat which is the loss of an ideal, as well as the loss of the world—both grow, paradoxically, more gentle, more human, and more wholly sympathetic. But both choose the "Roman" death of suicide, which is itself a last affirmation of pride in themselves and a refusal of the humiliation of walking in Caesar's triumph. Cleopatra places on her head the crown of a country she no longer rules, prepares to join a husband she never had, and rejects with contempt a world which has humiliated her, dying a death

> fitting for a princess
> Descended of so many royal kings. (V.ii.326–27)

This tragic subject Shakespeare has created out of his historical and political materials; and it is a subject that merits Caesar's words at the close of the play:

> High events as these
> Strike those that make them; and their story is
> No less in pity, than his glory which
> Brought them to be lamented. (V.ii.359–62)

Yet there can be a large difference between a play's "subject," summarized in detachment, and the full effect of the play itself; and this is true of *Antony and Cleopatra*. It certainly contains the "high events," the "pity" and "glory" that Caesar suggests as he closes the play on a fittingly high and sober note. But to leave the account of the play here would be as partial as to describe it, simply, as a historical and political drama.

In the first place, Antony's and Cleopatra's fates and

fortunes are not presented with the kind of tragic or dramatic intensity that such an outline might suggest. Rather, they and their world are presented in a series of leisurely—at first sight, almost casual—insights, that include in their range the great and the small, the significant and the insignificant: a fortunetelling and a great battle, a political conference and a wild party, a memory of the lovers' first meeting and a death in a monument, a woman slapping a messenger and a countryman giving a lecture on the nature of asps. Instead of the cumulative intensity of the earlier tragedies, which speed and slacken and speed again to their catastrophic climaxes, the play presents something more leisurely, more spacious, and more impassive; its structure lies in the panoramic or kaleidoscopic display of diverse aspects of a world, seen in all its variety. At one moment, we watch a conference of world leaders, attempting with some dignity and seriousness to come to terms with each other—an attempt that justifies Antony's earlier bitter self-accusations; after the briefest of pauses, they are all celebrating in a farcical party that ends with a Bacchic version of ring-a-ring-a-roses. Cleopatra speaks, over the dead Antony, her exquisite lament for the loss of all that is valuable in the world; shortly after, she is doing her best to cheat Caesar of her jewels. The whole play is constructed, in this manner, out of a pattern of juxtapositions and contrasts, with the point of view continually shifting and changing; and the effect is something very different from "tragic" intensity, though full of a complex and absorbing life.

Closely related to this fluid and changing dramatic vision is the presentation of the characters themselves; indeed, it might be more proper to say that the concept of "character" itself is transformed. The earlier tragic heroes change, where they change at all in the course of the play, by a process of development; inner potentialities for good and evil are gradually brought to the view as the play proceeds. This is only very partially true of Antony and Cleopatra. They display, rather, a succession of different moods and impulses, continually changing. This is, of course, most true of Cleopatra, who is "infinite variety" itself; but there is hardly a character in the play who is not capable, to some degree, of being and doing the unexpected. The result is that a quick fluidity and changeableness of character becomes the norm, almost the rule: and in such a world, tragic motivation becomes impossible, and tragic responsibility is largely absent. Men seem to be moved by impulse and instinct, chance and expediency; and the guilts and terrors, shames and miseries of the earlier tragedies are very largely absent.

This is to suggest a world that relatively lacks psychological and metaphysical depth. It would be truer to say that *Antony and Cleopatra* creates a physical rather than a metaphysical world and that its density of substance rather than its depth of treatment commands the attention. It creates a world that is triumphantly "natural" rather than "supernatural"—although the natural is not, in this play, without its mysteries. The soothsayer reads, and reads correctly, in "Nature's infinite book of secrecy"; and when the soldiers, on guard by night in the streets of Alexandria, hear "Music i' th' air," they recognize it as the departure of a god from a defeated man:

> 'Tis the god Hercules, whom Antony loved,
> Now leaves him.   (IV.iii.15–16)

To say that the world of *Antony and Cleopatra* is "natural" is to say that it presents all experiences and all events as rooted in the "dungy earth" or the "varying tide" of physical existence. And that physical existence is itself a "varying shore," subject to continual change in the battle of the elements. In politics as in love, the procession of time moves in a continual destruction; so Antony, in the proclamation of his love that challenges the power of the great Roman Empire, is making a proclamation and a challenge that time itself will silently verify:

> Let Rome in Tiber melt, and the wide arch
> Of the ranged empire fall! Here is my space:
> Kingdoms are clay . . .   (I.i.33–35)

The great lyrical image for the triumph of time is the image of the setting of the sun and the coming on of night; and this image fittingly colors the close of the play. The suicide of both Antony and Cleopatra is prefaced by the same echoing image:

> Unarm, Eros. The long day's task is done,
> And we must sleep. . . . (IV.xiv.35–36)

> Finish, good lady, the bright day is done,
> And we are for the dark. (V.ii.193–94)

Wherever such imagery occurs in the play, it has an effect that is undoubtedly complex. One of the many things it does is to suggest that Antony's political defeat and his and Cleopatra's individual tragedy are both set within the context of a larger process, simpler and more universal. All that happens in the play—the reversals of fortune, the victories and defeats, the alienations and reconciliations—all are a part of the "interchange of state" that rules the whole natural world,

> Increasing store with loss, and loss with store.
> (Sonnet 64)

Antony, in his "dotage," and Cleopatra, "wrinkled deep in time," suffer a defeat at the hands of a power greater than Caesar; and the cold politician Caesar himself has fought his way to the possession of an empire that will crumble in his hands to "dungy earth."

This fact Antony and Cleopatra know, and Caesar does not; their wisdom and their folly derives from their knowledge of it, and Caesar's power and his limitations derive from his ignorance or denial of it. Caesar's ambition is to "possess the time," by possessing the world for a while; Antony and Cleopatra live only in the present instant, and lose the world for good:

> There's not a minute of our lives should stretch
> Without some pleasure now. (I.i.46–47)

To give up the battle with Time and live intensely in the present instant; to create a small and circumscribed area in which to exist, in an exhilarated moment of freedom and vitality—this is a way or vision of life more native to comedy than to tragedy. And it is the way of life that Cleopatra, above all, represents.

> That time—O, times!—
> I laughed him out of patience; and that night
> I laughed him into patience; and next morn,
> Ere the ninth hour, I drunk him to his bed;
> Then put my tires and mantles on him, whilst
> I wore his sword Philippan.   (II.v.18–23)

Cleopatra's world is essentially a world of "play": a world, that is, that studies to find fit expression for the exuberance of natural energies and needs no justification for what it does. Her world is self-justifying, self-delighting, perhaps self-destroying; as such it is a perpetual challenge and threat to Caesar's vision of universal power and universal peace. The two cannot coexist: and in any battle between Cleopatra's devious wits and Caesar's steady will-to-power, the latter must triumph. Yet Cleopatra will live out even defeat on her own terms, as though it were an exuberant and triumphant game, the rules of which are her own and no one else's; her image of the dead Antony is of a god who has eluded, by the play of his intense natural energies, the restraining world of time:

> For his bounty,
> There was no winter in't: an autumn 'twas
> That grew the more by reaping. His delights
> Were dolphinlike, they showed his back above
> The element they lived in. . . .   (V.ii.86–90)

Just such an image she makes of her own death: she "plays till doomsday," secure and free within the limited dream she has created.

Certainly that dream is a limited one, always circumscribed by the opposed realities of Caesar and of Time:

Think you there was or might be such a man
As this I dreamt of?

> Gentle madam, no. (V.ii.93–94)

In presenting these realities side by side, and involved with each other—the comic and tragic deeply interfused—*Antony and Cleopatra* creates a world that is as complex as it is profoundly original. One phrase of Cleopatra's—her "Here's sport indeed," as she draws the dying Antony to her—bears all the profound comic pathos and tragic irony that fills and characterizes the play. Yet this mingled experience is as strong as it is complex; it has a power and vitality that is Antony's when, in defeat, he "mocks the midnight bell":

> Let's have one other gaudy night: call to me
> All my sad captains; fill our bowls once more;
> Let's mock the midnight bell. (III.xiii.183–85)

Barbara Everett
Newnham College
Cambridge

The Tragedy of
ANTONY
and
CLEOPATRA

The Tragedy of Antony and Cleopatra

ACT I

Scene I. [*Alexandria. Cleopatra's palace.*]

Enter Demetrius and Philo.

Philo. Nay, but this dotage of our general's
    O'erflows the measure. Those his goodly eyes
    That o'er the files and musters of the war
    Have glowed like plated°¹ Mars, now bend, now
      turn
    The office° and devotion of their view   5
    Upon a tawny front.° His captain's heart,
    Which in the scuffles of great fights hath burst
    The buckles on his breast, reneges all temper°
    And is become the bellows and the fan
    To cool a gypsy's° lust.

    Flourish.° Enter Antony, Cleopatra, her Ladies,
       the Train, with Eunuchs fanning her.

                        Look where they come: 10

¹ The degree sign (°) indicates a footnote, which is keyed to the
text by line number. Text references are printed in *italic* type; the
annotation follows in roman type.
I.i.4 *plated* armored   5 *office* service   6 *tawny front* dark face
(with a pun on the military sense of *front,* "first line of battle")
8 *reneges all temper* gives up all self-control   10 *gypsy's* (gypsies
were believed to have come from Egypt, hence " 'gyptians"; they had
a reputation for trickery, sorcery, and lechery)   10 s.d. *Flourish*
fanfare of trumpets

Take but good note, and you shall see in him
The triple pillar° of the world transformed
Into a strumpet's fool. Behold and see.

Cleopatra. If it be love indeed, tell me how much.

Antony. There's beggary in the love that can be
15   reckoned.

Cleopatra. I'll set a bourn° how far to be beloved.

Antony. Then must thou needs find out new heaven,
new earth.

Enter a Messenger.

Messenger. News, my good lord, from Rome.

Antony.   Grates me! The sum.°

Cleopatra. Nay, hear them, Antony.
20   Fulvia° perchance is angry; or who knows
If the scarce-bearded Caesar° have not sent
His pow'rful mandate to you, "Do this, or this;
Take in° that kingdom, and enfranchise° that.
Perform't, or else we damn thee."

Antony.   How,° my love?

25   *Cleopatra.* Perchance? Nay, and most like:
You must not stay here longer, your dismission°
Is come from Caesar; therefore hear it, Antony.
Where's Fulvia's process?° Caesar's I would say?
Both?
Call in the messengers. As I am Egypt's Queen,
30   Thou blushest, Antony, and that blood of thine
Is Caesar's homager:° else so° thy cheek pays shame
When shrill-tongued Fulvia scolds. The messengers!

12 *The triple pillar* i.e., one of the triumvirs who ruled the world
16 *bourn* limit   18 *Grates me! The sum* It's irritating! Be brief
20 *Fulvia* Antony's wife   21 *scarce-bearded Caesar* (Octavius, then
twenty-three, was some twenty years younger than Antony)   23
Take in occupy   23 *enfranchise* set free from slavery   24 *How* (a
common   exclamation,   like   "What!")   26 *dismission* dismissal
28 *process* summons (i.e., to appear in court)   31 *homager* vassal
31 *else so* or else

Antony. Let Rome in Tiber melt, and the wide arch
 Of the ranged empire fall! Here is my space,
 Kingdoms are clay: our dungy earth alike   35
 Feeds beast as man. The nobleness of life
 Is to do thus;° when such a mutual pair
 And such a twain can do't, in which I bind,
 On pain of punishment, the world to weet°
 We stand up peerless.

Cleopatra.   Excellent falsehood!   40
 Why did he marry Fulvia, and not love her?
 I'll seem the fool I am not. Antony
 Will be—himself.°

Antony.   But stirred° by Cleopatra.
 Now for the love of Love and her soft hours,
 Let's not confound° the time with conference harsh.   45
 There's not a minute of our lives should stretch
 Without some pleasure now. What sport tonight?

Cleopatra. Hear the ambassadors.

Antony.   Fie, wrangling queen!
 Whom everything becomes—to chide, to laugh,
 To weep; whose every passion fully° strives   50
 To make itself, in thee, fair and admired.
 No messenger but thine; and all alone
 Tonight we'll wander through the streets and note
 The qualities of people. Come, my queen;
 Last night you did desire it. [*To Attendants*] Speak
   not to us.   55
     Exeunt [*Antony and Cleopatra*] *with the Train.*

Demetrius. Is Caesar with° Antonius prized so slight?

Philo. Sir, sometimes, when he is not Antony,
 He comes too short of that great property°
 Which still° should go with Antony.

37 *thus* (perhaps they embrace, but perhaps *thus* alludes to their
way of life) 39 *weet* know 43 *himself* (1) the peerless Antony
(2) the fool he is 43 *stirred* (1) angered (2) inspired, inflamed
45 *confound* waste 50 *fully* absolutely and successfully 56 *with*
by 58 *property* quality 59 *still* always

Demetrius.   I am full sorry
60   That he approves° the common liar, who
        Thus speaks of him at Rome; but I will hope
        Of better deeds tomorrow. Rest you happy! *Exeunt.*

        [Scene II. *Alexandria. Cleopatra's palace.*]

        *Enter Enobarbus, Lamprius, a Soothsayer, Ran-
        nius, Lucillius, Charmian, Iras, Mardian the
                    Eunuch, and Alexas.*

Charmian. Lord Alexas, sweet Alexas, most anything
        Alexas, almost most absolute Alexas, where's the
        soothsayer that you praised so to th' Queen? O, that
        I knew this husband, which, you say, must charge
5   his horns with garlands!°

Alexas. Soothsayer!

Soothsayer. Your will?

Charmian. Is this the man? Is't you, sir, that know
        things?

Soothsayer. In Nature's infinite book of secrecy
        A little I can read.

10 *Alexas.*   Show him your hand.

Enobarbus. Bring in the banquet° quickly: wine enough
        Cleopatra's health to drink.

Charmian. Good sir, give me good fortune.

60 *approves* corroborates   I.ii.4–5 *charge his horns with garlands*
be a blindly happy cuckold of a husband (*charge* = load; *horns* =
symbol of a cuckold; *garlands* = bridegroom's chaplet, and sign of
happy prosperity)   11 *banquet* light refreshment of fruit and wine

Soothsayer. I make not, but foresee.

Charmian. Pray then, foresee me one.　　15

Soothsayer. You shall be yet far fairer° than you are.

Charmian. He means in flesh.

Iras. No, you shall paint when you are old.

Charmian. Wrinkles forbid!

Alexas. Vex not his prescience; be attentive.　　20

Charmian. Hush!

Soothsayer. You shall be more beloving than beloved.

Charmian. I had rather heat my liver° with drinking.

Alexas. Nay, hear him.

Charmian. Good now, some excellent fortune! Let me　　25
be married to three kings in a forenoon and widow
them all; let me have a child at fifty, to whom Herod
of Jewry° may do homage; find me to marry me
with Octavius Caesar, and companion me with my
mistress.　　30

Soothsayer. You shall outlive the lady whom you
serve.

Charmian. O excellent! I love long life better than
figs.°

Soothsayer. You have seen and proved a fairer former
fortune
Than that which is to approach.　　35

Charmian. Then belike my children shall have no
names.° Prithee, how many boys and wenches must
I have?

16 *fairer* more beautiful (though in the next line Charmian pretends
to take it another way, "plumper")　23 *liver* (believed to be the
seat of sexual desire)　27–28 *Herod of Jewry* i.e., even that bluster-
ing tyrant who slaughtered the innocents of Judea　33 *figs* (phallic
allusion)　36–37 *have no names* be bastards

Soothsayer. If every of your wishes had a womb,
40 And fertile every wish, a million.

Charmian. Out, fool! I forgive thee for a witch.°

Alexas. You think none but your sheets are privy to
your wishes.

Charmian. Nay, come, tell Iras hers.

45 *Alexas.* We'll know all our fortunes.

Enobarbus. Mine, and most of our fortunes, tonight,
shall be—drunk to bed.

Iras. There's a palm presages chastity, if nothing else.

Charmian. E'en as the o'erflowing Nilus presageth
50 famine.

Iras. Go, you wild bedfellow, you cannot soothsay.

Charmian. Nay, if an oily palm° be not a fruitful prognostication,° I cannot scratch mine ear. Prithee,
tell her but a workyday° fortune.

55 *Soothsayer.* Your fortunes are alike.

Iras. But how, but how? Give me particulars.

Soothsayer. I have said.

Iras. Am I not an inch of fortune better than she?

Charmian. Well, if you were but an inch of fortune
60 better than I, where would you choose it?

Iras. Not in my husband's nose.°

Charmian. Our worser thoughts Heavens mend!
Alexas—come, his fortune, his fortune! O, let him
marry a woman that cannot go,° sweet Isis,° I

---

41 *I forgive thee for a witch* (1) you have no power of prophecy,
so I absolve you from the charge of being a witch (2) a sorcerer
like you is allowed to be outspoken 52 *oily palm* (sign of a
lascivious nature) 52–53 *fruitful prognostication* omen of fertility
54 *workyday* commonplace 61 *husband's nose* (bawdy, hence
worser thoughts in next line) 64 *go* satisfactorily copulate (?) bear
children (?) 64 *Isis* goddess of fertility and the moon

beseech thee, and let her die too, and give him a 65
worse, and let worse follow worse till the worst of
all follow him laughing to his grave, fiftyfold a
cuckold! Good Isis, hear me this prayer, though
thou deny me a matter of more weight: good Isis,
I beseech thee! 70

Iras. Amen. Dear goddess, hear that prayer of the
people! For, as it is a heartbreaking to see a handsome man loose-wived,° so it is a deadly sorrow to
behold a foul° knave uncuckolded. Therefore, dear
Isis, keep decorum,° and fortune him accordingly! 75

Charmian. Amen.

Alexas. Lo, now, if it lay in their hands to make me a
cuckold, they would make themselves whores but
they'd do't.

Enobarbus. Hush, here comes Antony.

Charmian.　　　　　　　　　　Not he, the Queen. 80

Enter Cleopatra.

Cleopatra. Saw you my lord?

Enobarbus.　　　　　　　No, lady.

Cleopatra.　　　　　　　　　　　Was he not here?

Charmian. No, madam.

Cleopatra. He was disposed to mirth; but on the sudden
A Roman thought° hath struck him. Enobarbus!

Enobarbus. Madam? 85

Cleopatra. Seek him, and bring him hither. Where's
Alexas?

Alexas. Here at your service. My lord approaches.

Enter Antony with a Messenger [and Attendants].

73 *loose-wived* with a faithless, lecherous wife　74 *foul* ugly　75
keep decorum i.e., act like a just goddess　84 *Roman thought*
(1) thought of Rome (2) serious reflection

Cleopatra. We will not look upon him. Go with us.
　　　　　Exeunt [all but Antony, Messenger, and
　　　　　　　　　　　　　　　　　Attendants].

Messenger. Fulvia thy wife first came into the field.

90　*Antony.* Against my brother Lucius?

Messenger. Ay.
　　But soon that war had end, and the time's state
　　Made friends of them, jointing their force 'gainst
　　　　Caesar,
　　Whose better issue° in the war, from Italy
　　Upon the first encounter drave them.

95　*Antony.*　　　　　　　　　　　　　Well, what worst?

Messenger. The nature of bad news infects the teller.

Antony. When it concerns the fool or coward. On.
　　Things that are past are done, with me. 'Tis thus:
　　Who tells me true, though in his tale lie death,
　　I hear him as° he flattered.

100　*Messenger.*　　　　　　　　Labienus—
　　This is stiff news—hath with his Parthian force
　　Extended° Asia: from Euphrates°
　　His conquering banner shook, from Syria
　　To Lydia and to Ionia,
　　Whilst——

Antony.　　　Antony, thou wouldst say——

105　*Messenger.*　　　　　　　　　　　　O, my lord.

Antony. Speak to me home, mince not the general
　　　　tongue:°
　　Name Cleopatra as she is called in Rome;
　　Rail thou in Fulvia's phrase, and taunt my faults
　　With such full license as both truth and malice
110　Have power to utter. O, then we bring forth weeds

---

94 *better issue* greater success　100 *as* as if　102 *Extended* seized
upon　102 *Euphrates* (accented on first syllable)　106 *Speak . . .
tongue* be blunt, don't diminish what everyone is saying

When cur quick winds° lie still, and our ills told us
Is as our earing.° Fare thee well awhile.

Messenger. At your noble pleasure.   *Exit Messenger.*

Antony. From Sicyon, ho, the news! Speak there!

First Attendant. The man from Sicyon—is there such
an one?   115

Second Attendant. He stays upon your will.°

Antony.   Let him appear.
These strong Egyptian fetters I must break
Or lose myself in dotage.

    Enter another Messenger, with a letter.

                    What are you?

Messenger. Fulvia thy wife is dead.

Antony.   Where died she?

Messenger. In Sicyon.   120
Her length of sickness, with what else more serious
Importeth thee to know, this bears.   [*Gives a letter.*]

Antony.   Forbear me.° [*Exit Messenger.*]
There's a great spirit gone! Thus did I desire it:
What our contempts doth often hurl from us,
We wish it ours again. The present pleasure,   125
By revolution low'ring,° does become
The opposite of itself: she's good, being gone;
The hand could° pluck her back that shoved her on.
I must from this enchanting° queen break off:
Ten thousand harms, more than the ills I know,   130
My idleness doth hatch. Ho now, Enobarbus!

---

111 *quick winds* lively winds (that ventilate the soil)   111–12 *our
ills . . . earing* i.e., when our faults are told to us, it is like plowing
(that makes the ground fertile)   116 *stays upon your will* awaits
your pleasure   122 *Forbear me* leave me   126 *By revolution low'r-
ing* sinking in our estimation (as the wheel of time turns and spins
the present moment downward)   128 *could* would like to   129 *enchanting* spellbinding

Enter Enobarbus.

Enobarbus. What's your pleasure, sir?

Antony. I must with haste from hence.

Enobarbus. Why, then we kill all our women. We see
135   how mortal an unkindness is to them. If they suffer
       our departure, death's the word.

Antony. I must be gone.

Enobarbus. Under a compelling occasion let women
       die.° It were pity to cast them away for nothing,
140   though between them and a great cause they should
       be esteemed nothing. Cleopatra, catching but the
       least noise of this, dies instantly; I have seen her
       die twenty times upon far poorer moment.° I do
       think there is mettle° in death, which commits some
145   loving act upon her, she hath such a celerity in
       dying.

Antony. She is cunning past man's thought.

Enobarbus. Alack, sir, no; her passions are made of
       nothing but the finest part of pure love. We cannot
150   call her winds and waters sighs and tears; they are
       greater storms and tempests than almanacs can re-
       port. This cannot be cunning in her; if it be, she
       makes a show'r of rain as well as Jove.

Antony. Would I had never seen her!

155 *Enobarbus.* O, sir, you had then left unseen a wonder-
       ful piece of work, which not to have been blest
       withal would have discredited your travel.

Antony. Fulvia is dead.

Enobarbus. Sir?

160 *Antony.* Fulvia is dead.

Enobarbus. Fulvia?

139 *die* (throughout this speech Enobarbus puns on a second meaning of *die,* "to experience sexual orgasm")   143 *moment* cause
144 *mettle* strength

Antony. Dead.

Enobarbus. Why, sir, give the gods a thankful sacrifice. When it pleaseth their deities to take the wife
of a man from him, it shows to man the tailors of   165
the earth; comforting therein, that when old robes
are worn out, there are members to make new. If
there were no more women but Fulvia, then had
you indeed a cut,° and the case to be lamented.
This grief is crowned with consolation: your old   170
smock brings forth a new petticoat, and indeed the
tears live in an onion that should water this sorrow.

Antony. The business she hath broachèd in the state
Cannot endure my absence.

Enobarbus. And the business you have broached here 175
cannot be without you; especially that of Cleopatra's, which wholly depends on your abode.°

Antony. No more light° answers. Let our° officers
Have notice what we purpose. I shall break°
The cause of our expedience° to the Queen   180
And get her leave to part. For not alone
The death of Fulvia, with more urgent touches,°
Do strongly speak to us, but the letters too
Of many our contriving friends° in Rome
Petition us at home. Sextus Pompeius   185
Hath given the dare to Caesar and commands
The empire of the sea. Our slippery people,
Whose love is never linked to the deserver
Till his deserts are past, begin to throw
Pompey the Great and all his dignities   190
Upon° his son; who, high in name and power,

169 *cut* (1) severe blow (2) pudendum (the entire speech infuses
bawdy meanings [e.g., of *tailors* and *members*] into the conceit of
the world as a tailor's shop, with the gods as tailors cutting new
clothes out of old, replacing old people with new; the tailor's shop
is where men make love and breed)   175–77 *And the business . . .
abode* (bawdy again)   178 *light* indecent   178 *our* (royal plural)
179 *break* tell   180 *expedience* (1) haste (2) expedition   182 *more
urgent touches* more pressing reasons   184 *many our contriving
friends* many who plot on my behalf   189–91 *throw . . . /Upon*
transfer . . . to

Higher than both in blood and life,° stands up
For the main soldier;° whose quality, going on,
The sides o' th' world may danger.° Much is breed-
 ing,
195 Which, like the courser's hair,° hath yet but life
And not a serpent's poison. Say our pleasure,
To such whose places under us require,
Our quick remove from hence.

Enobarbus. I shall do't.   *[Exeunt.]*

[Scene III. *Alexandria. Cleopatra's palace.*]

Enter Cleopatra, Charmian, Alexas, and Iras.

Cleopatra. Where is he?

Charmian.   I did not see him since.°

Cleopatra. See where he is, who's with him, what he
 does:
I did not send you. If you find him sad,°
Say I am dancing; if in mirth, report
5 That I am sudden sick. Quick, and return.
          [Exit Alexas.]

Charmian. Madam, methinks, if you did love him
 dearly,
You do not hold the method to enforce
The like from him.

Cleopatra.   What should I do, I do not?

192 *blood and life* courage and energy   192–93 *stands . . . soldier*
sets himself up as the greatest soldier in the world   193–94 *whose
quality . . . danger* whose character may, if his fortunes prosper,
threaten the structure of the world   195 *courser's hair* (a horse's
hair placed in water was thought to turn into a serpent)   I.iii.1 *since*
recently   3 *sad* serious

Charmian. In each thing give him way, cross him in
nothing.

Cleopatra. Thou teachest like a fool: the way to lose
him!   10

Charmian. Tempt° him not so too far. I wish, forbear.
In time we hate that which we often fear.

Enter Antony.

But here comes Antony.

Cleopatra.   I am sick and sullen.

Antony. I am sorry to give breathing° to my purpose—

Cleopatra. Help me away, dear Charmian! I shall fall.   15
It cannot be thus long; the sides of nature
Will not sustain it.°

Antony.   Now, my dearest queen—

Cleopatra. Pray you, stand farther from me.

Antony.   What's the matter?

Cleopatra. I know by that same eye there's some good
news.
What, says the married woman you may go?   20
Would she had never given you leave to come!
Let her not say 'tis I that keep you here.
I have no power upon you; hers you are.

Antony. The gods best know——

Cleopatra.   O, never was there queen
So mightily betrayed! Yet at the first
I saw the treasons planted.°   25

Antony.   Cleopatra—

Cleopatra. Why should I think you can be mine, and
true

11 *Tempt* try   14 *breathing* utterance   16–17 *the sides . . . it* the
human frame will not stand it   26 *planted* (like seeds, and like
mines)

(Though you in swearing shake the thronèd gods)
Who have been false to Fulvia? Riotous madness,
30   To be entangled with those mouth-made vows
Which break themselves in swearing.°

Antony.   Most sweet queen—

Cleopatra. Nay, pray you seek no color° for your
        going,
But bid farewell, and go. When you sued staying,°
Then was the time for words: no going then;
35   Eternity was in our lips and eyes,
Bliss in our brows' bent,° none our parts so poor
But was a race of heaven;° they are so still,
Or thou, the greatest soldier of the world,
Art turned the greatest liar.

Antony.   How now, lady?

Cleopatra. I would I had thy inches; thou shouldst
40   know
There were a heart in Egypt.°

Antony.   Hear me, Queen:
The strong necessity of time commands
Our services awhile; but my full heart
Remains in use with you.° Our Italy
45   Shines o'er with civil swords;° Sextus Pompeius
Makes his approaches to the port of Rome;
Equality of two domestic powers
Breed scrupulous faction;° the hated, grown to
        strength,
Are newly grown to love;° the condemned Pompey,
50   Rich in his father's honor, creeps apace

---

31 *Which . . . swearing* which are broken the second they are uttered
32 *color* pretext   33 *sued staying* pleaded to stay   36 *brows' bent*
eyebrows' arch   37 *a race of heaven* (1) of heavenly flavor (2) of
heavenly origin, rooted in heaven   41 *Egypt* (here, as elsewhere,
Cleopatra as well as the country)   44 *in use with you* for you to
possess   45 *civil swords* swords drawn in civil war   47–48 *Equality
. . . faction* where the rule at home is equally divided between two,
parties grow up, quarreling over tiny points   48–49 *the hated . . .
to love* the hated begin to be loved as they gain power

Into the hearts of such as have not thrived
Upon the present state, whose numbers threaten;
And quietness, grown sick of rest, would purge
By any desperate change.° My more particular,°
And that which most with you should safe my
    going,   55
Is Fulvia's death.

Cleopatra. Though age from folly could not give me
    freedom,
    It does from childishness. Can Fulvia die?

Antony. She's dead, my queen.
    Look here, and at thy sovereign leisure read
    The garboils° she awaked. At the last, best,°   60
    See when and where she died.

Cleopatra.   O most false love!
    Where be the sacred vials° thou shouldst fill
    With sorrowful water? Now I see, I see,
    In Fulvia's death, how mine received shall be.   65

Antony. Quarrel no more, but be prepared to know
    The purposes I bear; which are, or cease,
    As you shall give th' advice. By the fire
    That quickens Nilus' slime,° I go from hence
    Thy soldier-servant, making peace or war   70
    As thou affects.°

Cleopatra.   Cut my lace,° Charmian, come—
    But let it be: I am quickly ill, and well,
    So Antony loves.°

Antony.   My precious queen, forbear,

53–54 *quietness . . . change* i.e., a long peace has developed disease
in the body politic, which demands to be made well by the blood-
letting of war and revolution   54 *My more particular* my own more
personal reason   61 *garboils* commotion   61 *best* i.e., best news of
all   63 *sacred vials* (the bottles of tears supposedly placed by
Romans in friends' tombs)   68–69 *By the fire . . . slime* by the sun
that generates life in the Nile's mud   71 *affects* choosest   71 *Cut
my lace* (of her tight bodice, i.e., "Give me air")   73 *So Antony
loves* (1) if Antony loves me (2) in just such a changeable way does
Antony love me

And give true evidence to his love, which stands°
An honorable trial.

75 *Cleopatra.*   So Fulvia told me.
I prithee turn aside and weep for her;
Then bid adieu to me, and say the tears
Belong to Egypt. Good now, play one scene
Of excellent dissembling, and let it look
Like perfect honor.

80 *Antony.*   You'll heat my blood: no more.

Cleopatra. You can do better yet; but this is meetly.°

Antony. Now by my sword—

Cleopatra.   And target.° Still he mends.
But this is not the best. Look, prithee, Charmian,
How this Herculean Roman does become
The carriage of his chafe.°

85 *Antony.*   I'll leave you, lady.

Cleopatra. Courteous lord, one word.
Sir, you and I must part, but that's not it:
Sir, you and I have loved, but there's not it:
That you know well. Something it is I would—
90 O, my oblivion is a very Antony,
And I am all forgotten.°

Antony.   But that your royalty
Holds idleness your subject,° I should take you
For idleness itself.

Cleopatra.   'Tis sweating labor
To bear° such idleness so near the heart
95 As Cleopatra this. But, sir, forgive me,
Since my becomings° kill me when they do not

74 *stands* sustains   81 *meetly* suitable   82 *target* small shield   84–
85 *How this . . . his chafe* how gracefully this descendant of Hercules
acts out his rage   90–91 *my oblivion . . . forgotten* (1) my forgetful
memory is like Antony and has deserted me (2) my forgetfulness
even, like my memory, is consumed by the image of Antony, and my
mind is empty of all else   91–92 *But that . . . subject* if you were
not queen over trifling   93–94 *labor/To bear* (pun on childbirth)
96 *becomings* graces

Eye well to you. Your honor calls you hence;
Therefore be deaf to my unpitied folly,
And all the gods go with you. Upon your sword
Sit laurel victory, and smooth success   100
Be strewed before your feet!

Antony.   Let us go. Come:
Our separation so abides and flies
That thou residing here goes yet with me,
And I hence fleeting here remain with thee.
Away!   *Exeunt.* 105

[Scene IV. *Rome. Caesar's house.*]

*Enter   Octavius   [Caesar],   reading   a   letter,
Lepidus, and their Train.*

Caesar. You may see, Lepidus, and henceforth know
It is not Caesar's natural vice to hate
Our great competitor.° From Alexandria
This is the news: he fishes, drinks, and wastes
The lamps of night in revel; is not more manlike   5
Than Cleopatra, nor the queen of Ptolemy°
More womanly than he; hardly gave audience, or
Vouchsafed to think he had partners. You shall
     find there
A man who is th' abstract of all faults
That all men follow.°

Lepidus.   I must not think there are   10
Evils enow° to darken all his goodness;
His faults, in him, seem as the spots of heaven,
More fiery by night's blackness, hereditary

I.iv.3 *competitor* partner   6 *queen of Ptolemy* (Cleopatra had
nominally married her brother Ptolemy, who was only a child, at the
command of Julius Caesar)   9–10 *abstract . . . follow* symbol of
universal weakness   11 *enow* enough

Rather than purchased,° what he cannot change
15   Than what he chooses.

Caesar. You are too indulgent. Let's grant it is not
Amiss to tumble on the bed of Ptolemy,
To give a kingdom for a mirth, to sit
And keep the turn of tippling° with a slave,
20   To reel the streets at noon, and stand the buffet
With knaves that smells of sweat. Say this becomes
him
(As his composure° must be rare indeed
Whom these things cannot blemish); yet must Antony
tony
No way excuse his foils° when we do bear
25   So great weight in his lightness.° If he filled
His vacancy° with his voluptuousness,
Full surfeits and the dryness of his bones
Call on him for't.° But to confound° such time
That drums him from his sport and speaks as loud
30   As his own state and ours, 'tis to be chid
As we rate boys who, being mature in knowledge,
Pawn their experience to their present pleasure
And so rebel to judgment.°

Enter a Messenger.

Lepidus.   Here's more news.

Messenger. Thy biddings have been done, and every
hour,
35   Most noble Caesar, shalt thou have report
How 'tis abroad. Pompey is strong at sea,
And it appears he is beloved of those
That only have feared Caesar: to the ports

14 *purchased* acquired   19 *keep the turn of tippling* exchange toasts
22 *composure* character   24 *foils* stains   24–25 *when we . . . lightness* when his triviality throws such a burden on us   26 *vacancy* leisure   27–28 *Full . . . for't* let him pay the price in sickness and syphilis   28 *confound* waste   30–33 *'tis to be . . . judgment* deserves the considered rebuke we give to boys who, though old enough to know better, give up all the wisdom they have learned in exchange for a moment's pleasure

    The discontents° repair, and men's reports
    Give him° much wronged.

Caesar.   I should have known no less.   40
    It hath been taught us from the primal state°
    That he which is was wished until he were;°
    And the ebbed man, ne'er loved till ne'er worth
      love,
    Comes deared by being lacked. This common
      body,°
    Like to a vagabond flag° upon the stream,   45
    Goes to and back, lackeying the varying tide,
    To rot itself with motion.

Messenger.   Caesar, I bring thee word
    Menecrates and Menas, famous pirates,
    Makes the sea serve them, which they ear° and
      wound
    With keels of every kind. Many hot inroads   50
    They make in Italy; the borders maritime
    Lack blood to think on't, and flush° youth revolt.
    No vessel can peep forth but 'tis as soon
    Taken as seen; for Pompey's name strikes more
    Than could his war resisted.

Caesar.   Antony,   55
    Leave thy lascivious wassails.° When thou once
    Was beaten from Modena,° where thou slew'st
    Hirtius and Pansa, consuls, at thy heel
    Did famine follow, whom thou fought'st against
    (Though daintily brought up) with patience more   60
    Than savages could suffer.° Thou didst drink
    The stale° of horses and the gilded° puddle
    Which beasts would cough at. Thy palate then did
      deign°

---

39 *discontents* malcontents   40 *Give him* say he is   41 *from the
primal state* since government began   42 *That he . . . were* that a
man in power had supporters until he gained power   44 *common
body* populace   45 *vagabond flag* aimlessly drifting iris   49 *ear*
plow   52 *flush* vigorous, lusty   56 *wassails* revelry   57 *Modena*
(accented on second syllable)   61 *suffer* summon up   62 *stale*
urine   62 *gilded* i.e., yellow with scum   63 *deign* not disdain

The roughest berry on the rudest hedge.
65 Yea, like the stag when snow the pasture sheets,
The barks of trees thou browsed. On the Alps
It is reported thou didst eat strange flesh,
Which some did die to look on. And all this
(It wounds thine honor that I speak it now)
70 Was borne so like a soldier that thy cheek
So much as lanked° not.

Lepidus.   'Tis pity of him.

Caesar. Let his shames quickly
Drive him to Rome. 'Tis time we twain
Did show ourselves i' th' field; and to that end
75 Assemble we immediate council. Pompey
Thrives in our idleness.

Lepidus.   Tomorrow, Caesar,
I shall be furnished to inform you rightly
Both what by sea and land I can be able°
To front° this present time.

Caesar.   Till which encounter,
80 It is my business too. Farewell.

Lepidus. Farewell, my lord. What you shall know
       meantime
Of stirs abroad, I shall beseech you, sir,
To let me be partaker.

Caesar.   Doubt not, sir;
I knew it for my bond.°   *Exeunt.*

71 *lanked* thinned   **78** *I can be able* my powers can be   **79** *front*
confront   **84** *bond* duty

[Scene V. *Alexandria. Cleopatra's palace.*]

Enter Cleopatra, Charmian, Iras, and Mardian.

Cleopatra. Charmian!

Charmian. Madam?

Cleopatra. [*Yawning*] Ha, ha.
  Give me to drink mandragora.°

Charmian.   Why, madam?

Cleopatra. That I might sleep out this great gap of time   5
  My Antony is away.

Charmian.   You think of him too much.

Cleopatra. O, 'tis treason!

Charmian.   Madam, I trust, not so.

Cleopatra. Thou, eunuch Mardian!

Mardian.   What's your Highness' pleasure?

Cleopatra. Not now to hear thee sing. I take no
    pleasure
  In aught an eunuch has: 'tis well for thee   10
  That, being unseminared,° thy freer thoughts
  May not fly forth of Egypt. Hast thou affections?°

Mardian. Yes, gracious madam.

Cleopatra. Indeed?

Mardian. Not in deed, madam; for I can do nothing   15
  But what indeed is honest° to be done:

I.v.4 *mandragora* mandrake (a strong narcotic)   11 *unseminared*
unsexed   12 *affections* passions   16 *honest* chaste

Yet have I fierce affections, and think
What Venus did with Mars.°

Cleopatra.   O, Charmian,
Where think'st thou he is now? Stands he, or sits he?
Or does he walk? Or is he on his horse?
O happy horse, to bear the weight of Antony!
Do bravely, horse, for wot'st° thou whom thou
      mov'st?
The demi-Atlas° of this earth, the arm
And burgonet° of men. He's speaking now,
Or murmuring, "Where's my serpent of old Nile?"
(For so he calls me.) Now I feed myself
With most delicious poison. Think on me,
That am with Phoebus'° amorous pinches black
And wrinkled deep in time. Broad-fronted Caesar,°
When thou wast here above the ground, I was
A morsel for a monarch; and great Pompey°
Would stand and make his eyes grow in my brow;
There would he anchor his aspect,° and die
With looking on his life.

Enter Alexas from Antony.

Alexas.   Sovereign of Egypt, hail!

Cleopatra. How much unlike art thou Mark Antony!
Yet, coming from him, that great med'cine hath
With his tinct gilded thee.°
How goes it with my brave Mark Antony?

Alexas. Last thing he did, dear Queen,
He kissed—the last of many doubled kisses—
This orient° pearl. His speech sticks in my heart.

18 *Venus . . . Mars* (Venus, goddess of love, and Mars, god of war,
were lovers)   22 *wot'st* knowest   23 *demi-Atlas* (the Titan Atlas
supported the heavens on his shoulders)   24 *burgonet* visored
helmet   28 *Phoebus'* the sun's   29 *Broad-fronted Caesar* wide-
browed Caesar (i.e., Julius Caesar, whose mistress she had been
in youth)   31 *great Pompey* Cneius Pompeius (son of Pompey the
Great)   33 *aspect* gaze (accented on second syllable)   36–37 *that
great med'cine . . . thee* (alchemists long tried to make or discover
the "philosopher's stone" or *elixir vitae*—known as the "great medi-
cine" and the "tincture"—which had the property of turning base
metals to gold, and of restoring youth)   41 *orient* eastern, bright

Cleopatra. Mine ear must pluck it thence.

Alexas.   "Good friend," quoth he,
"Say the firm° Roman to great Egypt sends
This treasure of an oyster; at whose foot,
To mend the petty present, I will piece°   45
Her opulent throne with kingdoms. All the East
(Say thou) shall call her mistress." So he nodded,
And soberly did mount an arm-gaunt° steed,
Who neighed so high that what I would have spoke
Was beastly dumbed° by him.

Cleopatra.   What was he, sad or merry?   50

Alexas. Like to the time o' th' year between the ex-
        tremes
    Of hot and cold, he was nor sad nor merry.

Cleopatra. O well-divided disposition!° Note him,
    Note him, good Charmian, 'tis the man;° but note
        him.
    He was not sad, for he would shine on those   55
    That make their looks by his; he was not merry,
    Which seemed to tell them his remembrance lay
    In Egypt with his joy; but between both.
    O heavenly mingle! Be'st thou sad or merry,
    The violence of either thee becomes,   60
    So does it no man else. —Met'st thou my posts?°

Alexas. Ay, madam, twenty several° messengers.
    Why do you send so thick?

Cleopatra.   Who's born that day
    When I forget to send to Antony
    Shall die a beggar. Ink and paper, Charmian.   65
    Welcome, my good Alexas. Did I, Charmian,
    Ever love Caesar so?

Charmian.   O, that brave° Caesar!

---

43 *firm* constant   45 *piece* add to   48 *arm-gaunt* battle-worn (?)
battle-hungry (?)   50 *beastly dumbed* silenced by a beast   53 *disposition* temperament   54 *'tis the man* that's exactly what he is like
61 *posts* messengers   62 *several* separate   67 *brave* splendid, fine

Cleopatra. Be choked with such another emphasis!°
Say "the brave Antony."

Charmian.   The valiant Caesar!

70 *Cleopatra.* By Isis, I will give thee bloody teeth
If thou with Caesar paragon° again
My man of men.

Charmian.   By your most gracious pardon,
I sing but after you.

Cleopatra.   My salad days,
When I was green° in judgment, cold in blood,
75 To say as I said then. But come, away,
Get me ink and paper.
He shall have every day a several greeting,
Or I'll unpeople Egypt.   *Exeunt.*

---

68 *emphasis* forceful statement   71 *paragon* compare   74 *green*
young, silly

[ACT II

Scene I. *Messina. Pompey's house.*]

*Enter Pompey, Menecrates, and Menas, in war-
like manner.*

Pompey. If the great gods be just, they shall° assist
The deeds of justest men.

Menecrates.   Know, worthy Pompey,
That what they do delay, they not deny.°

Pompey. Whiles we are suitors to their throne, decays
The thing we sue° for.

Menecrates.   We, ignorant of ourselves   5
Beg often our own harms, which the wise pow'rs
Deny us for our good; so find we profit
By losing of our prayers.

Pompey.   I shall do well:
The people love me, and the sea is mine;
My powers are crescent,° and my auguring° hope   10

II.i.1 *shall* surely must   3 *what they . . . deny* i.e., delay in perform-
ing does not necessarily imply a refusal   5 *sue* beg   10 *crescent*
growing (i.e., waxing like the moon—hence the following image)
10 *auguring* prophesying

Says it will come to th' full. Mark Antony
In Egypt sits at dinner, and will make
No wars without doors.° Caesar gets money where
He loses hearts. Lepidus flatters both,
15   Of both is flattered, but he neither loves,
Nor either cares for him.

Menas.   Caesar and Lepidus
Are in the field;° a mighty strength they carry.

Pompey. Where have you this? 'Tis false.

Menas.   From Silvius, sir.

Pompey. He dreams: I know they are in Rome to-
    gether,
20   Looking for Antony. But all the charms° of love,
Salt° Cleopatra, soften thy waned° lip!
Let witchcraft join with beauty, lust with both!
Tie up the libertine in a field of feasts,
Keep his brain fuming. Epicurean cooks
25   Sharpen with cloyless sauce his appetite,
That sleep and feeding may prorogue° his honor
Even till a Lethe'd° dullness—

                    Enter Varrius.

                              How now, Varrius?

Varrius. This is most certain, that I shall deliver:
Mark Antony is every hour in Rome
30   Expected. Since he went from Egypt 'tis
A space for farther travel.°

Pompey.   I could have given less matter
A better ear. Menas, I did not think
This amorous surfeiter would have donned his helm
For such a petty war. His soldiership

---

13 *without doors* out-of-doors (contrasted with the indoor "wars" of love)   17 *in the field* ready for battle   20 *charms* spells   21 *Salt* lustful   21 *waned* pale and thin (like the old moon)   26 *prorogue* suspend   27 *Lethe'd* oblivious (from Lethe, a river in Hades; those who drank of the water forgot all)   30–31 *'tis . . . travel* there has been time for an even longer journey

Is twice the other twain; but let us rear   35
The higher our opinion,° that our stirring
Can from the lap of Egypt's widow pluck
The ne'er-lust-wearied Antony.

Menas.   I cannot hope°
Caesar and Antony shall well greet° together;
His wife that's dead did trespasses to Caesar;   40
His brother warred upon him—although I think
Not moved° by Antony.

Pompey.   I know not, Menas,
How lesser enmities may give way to greater.
Were't not that we stand up against them all,
'Twere pregnant they should square between them-
    selves,°
                                                              45
For they have entertainèd cause enough
To draw their swords; but how the fear of us
May cement° their divisions and bind up
The petty difference, we yet not know.
Be't as our gods will have't! It only stands   50
Our lives upon,° to use our strongest hands.
Come, Menas.   *Exeunt.*

[Scene II. *Rome. Lepidus' house.*]

Enter Enobarbus and Lepidus.

Lepidus. Good Enobarbus, 'tis a worthy deed,
And shall become you well, to entreat your captain
To soft and gentle speech.

Enobarbus.   I shall entreat him

35–36 *let us . . . opinion* let us think all the better of ourselves
38 *hope* believe   39 *well greet* meet amiably   42 *moved* encouraged
44–45 *Were't not . . . themselves* had we not challenged them (and
thus united them) they would probably have quarreled among themselves   48 *cement* (accented on first syllable)   50–51 *It only . . .
upon* only, it is a matter of life and death to us all

To answer like himself: if Caesar move° him,
5 Let Antony look over Caesar's head
And speak as loud as Mars. By Jupiter,
Were I the wearer of Antonio's beard,
I would not shave't today!°

Lepidus.   'Tis not a time
For private stomaching.°

Enobarbus.   Every time
10 Serves for the matter that is then born in't.

Lepidus. But small to greater matters must give way.

Enobarbus. Not if the small come first.

Lepidus.   Your speech is passion;
But pray you stir no embers up. Here comes
The noble Antony.

      Enter Antony and Ventidius [in conversation].

Enobarbus.   And yonder, Caesar.

      Enter [from the other side] Caesar, Maecenas,
            and Agrippa [in conversation].

15 *Antony.* If we compose° well here, to Parthia.
Hark, Ventidius.

Caesar.   I do not know,
Maecenas; ask Agrippa.

Lepidus.   Noble friends,
That which combined us was most great, and let not
A leaner action rend us. What's amiss,
20 May it be gently heard. When we debate
Our trivial difference loud, we do commit
Murder in healing wounds. Then, noble partners,
The rather for I earnestly beseech,

II.ii.4 *move* irritate   8 *I would not shave't today* (1) I would not
do him the courtesy of clean-shaving (2) I would not remove the
temptation of plucking it (an incitement to fight)   9 *private stomaching* personal resentment   15 *compose* come to an agreement

Touch you the sourest points with sweetest terms,
Nor curstness grow to th' matter.°

Antony.   'Tis spoken well.   25
Were we before our armies, and to fight,
I should do thus.°
                                              Flourish.

Caesar. Welcome to Rome.

Antony. Thank you.

Caesar. Sit.
                                                                 30

Antony. Sit, sir.

Caesar. Nay then.   [*They sit.*]

Antony. I learn you take things ill which are not so,
Or being, concern you not.

Caesar.   I must be laughed at
If, or for nothing or° a little, I   35
Should say myself offended, and with you
Chiefly i' th' world; more laughed at that I should
Once name you derogately,° when to sound your
    name
It not concerned me.

Antony.   My being in Egypt, Caesar,
What was't to you?
                                                                 40

Caesar. No more than my residing here at Rome
Might be to you in Egypt: yet if you there
Did practice on my state,° your being in Egypt
Might be my question.

Antony.   How intend you? Practiced?

Caesar. You may be pleased to catch at mine intent   45
By what did here befall me. Your wife and brother

---

25 *Nor . . . matter* and do not let ill temper be added to the problem
at hand   27 *thus* (perhaps Antony embraces Caesar, but perhaps
he means his words would be temperate in any circumstance)
35 *or . . . or* either . . . or   38 *derogately* disparagingly   43 *practice
on my state* plot against my rule

Made wars upon me, and their contestation
Was theme for you;° you were the word of war.°

Antony. You do mistake your business: my brother never

50 Did urge me° in his act. I did inquire it
And have my learning from some true reports°
That drew their swords with you. Did he not rather
Discredit my authority with yours,
And make the wars alike against my stomach,°

55 Having alike your cause? Of this, my letters
Before did satisfy you. If you'll patch a quarrel,
As matter whole you have to make it with,°
It must not be with this.

Caesar.   You praise yourself
By laying defects of judgment to me, but
You patched up your excuses.

60 *Antony.*   Not so, not so:
I know you could not lack, I am certain on't,
Very necessity of this thought, that I,
Your partner in the cause 'gainst which he fought,
Could not with graceful eyes attend° those wars

65 Which fronted° mine own peace. As for my wife,
I would you had her spirit in such another;°
The third o' th' world is yours, which with a snaffle
You may pace° easy, but not such a wife.

Enobarbus. Would we had all such wives, that the men
70 might go to wars with the women.

Antony. So much uncurbable, her garboils, Caesar,
Made out of her impatience—which not wanted
Shrewdness of policy too—I grieving grant

---

48 *Was theme for you* had you as root cause (?) provided you with
a pretext (?)   48 *you were the word of war* the war was about you
50 *Did urge me* made use of my name   51 *reports* reporters   54
stomach desire   56–57 *If you'll . . . with* if you want to fabricate
a quarrel out of odds and ends, though in fact you have more substantial materials for one   64 *with graceful eyes attend* look favor-
ably on   65 *fronted* attacked   66 *I would . . . another* I wish you
were married to just such a wife   68 *pace* train (used of horses)

Did you too much disquiet: for that you must
But° say, I could not help it.

Caesar.   I wrote to you;   75
When rioting in Alexandria you
Did pocket up my letters, and with taunts
Did gibe my missive° out of audience.

Antony.   Sir,
He fell upon me, ere admitted, then:
Three kings I had newly feasted, and did want   80
Of what I was i' th' morning; but next day
I told him of myself,° which was as much
As to have asked him pardon. Let this fellow
Be nothing of° our strife: if we contend,
Out of our question wipe him.

Caesar.   You have broken   85
The article° of your oath, which you shall never
Have tongue to charge me with.

Lepidus.   Soft,° Caesar!

Antony.   No,
Lepidus; let him speak.
The honor is sacred which he talks on now,
Supposing that I lacked it. But on, Caesar,
The article of my oath—   90

Caesar. To lend me arms and aid when I required
     them,
The which you both denied.

Antony.   Neglected rather:
And then when poisonèd hours had bound me up
From mine own knowledge. As nearly as I may,   95
I'll play the penitent to you: but mine honesty
Shall not make poor my greatness, nor my power
Work without it.° Truth is, that Fulvia,
To have me out of Egypt, made wars here,
For which myself, the ignorant motive, do   100

75 *But* only   78 *missive* messenger   82 *myself* my condition   84 *Be nothing of* have no place in   86 *article* precise terms   87 *Soft* be careful   98 *it* honesty (?)

So far ask pardon as befits mine honor
To stoop in such a case.

Lepidus.   'Tis noble spoken.

Maecenas. If it might please you, to enforce no further
The griefs° between ye: to forget them quite
105 Were to remember that the present need
Speaks to atone you.°

Lepidus.   Worthily spoken, Maecenas.

Enobarbus. Or, if you borrow one another's love for
the instant, you may, when you hear no more words
of Pompey, return it again: you shall have time to
110 wrangle in when you have nothing else to do.

Antony. Thou art a soldier only; speak no more.

Enobarbus. That truth should be silent I had almost
forgot.

Antony. You wrong this presence;° therefore speak no
more.

115 *Enobarbus.* Go to, then; your considerate stone.°

Caesar. I do not much dislike the matter, but
The manner of his speech; for't cannot be
We shall remain in friendship, our conditions°
So diff'ring in their acts. Yet if I knew
120 What hoop should hold us stanch, from edge to edge
O' th' world I would pursue it.

Agrippa.   Give me leave, Caesar.

Caesar. Speak, Agrippa.

Agrippa. Thou hast a sister by the mother's side,°
Admired Octavia: great Mark Antony
Is now a widower.

---

104 *griefs* grievances   106 *Speaks to atone you* demands your reconciliation   114 *presence* dignified company   115 *your considerate
stone* I will be silent as stone about what I am thinking   118 *conditions* temperaments   123 *by the mother's side* i.e., half sister (though
actually Octavia was a full sister of Octavius)

Caesar.   Say not so, Agrippa: 125
  If Cleopatra heard you, your reproof
  Were well deserved of rashness.°

Antony. I am not married, Caesar: let me hear
  Agrippa further speak.

Agrippa. To hold you in perpetual amity,   130
  To make you brothers, and to knit your hearts
  With an unslipping knot, take Antony
  Octavia to his wife; whose beauty claims
  No worse a husband than the best of men;
  Whose virtue and whose general graces speak   135
  That which none else can utter. By this marriage
  All little jealousies,° which now seem great,
  And all great fears, which now import° their
    dangers,
  Would then be nothing: truths would be tales,
  Where now half-tales be truths:° her love to both   140
  Would each to other, and all loves to both,
  Draw after her. Pardon what I have spoke;
  For 'tis a studied, not a present° thought,
  By duty ruminated.

Antony.   Will Caesar speak?

Caesar. Not till he hears how Antony is touched°   145
  With what is spoke already.

Antony.   What power is in Agrippa,
  If I would say, "Agrippa, be it so,"
  To make this good?

Caesar.   The power of Caesar, and
  His power unto Octavia.

Antony.   May I never
  To this good purpose, that so fairly shows,   150
  Dream of impediment! Let me have thy hand.

126–27 *your reproof . . . rashness* you would get a deserved reproof
for being foolhardy 137 *jealousies* suspicions 138 *import* bring
139–40 *truths would . . . truths* things true would be disbelieved,
whereas now half-truths are believed 143 *present* momentary
145 *touched* affected

Further this act of grace,° and from this hour
The heart of brothers govern in our loves
And sway our great designs.

Caesar.   There's my hand.
155 A sister I bequeath you, whom no brother
Did ever love so dearly. Let her live
To join our kingdoms and our hearts; and never
Fly off our loves° again.

Lepidus.   Happily, amen.

Antony. I did not think to draw my sword 'gainst
       Pompey,
160 For he hath laid strange courtesies and great
Of late upon me. I must thank him only,
Lest my remembrance° suffer ill report:
At heel of that,° defy him.

Lepidus.   Time calls upon's.
Of us must Pompey presently° be sought,
Or else he seeks out us.

165 *Antony*.   Where lies he?

Caesar. About the Mount Mesena.°

Antony. What is his strength by land?

Caesar. Great and increasing; but by sea
He is an absolute master.

Antony.   So is the fame.°
170 Would we had spoke together! Haste we for it,
Yet, ere we put ourselves in arms, dispatch we
The business we have talked of.

Caesar.   With most gladness;
And do invite you to my sister's view,
Whither straight I'll lead you.

---

152 *grace* reconciliation 158 *Fly off our loves* may our love for
each other desert us 162 *remembrance* memory (of kindnesses
done) 163 *At heel of that* immediately after 164 *presently* at
once 166 *Mesena* Misenum, an Italian port 169 *fame* report

Antony.   Let us, Lepidus,
Not lack your company.

Lepidus.   Noble Antony,   175
Not sickness should detain me.

                              Flourish. Exit [all but]
                              Enobarbus, Agrippa, Maecenas.

Maecenas. Welcome from Egypt, sir.

Enobarbus. Half the heart° of Caesar, worthy Maecenas. My honorable friend, Agrippa.

Agrippa. Good Enobarbus.   180

Maecenas. We have cause to be glad that matters are
so well disgested.° You stayed well by't° in Egypt.

Enobarbus. Ay, sir, we did sleep day out of counte-
nance° and made the night light with drinking.

Maecenas. Eight wild boars roasted whole at a break-   185
fast, and but twelve persons there; is this true?

Enobarbus. This was but as a fly by° an eagle: we
had much more monstrous matter of feast, which
worthily deserved noting.

Maecenas. She's a most triumphant lady, if report be   190
square° to her.

Enobarbus. When she first met Mark Antony, she
pursed up° his heart, upon the river of Cydnus.

Agrippa. There she appeared indeed; or my reporter
devised° well for her.   195

Enobarbus. I will tell you.
The barge she sat in, like a burnished throne,
Burned on the water: the poop was beaten gold;
Purple the sails, and so perfumèd that

---

178 *Half the heart* dear friend (though possibly the idea is that
Caesar is equally devoted to Agrippa and to Maecenas)   182 *disgested* digested   182 *stayed well by't* "lived it up"   183–84 *we did
. . . countenance* we disconcerted the day by sleeping through it
187 *by* compared with   191 *square* just, true   193 *pursed up* put
in her purse, took possession of   195 *devised* invented

The winds were lovesick with them; the oars were
200   silver,
Which to the tune of flutes kept stroke and made
The water which they beat to follow faster,
As amorous of their strokes. For her own person,
It beggared all description: she did lie
205   In her pavilion, cloth-of-gold of tissue,°
O'erpicturing that Venus where we see
The fancy outwork nature:° on each side her
Stood pretty dimpled boys, like smiling Cupids,
With divers-colored fans, whose wind did seem
210   To glow the delicate cheeks which they did cool,
And what they undid did.°

Agrippa.   O, rare for Antony.

Enobarbus. Her gentlewomen, like the Nereides,°
So many mermaids, tended her i' th' eyes,
And made their bends adornings.° At the helm
215   A seeming mermaid steers: the silken tackle
Swell with the touches of those flower-soft hands,
That yarely frame the office.° From the barge
A strange invisible perfume hits the sense
Of the adjacent wharfs.° The city cast
220   Her people out upon her; and Antony,
Enthroned i' th' marketplace, did sit alone,
Whistling to th' air; which, but for vacancy,°
Had gone to gaze on Cleopatra too,
And made a gap in nature.

Agrippa.   Rare Egyptian!

225 *Enobarbus.* Upon her landing, Antony sent to her,
Invited her to supper. She replied,

---

205 *cloth-of-gold of tissue* a rich fabric interwoven with gold threads
206–07 *O'erpicturing . . . nature* surpassing that painting of Venus
where we can see the imagination excelling nature itself in creative
ability   211 *And . . . did* i.e., and seemed to produce the warm
color they were cooling   212 *Nereides* sea nymphs   213–14 *tended
. . . adornings* stood before her and waited on her, their bowing
movements being works of art in themselves   217 *yarely frame the
office* deftly perform the task   219 *wharfs* banks   222 *but for
vacancy* i.e., but for the law that nature abhors a vacuum

It should be better he became her guest;
Which she entreated. Our courteous Antony,
Whom ne'er the word of "No" woman heard speak,
Being barbered ten times o'er, goes to the feast,   230
And, for his ordinary,° pays his heart
For what his eyes eat only.

Agrippa.   Royal wench!
She made great Caesar lay his sword to bed;
He plowed her, and she cropped.°

Enobarbus.   I saw her once
Hop forty paces through the public street;   235
And having lost her breath, she spoke, and panted,
That° she did make defect perfection,
And, breathless, pow'r breathe forth.

Maecenas. Now Antony must leave her utterly.

Enobarbus. Never; he will not: 240
Age cannot wither her, nor custom stale
Her infinite variety: other women cloy
The appetites they feed, but she makes hungry
Where most she satisfies; for vilest things
Become themselves° in her, that the holy priests   245
Bless her when she is riggish.°

Maecenas. If beauty, wisdom, modesty, can settle
The heart of Antony, Octavia is
A blessèd lottery° to him.

Agrippa.   Let us go.
Good Enobarbus, make yourself my guest   250
Whilst you abide here.

Enobarbus.   Humbly, sir, I thank you. *Exeunt.*

231 *ordinary* public dinner in a tavern   234 *she cropped* i.e., had a
child (Caesarion)   237 *That* so that   245 *Become themselves* are
becoming   246 *riggish* wanton   249 *lottery* allotment

[Scene III. *Rome. Caesar's house.*]

Enter Antony, Caesar, Octavia between them.

Antony. The world and my great office will sometimes
    Divide me from your bosom.

Octavia.   All which time
    Before the gods my knee shall bow my prayers
    To them for you.

Antony.   Good night, sir. My Octavia,
5   Read not my blemishes in the world's report:
    I have not kept my square,° but that to come
    Shall all be done by th' rule. Good night, dear lady.
    Good night, sir.

Caesar. Good night.   *Exit* [*with Octavia*].

Enter Soothsayer.

10 *Antony*. Now, sirrah: you do wish yourself in Egypt?

Soothsayer. Would I had never come from thence, nor
    you thither.

Antony. If you can, your reason?

Soothsayer. I see it in my motion,° have it not in my
15   tongue, but yet hie you to Egypt again.

Antony. Say to me, whose fortunes shall rise higher,
    Caesar's, or mine?

Soothsayer. Caesar's.
    Therefore, O Antony, stay not by his side.
20   Thy daemon,° that thy spirit which keeps thee, is

II.iii.6 *kept my square* kept straight   14 *motion* mind   20 *daemon*
guardian angel

Noble, courageous, high, unmatchable,
Where Caesar's is not. But near him thy angel
Becomes afeard, as being o'erpow'red: therefore
Make space enough between you.

Antony.   Speak this no more.

Soothsayer. To none but thee; no more but when to
    thee.   25
If thou dost play with him at any game,
Thou art sure to lose; and of° that natural luck
He beats thee 'gainst the odds. Thy luster thickens°
When he shines by: I say again, thy spirit
Is all afraid to govern thee near him;   30
But he away, 'tis noble.

Antony.   Get thee gone.
Say to Ventidius I would speak with him.

                  Exit [*Soothsayer*].
He shall to Parthia. Be it art or hap,°
He hath spoken true. The very dice obey him,
And in our sports my better cunning faints
Under his chance:° if we draw lots, he speeds;°   35
His cocks do win the battle still° of mine
When it is all to naught,° and his quails ever
Beat mine, inhooped,° at odds. I will to Egypt:
And though I make this marriage for my peace,
I' th' East my pleasure lies.   40

           Enter Ventidius.

            O, come, Ventidius,
You must to Parthia. Your commission's ready:
Follow me, and receive't.   *Exeunt.*

---

27 *of* by   28 *thickens* dims   33 *art or hap* skill or chance   36
chance luck   36 *speeds* is successful   37 *still* always   38 *it is all
to naught* the odds are all to nothing (against him)   39 *inhooped*
confined within a ring

[Scene IV. *Rome. A street.*]

Enter Lepidus, Maecenas, and Agrippa.

Lepidus. Trouble yourselves no further: pray you, hasten
   Your generals after.

Agrippa.   Sir, Mark Antony
   Will e'en but kiss Octavia, and we'll follow.

Lepidus. Till I shall see you in your soldier's dress,
   Which will become you both, farewell.

5 *Maecenas.*   We shall,
   As I conceive° the journey, be at Mount°
   Before you, Lepidus.

Lepidus.   Your way is shorter;
   My purposes do draw me much about:°
   You'll win two days upon me.

Both.   Sir, good success.

10 *Lepidus.* Farewell.   *Exeunt.*

II.iv.6 *conceive* understand   6 *Mount* i.e., Misenum   8 *My purposes . . . about* my plans take me the long way around

[Scene V. *Alexandria. Cleopatra's palace.*]

Enter Cleopatra, Charmian, Iras, and Alexas.

Cleopatra. Give me some music: music, moody° food
   Of us that trade in love.

Omnes.°   The music, ho!

Enter Mardian the Eunuch.

Cleopatra. Let it alone, let's to billiards: come, Charmian.

Charmian. My arm is sore; best play with Mardian.

Cleopatra. As well a woman with an eunuch played   5
   As with a woman. Come, you'll play with me, sir?

Mardian. As well as I can, madam.

Cleopatra. And when good will is showed, though't
      come too short,
   The actor may plead pardon. I'll none now.
   Give me mine angle,° we'll to th' river: there,   10
   My music playing far off, I will betray
   Tawny-finned fishes. My bended hook shall pierce
   Their slimy jaws; and as I draw them up,
   I'll think them every one an Antony,
   And say, "Ah, ha! y' are caught!"

Charmian.   'Twas merry when   15
   You wagered on your angling, when your diver
   Did hang a salt° fish on his hook, which he
   With fervency drew up.

II.v.1 *moody* melancholy (with pun on musical "mood" or key)
2 *Omnes* all (Latin)   10 *angle* fishing tackle   17 *salt* dried

Cleopatra.   That time—O times!—
I laughed him out of patience; and that night
20 I laughed him into patience; and next morn,
Ere the ninth hour, I drunk him to his bed;
Then put my tires° and mantles on him, whilst
I wore his sword Philippan.°

Enter a Messenger.

O, from Italy!
Ram thou thy fruitful tidings in mine ears,
That long time have been barren.

25 *Messenger.*   Madam, madam—

Cleopatra. Antonio's dead! If thou say so, villain,
Thou kill'st thy mistress: but well and free,
If thou so yield him. There is gold and here
My bluest veins to kiss, a hand that kings
30 Have lipped, and trembled kissing.

Messenger. First, madam, he is well.

Cleopatra.   Why, there's more gold.
But, sirrah, mark, we use
To say the dead are well:° bring it to that,
The gold I give thee will I melt and pour
35 Down thy ill-uttering throat.

Messenger. Good madam, hear me.

Cleopatra.   Well, go to, I will:
But there's no goodness in thy face if Antony
Be free and healthful; so tart a favor°
To trumpet such good tidings? If not well,
Thou shouldst come like a Fury crowned with
40   snakes,
Not like a formal° man.

Messenger.   Will't please you hear me?

22. *tires* headdresses   23 *Philippan* (Antony's sword is named after
Philippi, where he conquered Brutus and Cassius)   33 *well* i.e.,
in having gone to heaven   38 *tart a favor* sour an expression   41
formal (1) sane (2) normally shaped

Cleopatra. I have a mind to strike thee ere thou
 speak'st:
 Yet, if thou say Antony lives, is well,
 Or friends with Caesar, or not captive to him,
 I'll set thee in a shower of gold, and hail   *45*
 Rich pearls upon thee.

Messenger.   Madam, he's well.

Cleopatra.   Well said.

Messenger. And friends with Caesar.

Cleopatra.   Th' art an honest man.

Messenger. Caesar and he are greater friends than
 ever.

Cleopatra. Make thee a fortune from me.

Messenger.   But yet, madam—

Cleopatra. I do not like "But yet"; it does allay   *50*
 The good precedence:° fie upon "But yet";
 "But yet" is as a jailer to bring forth
 Some monstrous malefactor. Prithee, friend,
 Pour out the pack of matter to mine ear,
 The good and bad together: he's friends with
  Caesar,
 In state of health, thou say'st, and thou say'st, free.   *55*

Messenger. Free, madam, no: I made no such report;
 He's bound unto Octavia.

Cleopatra.   For what good turn?°

Messenger. For the best turn i' th' bed.

Cleopatra.   I am pale, Charmian.

Messenger. Madam, he's married to Octavia.   *60*

Cleopatra. The most infectious pestilence upon thee!
          Strikes him down.

50–51 *allay/The good precedence* qualify the good news before it
58 *For what good turn* (she takes his *bound* in the sense "indebted
to"; he then takes up her *turn*, or "act," in a sexual sense)

Messenger. Good madam, patience.

Cleopatra.   What say you?
                                     Strikes him.
                                             Hence,

Horrible villain! Or I'll spurn° thine eyes
Like balls before me: I'll unhair thy head,
                    She hales him up and down.
65   Thou shalt be whipped with wire and stewed in
      brine,
      Smarting in ling'ring pickle.°

Messenger.   Gracious madam,
I that do bring the news made not the match.

Cleopatra. Say 'tis not so, a province I will give thee,
And make thy fortunes proud: the blow thou hadst
70   Shall make thy peace for moving me to rage,
      And I will boot thee° with what gift beside
      Thy modesty° can beg.

Messenger.   He's married, madam.

Cleopatra. Rogue, thou hast lived too long.
                              Draw a knife.

Messenger.   Nay, then I'll run.
What mean you, madam? I have made no fault.
                                             Exit.

Charmian. Good madam, keep yourself within your-
75   self,
      The man is innocent.

Cleopatra. Some innocents 'scape not the thunderbolt.
Melt Egypt into Nile, and kindly creatures
Turn all to serpents! Call the slave again:
80   Though I am mad, I will not bite him. Call!

Charmian. He is afeard to come.

Cleopatra.   I will not hurt him.
                              [*Exit Charmian.*]

63 *spurn* kick   66 *pickle* pickling solution (of painful salt or acid)
71 *boot thee* compensate you   72 *modesty* humble rank

These hands do lack nobility, that they strike
A meaner than myself; since I myself
Have given myself the cause.°

Enter [Charmian and] the Messenger again.

                         Come hither, sir.
Though it be honest, it is never good   85
To bring bad news: give to a gracious message
An host of tongues, but let ill tidings tell
Themselves, when they be felt.

Messenger.   I have done my duty.

Cleopatra. Is he married?
I cannot hate thee worser than I do   90
If thou again say "Yes."

Messenger.   He's married, madam.

Cleopatra. The gods confound° thee! Dost thou hold
   there still?

Messenger. Should I lie, madam?

Cleopatra.   O, I would thou didst,
So° half my Egypt were submerged and made
A cistern for scaled snakes! Go get thee hence;   95
Hadst thou Narcissus in thy face,° to me
Thou wouldst appear most ugly. He is married?

Messenger. I crave your Highness' pardon.

Cleopatra.   He is married?

Messenger. Take no offense that I would not offend
   you:°
To punish me for what you make me do   100
Seems much unequal:° he's married to Octavia.

Cleopatra. O, that his fault should make a knave of
   thee,

---

84 *the cause* i.e., by loving Antony   92 *confound* destroy   94 *So*
even if   96 *Hadst . . . face* even if you were as handsome as
Narcissus (Greek youth of great beauty)   99 *Take . . . offend you*
do not be angry at me for hesitating to tell you what I know will
anger you   101 *unequal* unjust

That art not what th' art sure of!° Get thee hence,
The merchandise which thou hast brought from
   Rome
105 Are all too dear for me. Lie they upon thy hand,
And be undone° by 'em!   [*Exit Messenger.*]

Charmian.   Good your Highness, patience.

Cleopatra. In praising Antony I have dispraised
   Caesar.

Charmian. Many times, madam.

Cleopatra.   I am paid for't now.
Lead me from hence;
110 I faint. O, Iras, Charmian! 'Tis no matter.
Go to the fellow, good Alexas; bid him
Report the feature° of Octavia: her years,
Her inclination,° let him not leave out
The color of her hair. Bring me word quickly.
                              [*Exit Alexas.*]
115 Let him forever go!—let him not!—Charmian,
Though he be painted one way like a Gorgon,
The other way's a Mars.° [*To Mardian*] Bid you
   Alexas
Bring me word how tall she is. —Pity me, Char-
   mian,
But do not speak to me. Lead me to my chamber.
                              Exeunt.

103 *That art . . . sure of* who are not really as wicked as the news
you insist on   106 *undone* bankrupted   112 *feature* appearance
(not limited to facial characteristics)   113 *inclination* character
116–17 *Though he . . . Mars* (alluding to "perspective" pictures,
trick paintings that showed contrasted figures—here a monstrous
woman and the god of war—when looked at from opposite sides)

[Scene VI. *Near Misenum.*]

*Flourish. Enter Pompey [and Menas] at one
door, with Drum and Trumpet: at another,
Caesar, Lepidus, Antony, Enobarbus, Maecenas,
Agrippa, with Soldiers marching.*

Pompey. Your hostages I have, so have you mine;
And we shall talk before we fight.

Caesar.   Most meet°
That first we come to words, and therefore have we
Our written purposes before us sent;
Which, if thou hast considered, let us know   5
If 'twill tie up thy discontented sword
And carry back to Sicily much tall° youth
That else must perish here.

Pompey.   To you all three,
The senators alone of this great world,
Chief factors° for the gods: I do not know   10
Wherefore my father should revengers want,°
Having a son and friends, since Julius Caesar,
Who at Philippi the good Brutus ghosted,°
There saw you laboring for him. What was't
That moved pale Cassius to conspire? And what   15
Made all-honored, honest, Roman Brutus,
With the armed rest, courtiers of beauteous free-
    dom,
To drench the Capitol—but that they would
Have one man but a man?° And that is it
Hath made me rig my navy, at whose burden   20

II.vi.2 *meet* fit   7 *tall* brave   10 *factors* agents   11 *want* lack
13 *ghosted* haunted   19 *but a man* merely a man (and not a king
or demigod)

The angered ocean foams; with which I meant
To scourge th' ingratitude that despiteful Rome
Cast on my noble father.

Caesar.   Take your time.

Antony. Thou canst not fear° us, Pompey, with thy
    sails.
25 We'll speak with thee° at sea. At land thou know'st
How much we do o'ercount thee.

Pompey.   At land indeed
Thou dost o'ercount° me of my father's house:
But since the cuckoo builds not for himself,
Remain in't as thou mayst.°

Lepidus.   Be pleased to tell us
30 (For this is from the present)° how you take
The offers we have sent you.

Caesar.   There's the point.

Antony. Which do not be entreated to, but weigh
What it is worth embraced.°

Caesar.   And what may follow,
To try a larger fortune.°

Pompey.   You have made me offer
35 Of Sicily, Sardinia; and I must
Rid all the sea of pirates; then, to send
Measures of wheat to Rome; this 'greed upon,
To part with unhacked edges° and bear back
Our targes° undinted.

24 *fear* frighten   25 *speak with thee* meet you   27 *o'ercount* cheat
(Antony had used it in the sense of "outnumber," but Pompey
punningly alludes to a house Antony bought from the elder Pompey
but did not pay for)   28–29 *But since . . . mayst* but since cuckoos
can't build (and therefore have to steal other birds' nests), keep
it if you can hold on to it. (Pompey includes in this sentence a
jeering suggestion that Antony is a cuckold, a lover of a faithless
woman)   30 *from the present* beside the point   33 *embraced* if
accepted   33–34 *And what . . . fortune* (1) and what the result
may be, if you try to do better for yourself (i.e., risk war) (2) and
the even greater things you may gain, if you join us and our affairs
prosper   38 *edges* swords   39 *targes* shields

Omnes.°   That's our offer.

Pompey.   Know then
I came before you here a man prepared
To take this offer. But Mark Antony
Put me to some impatience. Though I lose
The praise of it by telling, you must know,
When Caesar and your brother were at blows,
Your mother came to Sicily and did find
Her welcome friendly.

Antony.   I have heard it, Pompey,
And am well studied for a liberal thanks,
Which I do owe you.°

Pompey.   Let me have your hand:
I did not think, sir, to have met you here.

Antony. The beds i' th' East are soft; and thanks to
    you,
That called me timelier° than my purpose hither;
For I have gained by't.

Caesar.   Since I saw you last
There's a change upon you.

Pompey.   Well, I know not
What counts° harsh fortune casts° upon my face,
But in my bosom shall she never come
To make my heart her vassal.

Lepidus.   Well met here.

Pompey. I hope so, Lepidus. Thus we are agreed.
I crave our composition° may be written,
And sealed between us.

Caesar.   That's the next to do.

---

39 *Omnes* i.e., Caesar, Antony, Lepidus   47–48 *am well . . . you*
I am ready indeed to give you the free and full thanks that I owe you
51 *timelier* earlier   54 *counts* reckonings   54 *casts* (1) throws (2)
sums up (the lines and wrinkles resulting from a hard life are compared to a bill of costs written out by a cruelly precise Fortune)
58 *composition* agreement

60 *Pompey.* We'll feast each other ere we part, and let's
   Draw lots who shall begin.

Antony.   That will I, Pompey.

Pompey. No, Antony, take the lot:
   But, first or last, your fine Egyptian cookery
   Shall have the fame. I have heard that Julius Caesar
   Grew fat with feasting there.

65 *Antony.*   You have heard much.

Pompey. I have fair meanings, sir.

Antony.   And fair words to them.

Pompey. Then so much have I heard:
   And I have heard Apollodorus carried—

Enobarbus. No more of that: he did so.

Pompey.   What, I pray you?

70 *Enobarbus.* A certain queen to Caesar in a mattress.

Pompey. I know thee now; how far'st thou, soldier?

Enobarbus.   Well;
   And well am like to do, for I perceive
   Four feasts are toward.°

Pompey.   Let me shake thy hand;
   I never hated thee: I have seen thee fight
   When I have envied thy behavior.

75 *Enobarbus.*   Sir,
   I never loved you much; but I ha' praised ye
   When you have well deserved ten times as much
   As I have said you did.

Pompey.   Enjoy thy plainness,
   It nothing ill becomes thee.°
80   Aboard my galley I invite you all:
   Will you lead, lords?

All.   Show's the way, sir.

73 *toward* in the offing (accented "tòward")   79 *It . . .thee* it suits
you very well

Pompey.　　　　　　　　　　　　　　　Come.
Exeunt. Manet° Enobarbus and Menas.

Menas. [*Aside*] Thy father, Pompey, would ne'er have
  made this treaty. —You and I have known,° sir.

Enobarbus. At sea, I think.

Menas. We have, sir.　　　　　　　　　　　　　　　85

Enobarbus. You have done well by water.

Menas. And you by land.

Enobarbus. I will praise any man that will praise me;
  though it cannot be denied what I have done by
  land.　　　　　　　　　　　　　　　　　　　　　　90

Menas. Nor what I have done by water.

Enobarbus. Yes, something you can deny for your
  own safety: you have been a great thief by sea.

Menas. And you by land.

Enobarbus. There I deny my land service.° But give　95
  me your hand, Menas: if our eyes had authority,°
  here they might take two thieves kissing.°

Menas. All men's faces are true,° whatsome'er their
  hands are.

Enobarbus. But there is never a fair woman has a true　100
  face.

Menas. No slander; they steal hearts.

Enobarbus. We came hither to fight with you.

Menas. For my part, I am sorry it is turned to a drinking. Pompey doth this day laugh away his fortune.　105

Enobarbus. If he do, sure he cannot weep't back again.

81 s.d. *Manet* (Latin for "remains"; the plural is properly *manent*,
but the singular is often used for the plural, just as "exit" is often
used for "exeunt")　83 *known* met　95 *deny my land service* (a
quibble: "I claim exemption from military service" and "I deny
that I have been a thief")　96 *authority* authority to arrest　97 *two
thieves kissing* (1) two crooks fraternizing (2) two thieving hands
clasping　98 *true* (1) honest (2) natural, without make-up

Menas. Y' have said, sir. We looked not for Mark
Antony here. Pray you, is he married to Cleopatra?

Enobarbus. Caesar's sister is called Octavia.

110 *Menas.* True, sir, she was the wife of Caius Marcellus.

Enobarbus. But she is now the wife of Marcus Antonius.

Menas. Pray ye,° sir?

Enobarbus. 'Tis true.

115 *Menas.* Then is Caesar and he forever knit together.

Enobarbus. If I were bound to divine of this unity, I
would not prophesy so.

Menas. I think the policy° of that purpose made more
in the marriage than the love of the parties.

120 *Enobarbus.* I think so too. But you shall find the band
that seems to tie their friendship together will be
the very strangler of their amity: Octavia is of a
holy, cold, and still conversation.°

Menas. Who would not have his wife so?

125 *Enobarbus.* Not he that himself is not so; which is
Mark Antony. He will to his Egyptian dish again:
then shall the sighs of Octavia blow the fire up in
Caesar, and, as I said before, that which is the
strength of their amity shall prove the immediate
130 author of their variance. Antony will use his affection where it is. He married but his occasion° here.

Menas. And thus it may be. Come, sir, will you
aboard? I have a health for you.

Enobarbus. I shall take it, sir: we have used our
135 throats in Egypt.

Menas. Come, let's away.   *Exeunt.*

---

113 *Pray ye* pardon me (incredulous)   118 *policy* political expediency 123 *still conversation* quiet manner 131 *occasion* convenience

[Scene VII. *On board Pompey's galley, off Misenum.*]

Music plays. Enter two or three Servants, with a banquet.

First Servant. Here they'll be, man. Some o' their plants° are ill-rooted already; the least wind i' th' world will blow them down.

Second Servant. Lepidus is high-colored.

First Servant. They have made him drink alms drink.°   5

Second Servant. As they pinch one another by the disposition, he cries out "No more";° reconciles them to his entreaty, and himself to th' drink.

First Servant. But it raises the greater war between him and his discretion.   10

Second Servant. Why, this it is to have a name in great men's fellowship. I had as lief have a reed that will do me no service, as a partisan° I could not heave.

First Servant. To be called into a huge sphere,° and not to be seen to move° in't, are the holes where   15 eyes should be, which pitifully disaster° the cheeks.

A sennet° sounded. Enter Caesar, Antony, Pompey, Lepidus, Agrippa, Maecenas, Enobarbus, Menas, with other Captains.

II.vii.2 *plants* (pun on foot or sole of foot)   5 *alms drink* (1) remains of liquor usually saved for alms people (2) drinking done kindly, i.e., toasts given to smooth over quarrels   7 *No more* (1) no more quarreling (2) no more to drink   13 *partisan* great long-handled spear   14 *sphere* (1) area of influence (2) revolving circle holding a star or planet, in the old astronomy   15 *move* (1) be active, influential (2) circle, like a planet   16 *disaster* ruin (with a suggestion of a star's malignant influence)   16 s.d. *sennet* trumpet call signaling the entrance of a great man

Antony. Thus do they, sir: they take° the flow o' th'
    Nile
    By certain scales i'° th' pyramid. They know
    By th' height, the lowness, or the mean, if dearth
20   Or foison° follow. The higher Nilus swells,
    The more it promises; as it ebbs, the seedsman
    Upon the slime and ooze scatters his grain,
    And shortly comes to harvest.

Lepidus. Y' have strange serpents there.

25 *Antony.* Ay, Lepidus.

Lepidus. Your° serpent of Egypt is bred now of your
    mud by the operation of your sun: so is your croco-
    dile.

Antony. They are so.

30 *Pompey.* Sit—and some wine! A health to Lepidus!

Lepidus. I am not so well as I should be, but I'll ne'er
    out.°

Enobarbus. Not till you have slept; I fear me you'll be
    in° till then.

35 *Lepidus.* Nay, certainly, I have heard the Ptolemies'
    pyramises° are very goodly things; without contra-
    diction I have heard that.

Menas. [*Aside to Pompey*] Pompey, a word.

Pompey. [*Aside to Menas*] Say in mine ear: what is't?

Menas. [*Aside to Pompey*] Forsake thy seat, I do be-
    seech thee, captain,
    And hear me speak a word.

---

17 *take* measure 18 *scales i'* degree marks on 19–20 *dearth/Or foison* famine or plenty 26 *Your* (a colloquialism suggesting casual knowledgeableness) 31–32 *I'll ne'er out* I won't give in 34 *in* (1) in the game (2) in liquor 36 *pyramises* (a false plural made up from the Latin singular; Lepidus is pretentious and drunk)

Pompey.   [*Aside to Menas*] Forbear me till anon.°   *40*
                    [*Menas*] *whispers in's ear.*
This wine for Lepidus!

Lepidus. What manner o' thing is your crocodile?

Antony. It is shaped, sir, like itself, and it is as broad
as it hath breadth; it is just so high as it is, and
moves with it° own organs. It lives by that which   *45*
nourisheth it, and the elements once out of it, it
transmigrates.

Lepidus. What color is it of?

Antony. Of it own color too.

Lepidus. 'Tis a strange serpent.   *50*

Antony. 'Tis so; and the tears of it are wet.

Caesar. Will this description satisfy him?

Antony. With the health that Pompey gives him; else
he is a very epicure.

Pompey. [*Aside to Menas*] Go hang, sir, hang! Tell
me of that? Away!   *55*
Do as I bid you. —Where's this cup I called for?

Menas. [*Aside to Pompey*] If for the sake of merit
thou wilt hear me,
Rise from thy stool.

Pompey. [*Aside to Menas*] I think th' art mad. The
matter?   [*Rises and walks aside.*]

Menas. I have ever held my cap off to° thy fortunes.

Pompey. Thou hast served me with much faith. What's
else to say?
Be jolly, lords.   *60*

Antony.   These quicksands, Lepidus,
Keep off them, for you sink.

40 *Forbear me till anon* leave me alone for a minute   45 *it* its
59 *held my cap off to* treated respectfully

Menas. Wilt thou be lord of all the world?

Pompey.   What say'st thou?

Menas. Wilt thou be lord of the whole world? That's
   twice.

Pompey. How should that be?

65 *Menas.*   But entertain it,°
   And though thou think me poor, I am the man
   Will give thee all the world.

Pompey.   Hast thou drunk well?

Menas. No, Pompey, I have kept me from the cup.
   Thou art, if thou dar'st be, the earthly Jove:
70 Whate'er the ocean pales,° or sky inclips,°
   Is thine, if thou wilt ha't.

Pompey.   Show me which way.

Menas. These three world-sharers, these competitors,°
   Are in thy vessel. Let me cut the cable;
   And when we are put off, fall to their throats.
   All there is thine.

75 *Pompey.*   Ah, this thou shouldst have done,
   And not have spoke on't. In me 'tis villainy,
   In thee't had been good service. Thou must know,
   'Tis not my profit that does lead mine honor;
   Mine honor, it. Repent that e'er thy tongue
80 Hath so betrayed thine act. Being done unknown,
   I should have found it afterwards well done,
   But must condemn it now. Desist, and drink.

Menas. [*Aside*] For this,
   I'll never follow thy palled° fortunes more.
85 Who seeks, and will not take when once 'tis offered,
   Shall never find it more.

Pompey.   This health to Lepidus!

---

65 *But entertain it* only accept it   70 *pales* fences in   70 *inclips*
embraces   72 *competitors* partners   84 *palled* decayed

Antony. Bear him ashore. I'll pledge it for him,
   Pompey.

Enobarbus. Here's to thee, Menas!

Menas.   Enobarbus, welcome.

Pompey. Fill till the cup be hid.

Enobarbus. There's a strong fellow, Menas.   *90*
     [*Points to the Servant who carries off Lepidus.*]

Menas. Why?

Enobarbus. 'A° bears the third part of the world, man;
   seest not?

Menas. The third part then is drunk. Would it were all,
   That it might go on wheels!°   *95*

Enobarbus. Drink thou: increase the reels.°

Menas. Come.

Pompey. This is not yet an Alexandrian feast.

Antony. It ripens towards it. Strike the vessels,° ho!
   Here's to Caesar!

Caesar.   I could well forbear't.   *100*
   It's monstrous labor when I wash my brain
   And it grows fouler.

Antony.   Be a child o' th' time.

Caesar. Possess it, I'll make answer;°
   But I had rather fast from all, four days,
   Than drink so much in one.

Enobarbus.   Ha, my brave emperor!   *105*
   Shall we dance now the Egyptian bacchanals°
   And celebrate our drink?

92 *'A* he   95 *go on wheels* (1) go easily (2) spin wildly   96 *reels*
(1) revels (2) staggering movements   99 *Strike the vessels* broach
the casks   103 *Possess . . . answer* master the time (rather than be
mastered by it) is my answer   106 *bacchanals* riotous salute to
Bacchus, god of wine

Pompey.   Let's ha't, good soldier.

Antony. Come, let's all take hands
Till that the conquering wine hath steeped our sense
In soft and delicate Lethe.°

110 *Enobarbus.*   All take hands:
Make battery to our ears with the loud music;
The while I'll place you; then the boy shall sing.
The holding° every man shall bear as loud
As his strong sides can volley.

Music plays. Enobarbus places them hand in hand.

The Song

115   Come, thou monarch of the vine,
             Plumpy Bacchus with pink eyne!°
             In thy fats° our cares be drowned,
             With thy grapes our hairs be crowned.
                 Cup us till the world go round,
120   Cup us till the world go round!

Caesar. What would you more? Pompey, good night.
    Good brother,
Let me request you off:° our graver business
Frowns at this levity. Gentle lords, let's part;
You see we have burnt our cheeks: strong Enobarb
125 Is weaker than the wine, and mine own tongue
Splits what it speaks: the wild disguise° hath almost
Anticked° us all. What needs more words? Good
    night.
Good Antony, your hand.

Pompey.   I'll try you° on the shore.

Antony. And shall, sir. Give's your hand.

110 *Lethe* forgetfulness   113 *holding* refrain   116 *pink eyne* half-
closed eyes   117 *fats* vats   122 *request you off* beg you leave the
ship with me   126 *disguise* drunken revelry   127 *Anticked* made
fools of   128 *try you* test your power (to hold liquor)

Pompey.   O, Antony,
  You have my father's house. But what, we are
    friends!   130
  Come down into the boat.
              [Exeunt all but Enobarbus and Menas.]

Enobarbus. [*To Menas*]   Take heed you fall not.

Menas. I'll not on shore; no, to my cabin!
  These drums! These trumpets, flutes! What!
  Let Neptune hear we bid a loud farewell
  To these great fellows. Sound and be hanged, sound
    out!   *Sound a flourish, with drums.* 135

Enobarbus. Hoo, says 'a. There's my cap.
                    [Throws his cap in the air.]

Menas. Hoa! Noble captain, come.   *Exeunt.*

[ACT III

Scene I. *A plain in Syria.*]

*Enter Ventidius as it were in triumph, the dead
body of Pacorus borne before him; [with Silius
and other Romans].*

Ventidius. Now, darting° Parthia, art thou struck; and
    now
Pleased fortune does of Marcus Crassus'° death
Make me revenger. Bear the King's son's body
Before our army. Thy Pacorus, Orodes,
Pays this for Marcus Crassus.

5 *Silius.*   Noble Ventidius,
Whilst yet with Parthian blood thy sword is warm,
The fugitive Parthians follow. Spur through Media,
Mesopotamia, and the shelters whither
The routed fly. So thy grand captain, Antony,
10 Shall set thee on triumphant chariots, and
Put garlands on thy head.

III.i.1 *darting* (the Parthians' method of attack was to fling
darts and then retreat swiftly, shooting arrows) 2 *Marcus Crassus*
(treacherously killed by Orodes, King of Parthia and father of
Pacorus)

Ventidius.   O Silius, Silius,
I have done enough: a lower place,° note well,
May make too great an act. For learn this, Silius,
Better to leave undone, than by our deed
Acquire too high a fame when him we serve's away.   15
Caesar and Antony have ever won
More in their officer than person. Sossius,
One of my place° in Syria, his° lieutenant,
For quick accumulation of renown,
Which he achieved by th' minute,° lost his favor.   20
Who does i' th' wars more than his captain can
Becomes his captain's captain; and ambition
(The soldier's virtue) rather makes choice of loss
Than gain which darkens him.
I could do more to do Antonius good,   25
But 'twould offend him, and in his offense
Should my performance perish.°

Silius.   Thou hast, Ventidius, that
Without the which a soldier and his sword
Grants scarce distinction.° Thou wilt write to
    Antony?

Ventidius. I'll humbly signify what in his name,   30
That magical word of war, we have effected;
How, with his banners and his well-paid ranks,
The ne'er-yet-beaten horse of Parthia
We have jaded° out o' th' field.

Silius.   Where is he now?

Ventidius. He purposeth to Athens; whither, with what
    haste
The weight we must convey with's will permit,   35
We shall appear before him. —On, there; pass along.
                                        Exeunt.

---

12 *lower place* subordinate   18 *place* rank   18 *his* i.e., Antony's
20 *by th' minute* every minute, incessantly   27 *perish* i.e., lose its
value to me   27–29 *that . . . distinction* that quality (i.e., discretion)
without which it is hard to see any difference between a soldier and
his sword   34 *jaded* driven like nags

[Scene II. *Rome. Caesar's house.*]

Enter Agrippa at one door, Enobarbus at another.

Agrippa. What, are the brothers parted?°

Enobarbus. They have dispatched with Pompey; he is
    gone;
    The other three are sealing.° Octavia weeps
    To part from Rome; Caesar is sad, and Lepidus
5   Since Pompey's feast, as Menas says, is troubled
    With the green-sickness.°

Agrippa.   'Tis a noble Lepidus.

Enobarbus. A very fine one. O, how he loves Caesar!

Agrippa. Nay, but how dearly he adores Mark Antony!

Enobarbus. Caesar? Why, he's the Jupiter of men.

10 *Agrippa.* What's Antony? The god of Jupiter.

Enobarbus. Spake you of Caesar? How! The non-
    pareil!°

Agrippa. O Antony! O thou Arabian bird!°

Enobarbus. Would you praise Caesar, say "Caesar":
    go no further.

Agrippa. Indeed, he plied them both with excellent
    praises.

Enobarbus. But he loves Caesar best, yet he loves
15   Antony:

III.ii.1 *parted* departed 3 *sealing* making the last arrangements
6 *green-sickness* anemia supposed to affect lovesick girls (Lepidus'
hangover is attributed to his love of Antony and Octavius) 11 *nonpareil* unequaled thing 12 *Arabian bird* phoenix (unique and immortal)

Hoo! Hearts, tongues, figures, scribes, bards, poets, cannot
Think, speak, cast,° write, sing, number—hoo!—
His love to Antony. But as for Caesar,
Kneel down, kneel down, and wonder.

Agrippa.   Both he loves.

Enobarbus. They are his shards,° and he their beetle.
[*Trumpet within.*] So—   20
This is to horse. Adieu, noble Agrippa.

Agrippa. Good fortune, worthy soldier, and farewell!

Enter Caesar, Antony, Lepidus, and Octavia.

Antony. No further, sir.

Caesar. You take from me a great part of myself;
Use me well in't. Sister, prove such a wife   25
As my thoughts make thee, and as my farthest band
Shall pass on thy approof.° Most noble Antony,
Let not the piece° of virtue which is set
Betwixt us as the cement° of our love
To keep it builded, be the ram to batter   30
The fortress of it: for better might we
Have loved without this mean,° if on both parts
This be not cherished.

Antony.   Make me not offended
In° your distrust.

Caesar.   I have said.

Antony.   You shall not find,
Though you be therein curious,° the least cause   35
For what you seem to fear. So the gods keep you
And make the hearts of Romans serve your ends!
We will here part.

Caesar. Farewell, my dearest sister, fare thee well.

17 *cast* count   20 *shards* wings   26–27 *As my thoughts . . . approof*
as I believe you to be, and such as I would give my utmost bond
that you will triumphantly prove to be   28 *piece* masterpiece
29 *cement* (accented on first syllable)   32 *mean* intermediary
34 *In* by   35 *curious* overscrupulous

40   The elements be kind to thee, and make
Thy spirits all of comfort. Fare thee well.

Octavia. My noble brother!

Antony. The April's in her eyes: it is love's spring,
And these the showers to bring it on. Be cheerful.

Octavia. Sir, look well to my husband's house; and—

45   *Caesar.*   What,
Octavia?

Octavia.   I'll tell you in your ear.

Antony. Her tongue will not obey her heart, nor can
Her heart inform her tongue; the swan's-down
    feather
That stands upon the swell at the full of tide,
50   And neither way inclines.°

Enobarbus. [*Aside to Agrippa*] Will Caesar weep?

Agrippa. [*Aside to Enobarbus*] He has a cloud in's
    face.

Enobarbus. [*Aside to Agrippa*] He were the worse for
    that, were he a horse;°
So is he, being a man.

Agrippa. [*Aside to Enobarbus*] Why, Enobarbus,
When Antony found Julius Caesar dead,
55   He cried almost to roaring; and he wept
When at Philippi he found Brutus slain.

Enobarbus. [*Aside to Agrippa*] That year indeed he
    was troubled with a rheum.°
What willingly he did confound° he wailed,
Believe't, till I wept too.

Caesar.   No, sweet Octavia,

48–50 *the swan's . . . inclines* (pressure of feeling urges Octavia to
speak but prevents her from finding the words; she hesitates—like a
feather held immobile by cross-currents at the turn of the tide—
between husband and brother, love and sorrow, speech and silence)
52 *horse* (a horse with a dark face, or without a white star on its face,
was less prized) 57 *rheum* watering at the eyes 58 *confound* destroy

You shall hear from me still: the time shall not   60
Outgo my thinking on you.

Antony.   Come, sir, come,
I'll wrestle with you in my strength of love:
Look, here I have you; thus I let you go,
And give you to the gods.

Caesar.   Adieu; be happy!

Lepidus. Let all the number of the stars give light   65
To thy fair way!

Caesar.   Farewell, farewell! *Kisses Octavia.*

Antony.   Farewell!
                    Trumpets sound. Exeunt.

[Scene III. *Alexandria. Cleopatra's palace.*]

Enter Cleopatra, Charmian, Iras, and Alexas.

Cleopatra. Where is the fellow?

Alexas.   Half afeard to come.

Cleopatra. Go to, go to.

            Enter the Messenger as before.°

                    Come hither, sir.

Alexas.   Good Majesty,
Herod of Jewry° dare not look upon you
But when you are well pleased.

Cleopatra.   That Herod's head
I'll have: but how, when Antony is gone   5
Through whom I might command it? Come thou
    near.

III.iii.2 s.d. *as before* i.e., nervously, as he left her   3 *Herod of
Jewry* i.e., even the fiercest of tyrants

Messenger. Most gracious Majesty!

Cleopatra. Didst thou behold Octavia?

Messenger. Ay, dread queen.

10   *Cleopatra.* Where?

Messenger. Madam, in Rome.
   I looked her in the face, and saw her led
   Between her brother and Mark Antony.

Cleopatra. Is she as tall as me?

Messenger.   She is not, madam.

Cleopatra. Didst hear her speak? Is she shrill-tongued
15   or low?

Messenger. Madam, I heard her speak; she is low-
   voiced.

Cleopatra. That's not so good.° He cannot like her
   long.

Charmian. Like her? O Isis! 'Tis impossible.

Cleopatra. I think so, Charmian. Dull of tongue, and
   dwarfish.
20   What majesty is in her gait? Remember,
   If e'er thou look'st on majesty.

Messenger.   She creeps:
   Her motion and her station are as one.°
   She shows a body rather than a life,
   A statue than a breather.

Cleopatra.   Is this certain?

Messenger. Or I have no observance.

25   *Charmian.*   Three in Egypt
   Cannot make better note.

Cleopatra.   He's very knowing,

17 *That's not so good* (1) that's a nuisance. Nevertheless . . . (2)
that's a bad thing to be   22 *Her motion . . . one* moving and standing still are the same thing with her

I do perceive't. There's nothing in her yet.
The fellow has good judgment.

Charmian.   Excellent.

Cleopatra. Guess at her years, I prithee.

Messenger.   Madam,
She was a widow—

Cleopatra.   Widow? Charmian, hark.   30

Messenger. And I do think she's thirty.°

Cleopatra. Bear'st thou her face in mind? Is't long or
round?

Messenger. Round, even to faultiness.

Cleopatra. For the most part, too, they are foolish that
are so.
Her hair, what color?   35

Messenger. Brown, madam; and her forehead
As low as she would wish it.°

Cleopatra.   There's gold for thee.
Thou must not take my former sharpness ill;
I will employ thee back again: I find thee
Most fit for business. Go, make thee ready;   40
Our letters are prepared.   [*Exit Messenger.*]

Charmian.   A proper° man.

Cleopatra. Indeed he is so: I repent me much
That so I harried him. Why, methinks, by him,
This creature 's no such thing.°

Charmian.   Nothing, madam.

Cleopatra. The man hath seen some majesty, and
should know.
                                                45
Charmian. Hath he seen majesty? Isis else defend,°
And serving you so long!

31 *thirty* (Cleopatra, being thirty-eight, lets this pass)   37 *As low
. . . it* (colloquial phrase: low enough, and I hope she's pleased
with it)   41 *proper* excellent   44 *no such thing* nothing very much
46 *Isis else defend* Isis forbid

Cleopatra. I have one thing more to ask him yet, good
           Charmian;
       But 'tis no matter, thou shalt bring him to me
50   Where I will write. All may be well enough.

Charmian. I warrant you, madam.   *Exeunt.*

[Scene IV. *Athens. Antony's house.*]

Enter Antony and Octavia.

Antony. Nay, nay, Octavia, not only that,
       That were excusable, that and thousands more
       Of semblable import°——but he hath waged
       New wars 'gainst Pompey; made his will, and read it
5   To public ear;°
       Spoke scantly of me: when perforce he could not
       But pay me terms of honor, cold and sickly
       He vented them, most narrow measure° lent me;
       When the best hint was given him, he not took't,
       Or did it from his teeth.°

10 *Octavia.*   O, my good lord,
       Believe not all; or, if you must believe,
       Stomach° not all. A more unhappy lady,
       If this division chance, ne'er stood between,
       Praying for both parts.
15   The good gods will mock me presently°
       When I shall pray "O, bless my lord and husband!"——
       Undo that prayer by crying out as loud
       "O, bless my brother!" Husband win, win brother,
       Prays, and destroys the prayer; no midway
       'Twixt these extremes at all.

III.iv.3 *semblable import* similar significance 4–5 *made . . . ear*
i.e., like Julius Caesar, made a will benefiting the people and so
worked up popular support 8 *narrow measure* little credit 10
from his teeth grudgingly 12 *Stomach* resent 15 *presently* immediately

Antony.   Gentle Octavia,
Let your best love draw to that point which seeks
Best to preserve it. If I lose mine honor,
I lose myself: better I were not yours
Than yours so branchless.° But, as you requested,
Yourself shall go between's: the meantime, lady,   25
I'll raise the preparation of a war
Shall stain° your brother. Make your soonest haste;
So your desires are yours.

Octavia.   Thanks to my lord.
The Jove of power make me, most weak, most weak,
Your reconciler! Wars 'twixt you twain would be   30
As if the world should cleave, and that slain men
Should solder up the rift.

Antony. When it appears to you where this begins,
Turn your displeasure that way, for our faults
Can never be so equal that your love   35
Can equally move with them. Provide your going;
Choose your own company, and command what cost
Your heart has mind to.   *Exeunt.*

[Scene V. *Athens. Antony's house.*]

Enter Enobarbus and Eros.

Enobarbus. How now, friend Eros?

Eros. There's strange news come, sir.

Enobarbus. What, man?

Eros. Caesar and Lepidus have made wars upon
   Pompey.   5

Enobarbus. This is old. What is the success?°

24 *branchless* mutilated   27 *stain* eclipse   (the reputation of)
III.v.6 *success* sequel

Eros. Caesar, having made use of him in the wars
    'gainst Pompey, presently denied him rivality,°
    would not let him partake in the glory of the action;
10 and not resting here, accuses him of letters he had
    formerly wrote to Pompey; upon his own appeal,°
    seizes him; so the poor third is up,° till death enlarge
    his confine.

Enobarbus. Then, world, thou hast a pair of chaps,°
    no more;
15 And throw between them all the food thou hast,
    They'll grind the one the other.° Where's Antony?

Eros. He's walking in the garden——thus, and spurns
    The rush that lies before him; cries "Fool Lepidus!"
    And threats the throat of that his officer
    That murd'red Pompey.°

20 *Enobarbus.*   Our great navy's rigged.

Eros. For Italy and Caesar. More, Domitius:
    My lord desires you presently. My news
    I might have told hereafter.

Enobarbus.   'Twill be naught;
    But let it be. Bring me to Antony.

Eros.   Come, sir. *Exeunt.*

8 *rivality* partnership   11 *upon his own appeal* on his (Caesar's)
own accusation   12 *up* shut up, imprisoned   14 *chaps* jaws   15–
16 *And throw . . . other* and feed them with all the victims in the
world, they (Caesar and Antony) will nevertheless meet, and one
consume the other   20 *Pompey* (Pompey has by now been mur-
dered, according to Plutarch by Antony's command; Pompey would
have proved useful to Antony in the coming war)

[Scene VI. *Rome. Caesar's house.*]

Enter Agrippa, Maecenas, and Caesar.

Caesar. Contemning° Rome, he has done all this and
    more
In Alexandria. Here's the manner of't:
I' th' marketplace on a tribunal silvered,
Cleopatra and himself in chairs of gold
Were publicly enthroned; at the feet sat   5
Caesarion, whom they call my father's° son,
And all the unlawful issue that their lust
Since then hath made between them. Unto her
He gave the stablishment° of Egypt; made her
Of lower Syria, Cyprus, Lydia,
Absolute queen.

Maecenas.   This in the public eye?

Caesar. I' th' common showplace, where they exercise.
His sons he there proclaimed the kings of kings:
Great Media, Parthia, and Armenia
He gave to Alexander; to Ptolemy he assigned   15
Syria, Cilicia, and Phoenicia. She
In th' habiliments of the goddess Isis
That day appeared, and oft before gave audience,
As 'tis reported, so.

Maecenas.   Let Rome be thus informed.

Agrippa. Who, queasy° with his insolence already,   20
    Will their good thoughts call from him.

III.vi.1 *Contemning* despising   6 *my father* (Octavius had been
adopted by Julius Caesar)   9 *stablishment* possession   20 *queasy*
disgusted

Caesar. The people knows it, and have now received
   His accusations.

Agrippa.   Who does he accuse?

Caesar. Caesar: and that, having in Sicily
25   Sextus Pompeius spoiled,° we had not rated° him
   His part o' th' isle. Then does he say he lent me
   Some shipping, unrestored. Lastly, he frets
   That Lepidus of the triumvirate
   Should be deposed; and, being, that we detain
   All his revenue.°

30 *Agrippa*.   Sir, this should be answered.

Caesar. 'Tis done already, and the messenger gone.
   I have told him Lepidus was grown too cruel,
   That he his high authority abused
   And did deserve his change; for what I have
      conquered,
35   I grant him part; but then in his Armenia,
   And other of his conquered kingdoms, I
   Demand the like.

Maecenas.   He'll never yield to that.

Caesar. Nor must not then be yielded to in this.

        Enter Octavia with her Train.

Octavia. Hail, Caesar, and my lord, hail, most dear
   Caesar!

40 *Caesar*. That ever I should call thee castaway!

Octavia. You have not called me so, nor have you
   cause.

Caesar. Why have you stol'n upon us thus? You come
   not
   Like Caesar's sister. The wife of Antony
   Should have an army for an usher, and
45   The neighs of horse to tell of her approach

---

25 *spoiled* despoiled   25 *rated* allotted   30 *revenue* (accented on
second syllable)

Long ere she did appear. The trees by th' way
Should have borne men, and expectation fainted,
Longing for what it had not. Nay, the dust
Should have ascended to the roof of heaven,
Raised by your populous troops. But you are come   50
A market maid to Rome, and have prevented
The ostentation° of our love; which, left unshown,
Is often left unloved.° We should have met you
By sea and land, supplying every stage
With an augmented greeting.

Octavia.   Good my lord,   55
To come thus was I not constrained, but did it
On my free will. My lord, Mark Antony,
Hearing that you prepared for war, acquainted
My grievèd ear withal; whereon I begged
His pardon for return.

Caesar.   Which soon he granted,   60
Being an abstract° 'tween his lust and him.

Octavia. Do not say so, my lord.

Caesar.   I have eyes upon him,
And his affairs come to me on the wind.
Where is he now?

Octavia.   My lord, in Athens.

Caesar. No, my most wrongèd sister, Cleopatra   65
Hath nodded him to her. He hath given his empire
Up to a whore, who now° are levying
The kings o' th' earth for war. He hath assembled
Bocchus, the King of Libya; Archelaus,
Of Cappadocia; Philadelphos, King   70
Of Paphlagonia; the Thracian king, Adallas;
King Mauchus of Arabia; King of Pont;
Herod of Jewry; Mithridates, King
Of Comagene; Polemon and Amyntas,

---

52 *ostentation* public display   53 *left unloved* (1) unrequited (2)
thought not to exist   61 *abstract* (1) immaterial, merely notional
thing (2) short cut (3) symbol (of what prevented him from in-
dulging his lust)   67 *who now* and they now

75   The Kings of Mede and Lycaonia;
    With a more larger list of scepters.

    Octavia.   Ay me most wretched,
    That have my heart parted betwixt two friends
    That does afflict each other!

    Caesar.   Welcome hither.
    Your letters did withhold our breaking forth,
80   Till we perceived both how you were wrong led
    And we in negligent danger.° Cheer your heart:
    Be you not troubled with the time, which drives
    O'er your content these strong necessities;
    But let determined things to destiny
85   Hold unbewailed their way. Welcome to Rome,
    Nothing more dear to me. You are abused°
    Beyond the mark° of thought: and the high gods,
    To do you justice, makes his ministers
    Of us° and those that love you. Best of comfort,
    And ever welcome to us.

90   *Agrippa.*   Welcome, lady.

    Maecenas. Welcome, dear madam.
    Each heart in Rome does love and pity you.
    Only th' adulterous Antony, most large°
    In his abominations, turns you off
95   And gives his potent regiment to a trull°
    That noises it° against us.

    Octavia.   Is it so, sir?

    Caesar. Most certain. Sister, welcome. Pray you
    Be ever known to patience. My dear'st sister!
                                     Exeunt.

---

81 *in negligent danger* endangered by doing nothing   86 *abused* deceived   87 *mark* reach   88–89 *makes . . . us* make us their agents of justice   93 *large* loose, licentious   95 *potent regiment to a trull* powerful authority to a prostitute   96 *noises it* is clamorous

[Scene VII. *Near Actium. Antony's camp.*]

Enter Cleopatra and Enobarbus.

Cleopatra. I will be even with thee, doubt it not.

Enobarbus. But why, why, why?

Cleopatra. Thou hast forspoke° my being in these
    wars,
And say'st it is not fit.

Enobarbus.   Well, is it, is it?

Cleopatra. Is't not denounced against us?° Why should
    not we   5
Be there in person?

Enobarbus.   [*Aside*] Well, I could reply:
If we should serve with horse and mares together,
The horse were merely° lost; the mares would bear
A soldier and his horse.

Cleopatra.   What is't you say?

Enobarbus. Your presence needs must puzzle° Antony;   10
    Take from his heart, take from his brain, from's
    time,
What should not then be spared. He is already
Traduced for levity; and 'tis said in Rome
That Photinus an eunuch and your maids
Manage this war.

Cleopatra.   Sink Rome, and their tongues rot   15
    That speak against us! A charge we bear i' th' war,

III.vii.3 *forspoke* spoken against   5 *denounced against us* (Caesar
had declared, or denounced—the technical term—war on Cleopatra
personally)   8 *merely* utterly   10 *puzzle* bewilder, bring to a
standstill

And as the president of my kingdom will
Appear there for a man. Speak not against it,
I will not stay behind.

Enter Antony and Canidius.

Enobarbus.   Nay, I have done.
Here comes the Emperor.

20   *Antony.*   Is it not strange, Canidius,
That from Tarentum and Brundusium
He could so quickly cut the Ionian sea
And take in° Toryne? —You have heard on't,
    sweet?

Cleopatra. Celerity is never more admired
Than by the negligent.

25   *Antony.*   A good rebuke,
Which might have well becomed the best of men
To taunt at slackness. Canidius, we
Will fight with him by sea.

Cleopatra.   By sea; what else?

Canidius. Why will my lord do so?

Antony.   For that° he dares us to't.

30   *Enobarbus.* So hath my lord dared him to single fight.

Canidius. Ay, and to wage this battle at Pharsalia,
Where Caesar fought with Pompey: but these offers,
Which serve not for his vantage, he shakes off;
And so should you.

Enobarbus.   Your ships are not well manned;
35   Your mariners are muleters,° reapers, people
Ingrossed by swift impress.° In Caesar's fleet
Are those that often have 'gainst Pompey fought;
Their ships are yare,° yours, heavy: no disgrace
Shall fall you for refusing him at sea,
Being prepared for land.

23 *take in* conquer   29 *For that* because   35 *muleters* mule drivers
36 *Ingrossed by swift impress* collected by hasty conscription
38 *yare* swift, nimble

Antony.   By sea, by sea.   40

Enobarbus. Most worthy sir, you therein throw away
    The absolute soldiership you have by land,
    Distract° your army, which doth most consist
    Of war-marked footmen, leave unexecuted
    Your own renownèd knowledge, quite forgo   45
    The way which promises assurance, and
    Give up yourself merely to chance and hazard
    From firm security.

Antony.   I'll fight at sea.

Cleopatra. I have sixty sails, Caesar none better.

Antony. Our overplus of shipping will we burn,   50
    And with the rest full-manned, from th' head of
        Actium
    Beat th' approaching Caesar. But if we fail,
    We then can do't at land.

                Enter a Messenger.

                    Thy business?

Messenger. The news is true, my lord, he is descried;
    Caesar has taken Toryne.   55

Antony. Can he be there in person? 'Tis impossible;
    Strange that his power° should be. Canidius,
    Our nineteen legions thou shalt hold by land
    And our twelve thousand horse. We'll to our ship.
    Away, my Thetis!°

                Enter a Soldier.

                    How now, worthy soldier?   60

Soldier. O noble Emperor, do not fight by sea,
    Trust not to rotten planks. Do you misdoubt
    This sword and these my wounds? Let th' Egyptians
    And the Phoenicians go a-ducking:° we

---

43 *Distract* (1) divide (2) confuse   57 *power* army   60 *Thetis* sea
goddess, mother of Achilles   64 *a-ducking* (1) swimming like ducks
(2) tipped underwater

65 Have used to conquer standing on the earth
    And fighting foot to foot.

Antony.   Well, well: away!
            Exit Antony, Cleopatra, and Enobarbus.

Soldier. By Hercules, I think I am i' th' right.

Canidius. Soldier, thou art; but his whole action grows
    Not in the power on't:° so our leader's led,
    And we are women's men.

70 *Soldier.*   You keep by land
    The legions and the horse whole, do you not?

Canidius. Marcus Octavius, Marcus Justeius,
    Publicola, and Caelius are for sea;
    But we keep whole by land. This speed of Caesar's
    Carries° beyond belief.

75 *Soldier.*   While he was yet in Rome,
    His power went out in such distractions° as
    Beguiled all spies.

Canidius.   Who's his lieutenant, hear you?

Soldier. They say, one Taurus.

Canidius.   Well I know the man.

            Enter a Messenger.

Messenger. The Emperor calls Canidius.

Canidius. With news the time's with labor, and throws
80   forth
    Each minute some.°   *Exeunt.*

68–69 *his whole . . . power on't* his entire plan of action has developed away from its sources of power   75 *Carries* shoots him
forward   76 *distractions* divisions   80–81 *With news . . . some* i.e.,
more news is born every minute

[Scene VIII. *A plain near Actium.*]

Enter Caesar, with his Army, marching.

Caesar. Taurus!

Taurus. My lord?

Caesar. Strike not by land; keep whole, provoke not
　　battle
　　Till we have done at sea. Do not exceed
　　The prescript of this scroll. Our fortune lies　　　5
　　Upon this jump.° *Exit [with Taurus and the Army].*

[Scene IX. *Another part of the plain.*]

Enter Antony and Enobarbus.

Antony. Set we our squadrons on yond side o' th' hill
　　In eye of Caesar's battle;° from which place
　　We may the number of the ships behold,
　　And so proceed accordingly. *Exit [with Enobarbus].*

III.viii.6 *jump* risk　III.ix.2 *battle* battle line

[Scene X. *Another part of the plain.*]

*Canidius marcheth with his land army one way
over the stage, and Taurus, the lieutenant of
Caesar, [with his army,] the other way. After their
going in is heard the noise of a sea fight. Alarum.
Enter Enobarbus.*

Enobarbus. Naught,° naught, all naught! I can behold
no longer.
Th' *Antoniad,* the Egyptian admiral,°
With all their sixty, fly and turn the rudder:
To see't mine eyes are blasted.

Enter Scarus.

Scarus.   Gods and goddesses,
All the whole synod° of them!

5 *Enobarbus.*   What's thy passion?

Scarus. The greater cantle° of the world is lost
With very ignorance;° we have kissed away
Kingdoms and provinces.

Enobarbus.   How appears the fight?

Scarus. On our side like the tokened pestilence,°
Where death is sure. Yon ribaudred° nag of
10   Egypt—
Whom leprosy o'ertake!—i' th' midst o' th' fight,
When vantage like a pair of twins appeared,

III.x.1 *Naught* i.e., all's come to nothing 2 *admiral* flagship
5 *synod* assembly 6 *cantle* segment of a sphere 7 *With very ignorance* by utter stupidity 9 *tokened pestilence* first fatal symp-
toms of the plague 10 *ribaudred* (apparently from "ribald," but
of uncertain meaning; probably just a cursing word; "filthy")

Both as the same, or rather ours the elder,°
The breese° upon her, like a cow in June,
Hoists sails, and flies.

Enobarbus.   That I beheld: 15
Mine eyes did sicken at the sight, and could not
Endure a further view.

Scarus.   She once being loofed,°
The noble ruin of her magic, Antony,
Claps on his sea wing, and (like a doting mallard)°
Leaving the fight in height, flies after her.   20
I never saw an action of such shame;
Experience, manhood, honor, ne'er before
Did violate so itself.

Enobarbus.   Alack, alack!

Enter Canidius.

Canidius. Our fortune on the sea is out of breath,
And sinks most lamentably. Had our general   25
Been what he knew himself,° it had gone well.
O, he has given example for our flight
Most grossly by his own.

Enobarbus.   Ay, are you thereabouts?°
Why then, good night indeed.

Canidius. Toward Peloponnesus are they fled.   30

Scarus. 'Tis easy to 't; and there I will attend
What further comes.

Canidius.   To Caesar will I render
My legions and my horse; six kings already
Show me the way of yielding.

---

13 *elder* greater 14 *breese* gadfly (with pun on "breeze," "wind")
17 *loofed* (1) luffed, i.e., with the head of a ship turned into the
wind (2) aloofed, rapidly departing 19 *mallard* wild duck 26
Been . . . himself been his true self—and he knew what that was
28 *are you thereabouts* is that where your thoughts are

Enobarbus.   I'll yet follow
      The wounded chance° of Antony, though my rea-
35   son
      Sits in the wind against me.°   [*Exeunt.*]

[Scene XI. *Alexandria. Cleopatra's palace.*]

Enter Antony with Attendants.

Antony. Hark! The land bids me tread no more upon't,
      It is ashamed to bear me. Friends, come hither.
      I am so lated° in the world that I
      Have lost my way forever. I have a ship
5   Laden with gold: take that, divide it; fly,
      And make your peace with Caesar.

Omnes.   Fly? Not we.

Antony. I have fled myself, and have instructed cow-
      ards
      To run and show their shoulders. Friends, be gone.
      I have myself resolved upon a course
10   Which has no need of you. Be gone.
      My treasure's in the harbor. Take it. O,
      I followed that° I blush to look upon.
      My very hairs do mutiny, for the white
      Reprove the brown for rashness,° and they them
15   For fear and doting. Friends, be gone; you shall
      Have letters from me to some friends that will
      Sweep your way for you. Pray you, look not sad,
      Nor make replies of loathness; take the hint°
      Which my despair proclaims. Let that be left

---

35 *wounded chance* broken fortunes   36 *Sits . . . me* is opposed to
me   III.xi.3 *lated* belated (as of a traveler, caught by the encroach-
ing night)   12 *that* what   14 *rashness* foolishness   18 *hint* opportunity

Which leaves itself.° To the seaside straightway!   20
I will possess you of that ship and treasure.
Leave me, I pray, a little: pray you now,
Nay, do so; for indeed I have lost command,°
Therefore I pray you. I'll see you by and by.

Sits down.

*Enter Cleopatra led by Charmian, [Iras,] and
Eros.*

Eros. Nay, gentle madam, to him, comfort him.   25

Iras. Do, most dear queen.

Charmian. Do: why, what else?

Cleopatra. Let me sit down. O, Juno!

Antony. No, no, no, no, no.

Eros. See you here, sir?   30

Antony. O, fie, fie, fie!

Charmian. Madam!

Iras. Madam, O, good empress!

Eros. Sir, sir!

Antony. Yes, my lord, yes. He° at Philippi kept   35
His sword e'en like a dancer,° while I struck
The lean and wrinkled Cassius; and 'twas I
That the mad Brutus ended: he alone
Dealt on lieutenantry,° and no practice had
In the brave squares° of war: yet now—— No
matter.   40

Cleopatra. Ah, stand by.

Eros. The Queen, my lord, the Queen.

19–20 *Let that . . . itself* leave the man who has taken leave of his
senses (?); leave the man who has given himself up for lost (?)
23 *I have lost command* (1) my feelings are becoming uncontrollable
(2) I have lost the right to order you   35 *He* i.e., Octavius   36 *like
a dancer* i.e., for ornament only   39 *Dealt on lieutenantry* told his
subordinates how to fight   40 *squares* squadrons

Iras. Go to him, madam, speak to him;
    He is unqualitied° with very shame.

45 *Cleopatra.* Well then, sustain me. O!

Eros. Most noble sir, arise. The Queen approaches.
    Her head's declined, and death will seize her, but°
    Your comfort makes the rescue.

Antony. I have offended reputation,°
    A most unnoble swerving.

50 *Eros.*   Sir, the Queen.

Antony. O, whither hast thou led me, Egypt? See
    How I convey my shame out of thine eyes
    By looking back° what I have left behind
    'Stroyed in dishonor.

Cleopatra.   O my lord, my lord,
55   Forgive my fearful sails! I little thought
    You would have followed.

Antony.   Egypt, thou knew'st too well
    My heart was to thy rudder tied by th' strings,
    And thou shouldst tow me after. O'er my spirit
    Thy full supremacy thou knew'st, and that
60   Thy beck might from the bidding of the gods
    Command me.

Cleopatra.   O, my pardon!

Antony.   Now I must
    To the young man send humble treaties, dodge
    And palter in the shifts of lowness,° who
    With half the bulk o' th' world played as I pleased,
65   Making and marring fortunes. You did know
    How much you were my conqueror, and that
    My sword, made weak by my affection,° would
    Obey it on all cause.

---

44 *unqualitied* beside himself 47 *but* unless 49 *reputation* honor
53 *By looking back* i.e., by averting my eyes and by lonely meditation
on 63 *palter . . . lowness* employ the tricks of a man brought low
67 *affection* love

Cleopatra.   Pardon, pardon!

Antony. Fall° not a tear, I say; one of them rates°
  All that is won and lost. Give me a kiss;
  Even this repays me. We sent our schoolmaster:°   70
  Is 'a come back? Love, I am full of lead.
  Some wine, within there, and our viands! Fortune
    knows
  We scorn her most when most she offers blows.
                             Exeunt.

[Scene XII. *Egypt. Caesar's camp.*]

*Enter Caesar, Agrippa, Dolabella, [Thidias,] with
others.*

Caesar. Let him appear that's come from Antony.
  Know you him?

Dolabella.   Caesar, 'tis his schoolmaster:
  An argument that he is plucked, when hither
  He sends so poor a pinion of his wing,
  Which had superfluous kings for messengers   5
  Not many moons gone by.

        Enter Ambassador from Antony.

Caesar.   Approach and speak.

Ambassador. Such as I am, I come from Antony.
  I was of late as petty to his ends
  As is the morn-dew on the myrtle leaf
  To his grand sea.°

---

69 *Fall* let fall   69 *rates* (1) is worth (2) berates, rebukes as unimportant   71 *our schoolmaster* i.e., the tutor of his and Cleopatra's
children   III.xii.10 *To his grand sea* (1) to the great sea that is its
source and end (2) to the great sea that is Antony

10 *Caesar.*   Be't so. Declare thine office.

    Ambassador. Lord of his fortunes he salutes thee, and
      Requires° to live in Egypt; which not granted,
      He lessons° his requests, and to thee sues
      To let him breathe between the heavens and earth,
15   A private man in Athens: this for him.
      Next, Cleopatra does confess thy greatness,
      Submits her to thy might, and of thee craves
      The circle° of the Ptolemies for her heirs,
      Now hazarded to thy grace.°

    Caesar.   For Antony,
20   I have no ears to his request. The Queen
      Of audience nor desire shall fail, so° she
      From Egypt drive her all-disgracèd friend
      Or take his life there. This if she perform,
      She shall not sue unheard. So to them both.

    Ambassador. Fortune pursue thee!

25 *Caesar.*   Bring him through the bands.
                      [Exit Ambassador.]
    [To Thidias] To try thy eloquence now 'tis time.
      Dispatch.
      From Antony win Cleopatra: promise,
      And in our name, what she requires; add more,
      From thine invention, offers.° Women are not
30   In their best fortunes strong, but want will perjure°
      The ne'er-touched vestal.° Try thy cunning,
      Thidias;
      Make thine own edict° for thy pains, which we
      Will answer as a law.

    Thidias.   Caesar, I go.

---

12 *Requires* requests 13 *lessons* disciplines (though perhaps the word should be emended to "lessens") 18 *circle* crown 19 *Now hazarded to thy grace* now dependent for its fate on your favor 21 *so* provided that 27–29 *promise . . . offers* (possibly corrupt; rearranges to the much more lucid: "promise/What she requires; and in our name add more/Offers from thine invention") 30 *perjure* make a perjuror of 31 *ne'er-touched vestal* immaculate virgin 32 *Make thine own edict* decree what you think the right reward

Caesar. Observe how Antony becomes his flaw,°
And what thou think'st his very action speaks   35
In every power that moves.

Thidias.   Caesar, I shall. *Exeunt.*

[Scene XIII. *Alexandria. Cleopatra's palace.*]

Enter Cleopatra, Enobarbus, Charmian, and Iras.

Cleopatra. What shall we do, Enobarbus?

Enobarbus.   Think, and die.

Cleopatra. Is Antony, or we, in fault for this?

Enobarbus. Antony only, that would make his will°
Lord of his reason. What though you fled
From that great face of war, whose several ranges   5
Frighted each other? Why should he follow?
The itch of his affection° should not then
Have nicked° his captainship, at such a point,
When half to half the world opposed, he being
The merèd question.° 'Twas a shame no less   10
Than was his loss, to course° your flying flags
And leave his navy gazing.

Cleopatra.   Prithee, peace.

Enter the Ambassador, with Antony.

Antony. Is that his answer?

Ambassador. Ay, my lord.

Antony. The Queen shall then have courtesy, so° she   15

34 *becomes his flaw* takes his fall   III.xiii.3 *will* desire, lust   7 *affection* passion   8 *nicked* (1) maimed (2) got the better of   10 *merèd question* sole ground of dispute   11 *course* pursue   15 *so* if

Will yield us up.

Ambassador.   He says so.

Antony.   Let her know't.
To the boy Caesar send this grizzled head,
And he will fill thy wishes to the brim
With principalities.

Cleopatra.   That head, my lord?

20   *Antony.* To him again! Tell him he wears the rose
Of youth upon him; from which the world should
     note
Something particular.° His coin, ships, legions
May be a coward's, whose ministers would prevail
Under the service of a child as soon
25   As i' th' command of Caesar. I dare him therefore
To lay his gay comparisons° apart
And answer me declined,° sword against sword,
Ourselves alone. I'll write it: follow me.
               [*Exeunt Antony and Ambassador.*]

Enobarbus. [*Aside*] Yes, like enough: high-battled°
     Caesar will
30   Unstate his happiness and be staged to th' show
Against a sworder!° I see men's judgments are
A parcel° of their fortunes, and things outward
Do draw the inward quality after them
To suffer all alike.° That he should dream,
35   Knowing all measures,° the full Caesar will
Answer his emptiness! Caesar, thou hast subdued
His judgment too.

               Enter a Servant.

Servant.   A messenger from Caesar.

22 *Something particular* i.e., a fact concerning Caesar   26 *comparisons* i.e., the ships, etc., which make him Antony's superior by comparison   27 *declined* i.e., in years and fortunes   29 *high-battled* elevated high by great armies   30–31 *Unstate . . . sworder* strip his good fortune of all its power, and make a public exhibition of himself against a gladiator   32 *parcel* part   34 *suffer all alike* deteriorate together   35 *knowing all measures* having experienced every measure of fortune

ENJOY THE COMPANY OF THREE OF THE WISEST MEN WHO EVER LIVED

(Continued from other side)

The selections themselves are remarkable values. They are carefully printed on expensive paper stock. They are hard-bound in matched sand-colored buckram, worked and stamped in crimson, black, and genuine gold. And through direct-to-the-public distribution, we are able to offer our members these deluxe editions for only $3.89 each, plus shipping.

Interested? We will send you the first three selections, Plato, Aristotle and Marcus Aurelius—all three

LET THESE 3 WISE MEN INTO YOUR HOME. LATER, YOU MIGHT LIKE TO INVITE THEIR FRIENDS.

Do you have room in your home for three wise men? They are Plato, Aristotle, and Marcus Aurelius . . . three of the wisest, wittiest, most stimulating minds that ever lived.

They still live . . . in the Five Great Dialogues of Plato, the Meditations of Marcus Aurelius, and Aristotle's On Man in the Universe.

All three books (regularly $11.67) can be yours for only $1.00 as your introduction to the Classics Club.

The Classics Club is quite unlike any other book club.

The Club does not offer best sellers that come and go. Instead, it offers its members a chance to stay

Cleopatra. What, no more ceremony? See, my women,
  Against the blown rose may they stop their nose
  That kneeled unto the buds. Admit him, sir.   40

                    [*Exit Servant.*]

Enobarbus. [*Aside*] Mine honesty and I begin to
    square.°
  The loyalty well held to fools does make
  Our faith° mere folly: yet he that can endure
  To follow with allegiance a fall'n lord
  Does conquer him that did his master conquer   45
  And earns a place i' th' story.

                Enter Thidias.

Cleopatra.   Caesar's will?

Thidias. Hear it apart.

Cleopatra.   None but friends: say boldly.

Thidias. So, haply,° are they friends to Antony.

Enobarbus. He needs as many, sir, as Caesar has,
  Or needs not us. If Caesar please, our master   50
  Will leap to be his friend; for us, you know,
  Whose he is we are, and that is Caesar's.

Thidias.   So.
  Thus then, thou most renowned: Caesar entreats
  Not to consider in what case thou stand'st
  Further than he is Caesar.°

Cleopatra.   Go on: right royal.   55

Thidias. He knows that you embraced not Antony
  As you did love, but as you feared him.

Cleopatra.   O!

Thidias. The scars upon your honor therefore he
  Does pity, as constrainèd blemishes,
  Not as deserved.

Cleopatra.   He is a god, and knows   60

41 *square* quarrel 43 *faith* faithfulness 48 *haply* perhaps 55
Caesar i.e., famous for generosity

What is most right. Mine honor was not yielded,
But conquered merely.°

Enobarbus.   [*Aside*] To be sure of that,
I will ask Antony. Sir, sir, thou art so leaky
That we must leave thee to thy sinking, for
Thy dearest quit thee.   *Exit Enobarbus.*

65 **Thidias.**   Shall I say to Caesar
What you require° of him? For he partly begs
To be desired to give. It much would please him
That of his fortunes you should make a staff
To lean upon. But it would warm his spirits
70 To hear from me you had left Antony,
And put yourself under his shroud,°
The universal landlord.

Cleopatra.   What's your name?

Thidias. My name is Thidias.

Cleopatra.   Most kind messenger,
Say to great Caesar this: in deputation°
75 I kiss his conqu'ring hand; tell him I am prompt
To lay my crown at's feet, and there to kneel.
Tell him, from his all-obeying° breath I hear
The doom of Egypt.°

Thidias.   'Tis your noblest course:
Wisdom and fortune combating together,
80 If that the former dare but what it can,°
No chance may shake it. Give me grace to lay
My duty° on your hand.

Cleopatra. [*Giving her hand*] Your Caesar's father oft,
When he hath mused of taking kingdoms in,

---

62 *merely* utterly   66 *require* request   71 *shroud* protection   74 *in
deputation* by proxy   77 *all-obeying* which all obey   78 *doom of
Egypt* judgment of the Queen of Egypt   80 *If that . . . it can* if a
wise man has the courage merely to go on being wise   82 *duty* i.e.,
a kiss

Bestowed his lips on that unworthy place,
As° it rained kisses.

Enter Antony and Enobarbus.

Antony.   Favors, by Jove that thunders!   85
What art thou, fellow?

Thidias.   One that but performs
The bidding of the fullest° man, and worthiest
To have command obeyed.

Enobarbus.   [*Aside*] You will be whipped.

Antony. [*Calling for Servants*] Approach there! —Ah,
   you kite!° Now, gods and devils!
Authority melts from me. Of late, when I cried
   "Ho!"
Like boys unto a muss° kings would start forth,   90
And cry "Your will?" Have you no ears? I am
Antony yet.

        Enter a Servant [*followed by others*].

                Take hence this Jack° and whip him.

Enobarbus. [*Aside*] 'Tis better playing with a lion's
   whelp
Than with an old one dying.

Antony.   Moon and stars!   95
Whip him! Were't twenty of the greatest tributaries
That do acknowledge Caesar, should I find them
So saucy with the hand of she here—what's her
   name
Since she was Cleopatra? Whip him, fellows,
Till like a boy you see him cringe his face   100
And whine aloud for mercy. Take him hence.

Thidias. Mark Antony—

Antony.   Tug him away. Being whipped,

85 *As* as if   87 *fullest* greatest (in character and fortunes)   89 *kite*
ignoble bird of prey   91 *muss* scramble; fighting heap of bodies
93 *Jack* fellow, knave

Bring him again. The Jack of Caesar's shall
Bear us an errand to him.

Exeunt [Servants] with Thidias.

105 You were half blasted° ere I knew you. Ha!
Have I my pillow left unpressed in Rome,
Forborne the getting° of a lawful race,
And by a gem of women, to be abused
By one that looks on feeders?°

Cleopatra.   Good my lord—

110 *Antony.* You have been a boggler° ever:
But when we in our viciousness grow hard
(O misery on't!) the wise gods seel° our eyes,
In our own filth drop our clear judgments, make us
Adore our errors, laugh at's while we strut
To our confusion.°

115 *Cleopatra.*   O, is't come to this?

Antony. I found you as a morsel cold upon
Dead Caesar's trencher:° nay, you were a fragment°
Of Gneius Pompey's, besides what hotter hours,
Unregist'red in vulgar fame,° you have
120 Luxuriously picked out.° For I am sure,
Though you can guess what temperance should be,
You know not what it is.

Cleopatra.   Wherefore is this?

Antony. To let a fellow that will take rewards
And say "God quit° you!" be familiar with
125 My playfellow, your hand, this kingly seal
And plighter of high hearts. O, that I were
Upon the hill of Basan to outroar

---

105 *blasted* worn out   107 *getting* begetting   109 *feeders* servants,
parasites   110 *boggler* waverer   112 *seel* blind (in falconry, a
hawk's eyelids are seeled, or sewn up, before it grows used to being
hooded)   115 *confusion* destruction   117 *trencher* wooden dish
117 *fragment* leftover   119 *vulgar fame* common knowledge, popular rumor   120 *Luxuriously picked out* lecherously selected   124
quit reward

The hornèd herd!° For I have savage cause,
And to proclaim it civilly were like
A haltered neck which does the hangman thank   130
For being yare° about him.

> *Enter a Servant with Thidias.*

Is he whipped?

Servant. Soundly, my lord.

Antony.   Cried he? And begged 'a pardon?

Servant. He did ask favor.

Antony. If that thy father live, let him repent
Thou wast not made his daughter; and be thou sorry   135
To follow Caesar in his triumph, since
Thou hast been whipped for following him. Hence-
    forth
The white hand of a lady fever thee,
Shake thou to look on't. Get thee back to Caesar,
Tell him thy entertainment:° look thou say   140
He makes me angry with him; for he seems
Proud and disdainful, harping on what I am,
Not what he knew I was. He makes me angry,
And at this time most easy 'tis to do't,
When my good stars that were my former guides   145
Have empty left their orbs° and shot their fires
Into th' abysm of hell. If he mislike
My speech and what is done, tell him he has
Hipparchus, my enfranchèd° bondman, whom
He may at pleasure whip, or hang, or torture,   150
As he shall like, to quit me. Urge it thou.
Hence with thy stripes, be gone!   *Exit Thidias.*

Cleopatra. Have you done yet?

Antony.   Alack, our terrene moon°

126–28 *O that . . . hornèd herd* i.e., Antony is so well provided with
the cuckold's horns that he should be among the "fat bulls of
Basan" of Psalm 22   131 *yare* deft   140 *entertainment* reception
146 *orbs* spheres   149 *enfranchèd* freed   153 *terrene moon* earthly
Isis (goddess of the moon)

Is now eclipsed, and it portends alone
The fall of Antony.

155 *Cleopatra.*   I must stay his time.°

Antony. To flatter Caesar, would you mingle eyes
With one that ties his points?°

Cleopatra.   Not know me yet?

Antony. Cold-hearted toward me?

Cleopatra.   Ah, dear, if I be so,
From my cold heart let heaven engender hail,
160 And poison it in the source, and the first stone
Drop in my neck: as it determines,° so
Dissolve my life! The next Caesarion smite,
Till by degrees the memory° of my womb,
Together with my brave Egyptians all,
165 By the discandying° of this pelleted storm,
Lie graveless, till the flies and gnats of Nile
Have buried them for prey!

Antony.   I am satisfied.
Caesar sits down in Alexandria, where
I will oppose his fate.° Our force by land
170 Hath nobly held; our severed navy too
Have knit again, and fleet,° threat'ning most sea-
     like.
Where hast thou been, my heart?° Dost thou hear,
     lady?
If from the field I shall return once more
To kiss these lips, I will appear in blood;°
175 I and my sword will earn our chronicle.°
There's hope in't yet.

Cleopatra. That's my brave lord!

---

155 *stay his time* i.e., wait till his rage ends   157 *one that ties his
points* one who laces up his clothes, i.e., a valet   161 *determines*
comes to an end, melts   163 *memory* memorials, heirs   165 *discandying* melting   169 *oppose his fate* challenge his destiny   171
fleet float   172 *heart* courage   174 *in blood* (1) covered with blood
(2) in full vigor   175 *chronicle* place in history

Antony. I will be treble-sinewed, hearted, breathed,°
And fight maliciously; for when mine hours
Were nice° and lucky, men did ransom lives   *180*
Of me for jests; but now I'll set my teeth
And send to darkness all that stop me. Come,
Let's have one other gaudy° night: call to me
All my sad captains; fill our bowls once more;
Let's mock the midnight bell.

Cleopatra.   It is my birthday.   *185*
I had thought t' have held it poor. But since my lord
Is Antony again, I will be Cleopatra.

Antony. We will yet do well.

Cleopatra. Call all his noble captains to my lord.

Antony. Do so, we'll speak to them; and tonight I'll
force
The wine peep through their scars. Come on, my   *190*
queen,
There's sap in't yet! The next time I do fight,
I'll make death love me, for I will contend
Even with his pestilent scythe.
                    Exeunt [all but Enobarbus].

Enobarbus. Now he'll outstare the lightning. To be
furious
Is to be frighted out of fear, and in that mood   *195*
The dove will peck the estridge;° and I see still
A diminution in our captain's brain
Restores his heart. When valor preys on reason,
It eats the sword it fights with. I will seek   *200*
Some way to leave him.   *Exit.*

178 *I will . . . breathed* I will have the strength, courage, and expertise
of three men   180 *nice* delicate, wanton   183 *gaudy* joyful   197
estridge goshawk (?) ostrich (?)

[ACT IV

Scene I. *Before Alexandria. Caesar's camp.*]

*Enter Caesar, Agrippa, and Maecenas, with his
Army, Caesar reading a letter.*

Caesar. He calls me boy, and chides as he had power
  To beat me out of Egypt. My messenger
  He hath whipped with rods; dares me to personal
    combat.
  Caesar to Antony: let the old ruffian know
5 I have many other ways to die; meantime
  Laugh at his challenge.

Maecenas.   Caesar must think,
  When one so great begins to rage,° he's hunted
  Even to falling. Give him no breath, but now
  Make boot of his distraction:° never anger
  Made good guard for itself.

10 *Caesar.*   Let our best heads
  Know that tomorrow the last of many battles
  We mean to fight. Within our files° there are,
  Of those that served Mark Antony but late,
  Enough to fetch him in.° See it done,

IV.i.7 *rage* grow mad   9 *Make boot of his distraction* profit from
his rage   12 *files* ranks   14 *fetch him in* capture him

And feast the army; we have store to do't,   15
And they have earned the waste. Poor Antony!

                                          Exeunt.

[Scene II. *Alexandria. Cleopatra's palace.*]

Enter Antony, Cleopatra, Enobarbus, Charmian,
        Iras, Alexas, with others.

Antony. He will not fight with me, Domitius?

Enobarbus.   No.

Antony. Why should he not?

Enobarbus. He thinks, being twenty times of better
     fortune,
He is twenty men to one.

Antony.   Tomorrow, soldier,
By sea and land I'll fight: or° I will live,   5
Or bathe my dying honor in the blood
Shall make it live again. Woo't° thou fight well?

Enobarbus. I'll strike, and cry "Take all!"°

Antony.   Well said, come on;
Call forth my household servants; let's tonight
Be bounteous at our meal.

            Enter three or four Servitors.

                          Give me thy hand,   10
Thou hast been rightly honest—so hast thou—
Thou—and thou—and thou: you have served me
     well,
And kings have been your fellows.°

Cleopatra.   [*Aside to Enobarbus*] What means this?

IV.ii.5 *or* either   7 *Woo't* wilt   8 *Take all* all or nothing   13 *kings
have been your fellows* kings have served me too, but no better

Enobarbus. [*Aside to Cleopatra*] 'Tis one of those
    odd tricks which sorrow shoots
  Out of the mind.

15 *Antony.*   And thou art honest too.
  I wish I could be made so many men,
  And all of you clapped up together in
  An Antony, that I might do you service
  So good as you have done.

Omnes.   The gods forbid!

20 *Antony.* Well, my good fellows, wait on me tonight:
  Scant not my cups, and make as much of me
  As when mine empire was your fellow too
  And suffered my command.°

Cleopatra. [*Aside to Enobarbus*] What does he mean?

Enobarbus. [*Aside to Cleopatra*] To make his fol-
    lowers weep.

Antony.   Tend me tonight;
25   May be it is the period° of your duty.
  Haply° you shall not see me more; or if,
  A mangled shadow. Perchance tomorrow
  You'll serve another master. I look on you
  As one that takes his leave. Mine honest friends,
30   I turn you not away, but like a master
  Married to your good service; stay till death.
  Tend me tonight two hours, I ask no more,
  And the gods yield° you for't!

Enobarbus.   What mean you, sir,
  To give them this discomfort? Look, they weep,
35   And I, an ass, am onion-eyed; for shame,
  Transform us not to women.

Antony.   Ho, ho, ho!
  Now the witch take me° if I meant it thus!

---

23 *suffered my command* served under my authority   25 *period* end
26 *Haply* perhaps   33 *yield* reward   37 *the witch take me* may I be
bewitched

Grace° grow where those drops fall! My hearty
  friends,
You take me in too dolorous a sense,
For I spake to you for your comfort, did desire you 40
To burn this night with torches. Know, my hearts,
I hope well of tomorrow, and will lead you
Where rather I'll expect victorious life
Than death and honor.° Let's to supper, come,
And drown consideration. *Exeunt.* 45

[Scene III. *Alexandria. Before Cleopatra's palace.*]

Enter a Company of Soldiers.

First Soldier. Brother, good night: tomorrow is the
  day.

Second Soldier. It will determine one way: fare you
  well.
  Heard you of nothing strange about the streets?

First Soldier. Nothing. What news?

Second Soldier. Belike° 'tis but a rumor. Good night
  to you. 5

First Soldier. Well, sir, good night.

They meet other Soldiers.

Second Soldier.   Soldiers, have careful watch.

Third Soldier. And you. Good night, good night.

They place themselves in every corner of the stage.

Second Soldier. Here we;° and if tomorrow

38 *Grace* (1) God's grace, favor (2) herb of grace, rue 44 *death
and honor* honorable death IV.iii.5 *Belike* probably 8 *Here we*
here is our post

Our navy thrive, I have an absolute hope
Our landmen will stand up.

10 *First Soldier.*   'Tis a brave army,
And full of purpose.
                    Music of the hautboys is under the stage.

Second Soldier.   Peace! What noise?

First Soldier.   List, list!

Second Soldier. Hark!

First Soldier.   Music i' th' air.

Third Soldier.   Under the earth.

Fourth Soldier. It signs° well, does it not?

Third Soldier.   No.

First Soldier.   Peace, I say!
What should this mean?

Second Soldier. 'Tis the god Hercules, whom Antony
15 loved,
Now leaves him.

First Soldier. Walk; let's see if other watchmen
Do hear what we do.

Second Soldier. How now, masters?

20 *Omnes.* (*Speak together*) How now? How now? Do
you hear this?

First Soldier. Ay. Is't not strange?

Third Soldier. Do you hear, masters? Do you hear?

First Soldier. Follow the noise so far as we have
quarter.
25 Let's see how it will give off.°

Omnes. Content. 'Tis strange.   *Exeunt.*

13 *signs* signifies   25 *give off* cease

[Scene IV. *Alexandria. Cleopatra's palace.*]

Enter Antony and Cleopatra, with [*Charmian and*] *others* [*attending*].

Antony. Eros! Mine armor, Eros!

Cleopatra.   Sleep a little.

Antony. No, my chuck.° Eros! Come, mine armor, Eros!

Enter Eros [*with armor*].

Come, good fellow, put thine iron° on.
If fortune be not ours today, it is
Because we brave her.° Come.

Cleopatra.   Nay, I'll help too.   5
What's this for?

Antony.   Ah, let be, let be! Thou art
The armorer of my heart. False,° false; this, this.   ‹

Cleopatra. Sooth, la, I'll help: thus it must be.

Antony.   Well, well,
We shall thrive now. Seest thou, my good fellow?
Go put on thy defenses.

Eros.   Briefly,° sir.   10

Cleopatra. Is not this buckled well?

Antony.   Rarely, rarely:
He that unbuckles this, till we do please
To daff't° for our repose, shall hear a storm.

IV.iv.2 *chuck* chick   3 *thine iron* that armor (of mine) you hold
4–5 *If fortune . . . brave her* (1) if fortune is not friendly to us today,
it will be because we defy her (2) we shall be fortunate today, or we
shall defy fortune   7 *False* i.e., wrong piece   10 *Briefly* soon   13
daff't put it off

Thou fumblest, Eros, and my queen's a squire
15   More tight° at this than thou. Dispatch. O, love,
That thou couldst see my wars today, and knew'st
The royal occupation:° thou shouldst see
A workman° in't.

Enter an armed Soldier.

Good morrow to thee; welcome:
Thou look'st like him that knows a warlike charge.°
20   To business that we love we rise betime
And go to't with delight.

Soldier.   A thousand, sir,
Early though't be, have on their riveted trim,°
And at the port° expect you.

*Shout. Trumpets flourish. Enter Captains and
Soldiers.*

Captain. The morn is fair. Good morrow, General.

All. Good morrow, General.

25   *Antony.*   'Tis well blown,° lads.
This morning, like the spirit of a youth
That means to be of note, begins betimes.
So, so. Come, give me that: this way; well said.°
Fare thee well, dame; whate'er becomes of me,
30   This is a soldier's kiss. Rebukable
And worthy shameful check° it were to stand
On more mechanic compliment.° I'll leave thee
Now like a man of steel. You that will fight,
Follow me close; I'll bring you to't. Adieu.
                Exeunt [all but Cleopatra and Charmian].

Charmian. Please you retire to your chamber?

35   *Cleopatra.*   Lead me.
He goes forth gallantly. That he and Caesar might

15 *tight* skilled   17 *royal occupation* kingly trade   18 *workman*
professional   19 *charge* duty   22 *riveted trim* armor   23 *port* gate
25 *well blown* (1) i.e., on the trumpets (2) in full flower (of the
morning)   28 *well said* well done   31 *shameful check* shaming
rebuke   31–32 *to stand ... compliment* to make a business of vulgar civilities

Determine this great war in single fight!
Then Antony—but now——. Well, on.　　　*Exeunt.*

[Scene V. *Alexandria. Antony's camp.*]

*Trumpets sound. Enter Antony and Eros, [a
soldier meeting them].*

Soldier. The gods make this a happy° day to Antony!

Antony. Would thou and those thy scars had once pre-
　　vailed
　To make me fight at land!

Soldier.　　　　　　　　　Hadst thou done so,
　The kings that have revolted, and the soldier
　That has this morning left thee, would have still　　　*5*
　Followèd thy heels.

Antony.　　　　　　　Who's gone this morning?

Soldier.　　　　　　　　　　　　　Who?
　One ever near thee: call for Enobarbus,
　He shall not hear thee, or from Caesar's camp
　Say "I am none of thine."

Antony.　　　　　　　What sayest thou?

Soldier.　　　　　　　　　　　　Sir,
　He is with Caesar.

Eros.　　　　　　Sir, his chests and treasure　　　*10*
　He has not with him.

Antony.　　　　　Is he gone?

Soldier.　　　　　　　　　　Most certain.

Antony. Go, Eros, send his treasure after; do it;
　Detain no jot, I charge thee. Write to him

IV.v.1 *happy* fortunate

(I will subscribe)° gentle adieus and greetings;
15   Say that I wish he never find more cause
To change a master. O, my fortunes have
Corrupted honest men! Dispatch. Enobarbus!

Exit [with Eros and Soldier].

[Scene VI. *Alexandria. Caesar's camp.*]

*Flourish. Enter Agrippa, Caesar, with Enobarbus,
and Dolabella.*

Caesar. Go forth, Agrippa, and begin the fight.
Our will is Antony be took alive:
Make it so known.

Agrippa. Caesar, I shall.   [*Exit.*]

5   *Caesar.* The time of universal peace is near.
Prove this a prosp'rous day, the three-nooked°
world
Shall bear the olive freely.

Enter a Messenger.

Messenger.   Antony
Is come into the field.

Caesar.   Go charge Agrippa
Plant those that have revolted in the vant,°
10   That Antony may seem to spend his fury
Upon himself.   *Exeunt [all but Enobarbus].*

Enobarbus. Alexas did revolt and went to Jewry on
Affairs of Antony; there did dissuade°
Great Herod to incline himself to Caesar
15   And leave his master Antony. For this pains

14 *subscribe* sign   IV.vi.6 *three-nooked* three-cornered (Europe,
Asia, Africa)   9 *vant* first lines   13 *dissuade* i.e., persuade to leave
Antony

Caesar hath hanged him. Canidius and the rest
That fell away have entertainment, but
No honorable trust. I have done ill,
Of which I do accuse myself so sorely
That I will joy no more.

Enter a Soldier of Caesar's.

Soldier.   Enobarbus, Antony   20
Hath after thee sent all thy treasure, with
His bounty overplus. The messenger
Came on my guard, and at thy tent is now
Unloading of his mules.

Enobarbus.   I give it you.

Soldier. Mock not, Enobarbus: 25
I tell you true: best you safed the bringer
Out of the host;° I must attend mine office
Or would have done't myself. Your emperor
Continues still a Jove.   *Exit.*

Enobarbus. I am alone the° villain of the earth,   30
And feel I am so most.° O, Antony,
Thou mine of bounty, how wouldst thou have paid
My better service, when my turpitude
Thou dost so crown with gold! This blows° my
    heart.
If swift thought° break it not, a swifter mean   35
Shall outstrike thought; but thought will do't, I feel.
I fight against thee! No, I will go seek
Some ditch wherein to die: the foul'st best fits
My latter part of life.   *Exit.*

26–27 *best . . . host* you had better see that the man who brought
them has safe-conduct through enemy lines   30 *alone the* the only
31 *And feel I am so most* and no one could be more bitterly aware
of it   34 *blows* swells   35 *thought* sorrow

[Scene VII. *Field of battle between the camps.*]

Alarum. Drums and Trumpets. Enter Agrippa
[*and Soldiers*].

Agrippa. Retire; we have engaged ourselves too far:
Caesar himself has work,° and our oppression°
Exceeds what we expected.   *Exit* [*with Soldiers*].

Alarums. Enter Antony, and Scarus wounded.

Scarus. O my brave emperor, this is fought indeed!
5   Had we done so at first, we had droven them home
With clouts° about their heads.

Antony.   Thou bleed'st apace.

Scarus. I had a wound here that was like a *T,*
But now 'tis made an *H.*°   [*Retreat sounded*] *far off.*

Antony.   They do retire.

Scarus. We'll beat 'em into bench holes.° I have yet
10   Room for six scotches° more.

                              Enter Eros.

Eros. They are beaten, sir, and our advantage serves
For a fair victory.

Scarus.   Let us score° their backs
And snatch 'em up, as we take hares, behind:
'Tis sport to maul a runner.

Antony.   I will reward thee

IV.vii.2 *has work* is hard-pressed   2 *our oppression* the pressure on
us   6 *clouts* (1) blows (2) bandages 8 *H* (pun on "ache," pronounced "aitch")   9 *bench holes* holes in a privy   10 *scotches*
gashes   12 *score* slash

Once for thy sprightly° comfort, and tenfold   15
For thy good valor. Come thee on.
Scarus.   I'll halt° after. *Exeunt.*

[Scene VIII. *Before Alexandria.*]

Alarum. Enter Antony again in a march; Scarus,
with others.

Antony. We have beat him to his camp. Run one
          before
And let the Queen know of our gests.° Tomorrow,
Before the sun shall see's, we'll spill the blood
That has today escaped. I thank you all,
For doughty-handed are you, and have fought   5
Not as you served the cause, but as't had been
Each man's like mine: you have shown all Hectors.
Enter the city, clip° your wives, your friends,
Tell them your feats, whilst they with joyful tears
Wash the congealment from your wounds, and kiss   10
The honored gashes whole.

            Enter Cleopatra.

            [*To Scarus*] Give me thy hand;

To this great fairy° I'll commend thy acts,
Make her thanks bless thee. —O thou day o' th'
          world,
Chain mine armed neck; leap thou, attire and all,
Through proof of harness° to my heart, and there   15
Ride on the pants triumphing.

15 *sprightly* high-hearted   16 *halt* limp   IV.viii.2 *gests* deeds   8 *clip* embrace   12 *fairy* enchantress   15 *proof of harness* impenetrable armor

Cleopatra.   Lord of lords!
O infinite virtue,° com'st thou smiling from
The world's great snare uncaught?

Antony.   Mine nightingale,
We have beat them to their beds. What, girl! Though
    gray
Do something mingle with our younger brown, yet
20   ha' we
A brain that nourishes our nerves, and can
Get goal for goal of youth.° Behold this man:
Commend unto his lips thy favoring hand.—
Kiss it, my warrior.— He hath fought today
25   As if a god in hate of mankind had
Destroyed in such a shape.

Cleopatra.   I'll give thee, friend,
An armor all of gold; it was a king's.

Antony. He has deserved it, were it carbuncled°
Like holy Phoebus' car.° Give me thy hand.
30   Through Alexandria make a jolly march;
Bear our hacked targets° like the men that owe°
    them.
Had our great palace the capacity
To camp this host, we all would sup together
And drink carouses to the next day's fate,
35   Which promises royal peril. Trumpeters,
With brazen din blast you the city's ear,
Make mingle with our rattling tabourines,°
That heaven and earth may strike their sounds
    together,
Applauding our approach.   *Exeunt.*

---

17 *virtue* valor   22 *Get goal for goal of youth* keep pace with every
point won by youth   28 *carbuncled* jeweled   29 *Phoebus' car* the
sun god's chariot   31 *targets* shields   31 *owe* own   37 *tabourines*
small drums

[Scene IX. *Caesar's camp.*]

Enter a Sentry and his Company. Enobarbus
follows.

Sentry. If we be not relieved within this hour,
We must return to th' court of guard. The night
Is shiny, and they say we shall embattle
By th' second hour i' th' morn.

First Watch.   This last day was
A shrewd° one to's.

Enobarbus.   O, bear me witness, night—   5

Second Watch. What man is this?

First Watch.   Stand close, and list him.

Enobarbus. Be witness to me, O, thou blessèd moon,
When men revolted shall upon record
Bear hateful memory, poor Enobarbus did
Before thy face repent!

Sentry.   Enobarbus?

Second Watch.   Peace: 10
Hark further.

Enobarbus. O sovereign mistress° of true melancholy,
The poisonous damp of night disponge° upon me,
That life, a very rebel to my will,
May hang no longer on me. Throw my heart   15
Against the flint and hardness of my fault,
Which, being dried with grief, will break to powder,
And finish all foul thoughts. O, Antony,
Nobler than my revolt is infamous,

IV.ix.5 *shrewd* curst, bad   12 *mistress* i.e., the moon   13 *disponge*
drip

20 Forgive me in thine own particular,°
    But let the world rank me in register°
    A master-leaver° and a fugitive.
    O, Antony! O, Antony!   [*Dies.*]

First Watch.   Let's speak to him.

Sentry. Let's hear him, for the things he speaks
    May concern Caesar.

25 *Second Watch.*   Let's do so. But he sleeps.

Sentry. Swoons rather, for so bad a prayer as his
    Was never yet for° sleep.

First Watch.   Go we to him.

Second Watch. Awake, sir, awake; speak to us.

First Watch.   Hear you, sir?

Sentry. The hand of death hath raught° him.
                            Drums afar off.
                        Hark! The drums
30 Demurely° wake the sleepers. Let us bear him
    To th' court of guard: he is of note. Our hour
    Is fully out.

Second Watch. Come on then; he may recover yet.
                    Exeunt [*with the body*].

[Scene X. *Between the two camps.*]

Enter Antony and Scarus, with their Army.

Antony. Their preparation is today by sea;
    We please them not by land.

20 *in thine own particular* yourself   21 *in register* in its records
22 *master-leaver* (1) supreme traitor (2) runaway servant   27 *for* a
prelude to   29 *raught* reached   30 *Demurely* soberly, with a low
sound

Scarus.   For both, my lord.

Antony. I would they'd fight i' th' fire or i' th' air;°
  We'd fight there too. But this it is: our foot
  Upon the hills adjoining to the city
  Shall stay with us—order for sea is given;   5
  They have put forth the haven—
  Where their appointment we may best discover
  And look on their endeavor.   *Exeunt.*

[Scene XI. *Between the two camps.*]

Enter Caesar and his Army.

Caesar. But being charged,° we will be still by land—
  Which, as I take't, we shall, for his best force
  Is forth to man his galleys. To the vales,
  And hold our best advantage.°   *Exeunt.*

[Scene XII. *Before Alexandria.*]

Enter Antony and Scarus.

Antony. Yet they are not joined.° Where yond pine
  does stand
  I shall discover all. I'll bring thee word

IV.x.3 *i' th' fire or i' th' air* i.e., as well as the other two elements,
earth and water (land and sea)   IV.xi.1 *But being charged* unless
we are attacked   4 *hold our best advantage* take up the best position
we can   IV.xii.1 *joined* i.e., in battle

Straight how 'tis like to go.   *Exit.*
         Alarum afar off, as at a sea fight.°

Scarus.   Swallows have built
    In Cleopatra's sails their nests. The augurers
5   Say they know not, they cannot tell, look grimly,
    And dare not speak their knowledge. Antony
    Is valiant, and dejected, and by starts
    His fretted° fortunes give him hope and fear
    Of what he has, and has not.

                 Enter Antony.

Antony.   All is lost!
10 This foul Egyptian hath betrayèd me:
    My fleet hath yielded to the foe, and yonder
    They cast their caps up and carouse together
    Like friends long lost. Triple-turned° whore! 'Tis
        thou
    Hast sold me to this novice, and my heart
15 Makes only wars on thee. Bid them all fly;
    For when I am revenged upon my charm,°
    I have done all. Bid them all fly, be gone.
                        [*Exit Scarus.*]
    O sun, thy uprise shall I see no more.
    Fortune and Antony part here, even here
20 Do we shake hands. All come to this? The hearts
    That spanieled me at heels, to whom I gave
    Their wishes, do discandy,° melt their sweets
    On blossoming Caesar; and this pine is barked,°
    That overtopped them all. Betrayed I am.
25 O this false soul of Egypt! This grave charm,°
    Whose eye becked forth my wars, and called them
        home,
    Whose bosom was my crownet, my chief end,°

3 s.d. *Alarum . . . sea fight* (the Folio prints this direction just before
the entrance of Antony and Scarus; if F's placement is correct, the
noise fills the otherwise empty stage for a moment and makes ironic
Antony's first line, but probably the direction should be placed
either in its present position or in the middle of line 9)   8 *fretted*
(1) checkered (2) worn, decayed   13 *Triple-turned* i.e., from Pompey, from Julius Caesar, from Antony   16 *charm* witch   22 *dis-
candy* dissolve   23 *barked* stripped bare   25 *grave charm* deadly
witch   27 *crownet, my chief end* crown and end of all I did

Like a right° gypsy hath at fast and loose°
Beguiled me, to the very heart of loss.
What, Eros, Eros!

Enter Cleopatra.

Ah, thou spell! Avaunt!°   30

Cleopatra. Why is my lord enraged against his love?

Antony. Vanish, or I shall give thee thy deserving
And blemish Caesar's triumph. Let him take thee
And hoist thee up to the shouting plebeians;°
Follow his chariot, like the greatest spot°   35
Of all thy sex: most monsterlike be shown
For poor'st diminutives,° for dolts, and let
Patient Octavia plow thy visage up
With her preparèd nails.   *Exit Cleopatra.*
                            'Tis well th' art gone,
If it be well to live; but better 'twere   40
Thou fell'st into my fury, for one death
Might have prevented many. Eros, ho!
The shirt of Nessus is upon me; teach me,
Alcides, thou mine ancestor, thy rage.
Let me lodge Lichas on the horns o' th' moon,°   45
And with those hands that grasped the heaviest club
Subdue my worthiest self. The witch shall die:
To the young Roman boy she hath sold me, and
    I fall
Under this plot: she dies for't. Eros, ho!   *Exit.*

28 *right* true   28 *fast and loose* (a cheating game played by gypsies,
in which the dupe inevitably fails to make fast a coiled rope)
30 *Avaunt* begone   34 *plebeians* (accented on first syllable)   35
spot blemish   37 *diminutives* little people, i.e., the populace   43–
45 *Nessus . . . moon* (the death of Antony's ancestor Hercules—
called Alcides in line 44—is here recalled. Hercules killed the
centaur Nessus with a poisoned arrow, for trying to rape his wife
Deianira; the dying Nessus in revenge gave his robe, soaked in
poisoned blood, to Deianira, pretending it would act as a love
charm. She sent it to her husband for this purpose; in his dying
agonies Hercules hurled the bringer of it, Lichas, high in the air)

[Scene XIII. *Alexandria. Cleopatra's palace.*]

Enter Cleopatra, Charmian, Iras, Mardian.

Cleopatra. Help me, my women! O, he's more mad
    Than Telamon° for his shield; the boar of Thessaly°
    Was never so embossed.°

Charmian.   To th' monument:
    There lock yourself, and send him word you are
        dead.
5   The soul and body rive° not more in parting
    Than greatness going off.

Cleopatra.   To th' monument!
    Mardian, go tell him I have slain myself:
    Say that the last I spoke was "Antony"
    And word it, prithee, piteously. Hence, Mardian,
10 And bring me how he takes my death. To th' monu-
        ment!   *Exeunt.*

IV.xiii.2 *Telamon* i.e., Ajax, who went mad and killed himself when
he lost the contest between himself and Odysseus for the arms and
shield of Achilles   2 *the boar of Thessaly* (sent by Artemis to
ravage the country of King Oeneus, and killed by his son Meleager)
3 *embossed* (of a hunted animal) foaming at the mouth from fury
and exhaustion   5 *rive* rend

[Scene XIV. *Alexandria. Cleopatra's palace.*]

Enter Antony and Eros.

Antony. Eros, thou yet behold'st me?

Eros.   Ay, noble lord.

Antony. Sometime we see a cloud that's dragonish,
A vapor sometime like a bear or lion,
A towered citadel, a pendant rock,
A forkèd mountain, or blue promontory   5
With trees upon't that nod unto the world
And mock our eyes with air. Thou hast seen these signs:
They are black vesper's pageants.°

Eros.   Ay, my lord.

Antony. That which is now a horse, even with a thought
The rack dislimns,° and makes it indistinct   10
As water is in water.

Eros.   It does, my lord.

Antony. My good knave° Eros, now thy captain is
Even such a body: here I am Antony,
Yet cannot hold this visible shape, my knave.
I made these wars for Egypt; and the Queen——   15
Whose heart I thought I had, for she had mine,
Which, whilst it was mine, had annexed unto't
A million moe,° now lost——she, Eros, has

IV.xiv.8 *black vesper's pageants* evening's brightly colored but unreal scenery (*pageants*=floats of the mystery plays, hence plays, masques, etc.)   9–10 *even . . . dislimns* as swift as thought the cloud formation (*rack*) obliterates   12 *knave* boy   18 *moe* more

Packed cards with Caesar, and false-played my glory
20   Unto an enemy's triumph.°
Nay, weep not, gentle Eros, there is left us
Ourselves to end ourselves.

Enter Mardian.

                    O, thy vile lady!
She has robbed me of my sword.°

Mardian.   No, Antony;
My mistress loved thee, and her fortunes mingled
With thine entirely.

25   *Antony.*   Hence, saucy eunuch, peace!
She hath betrayed me and shall die the death.

Mardian. Death of one person can be paid but once,
And that she has discharged. What thou wouldst do
Is done unto thy hand.° The last she spake
30   Was "Antony! most noble Antony!"
Then in the midst a tearing groan did break
The name of Antony; it was divided
Between her heart and lips: she rend'red° life,
Thy name so buried in her.

Antony.   Dead, then?

Mardian.   Dead.

35   *Antony.* Unarm, Eros. The long day's task is done,
And we must sleep. [*To Mardian*] That thou depart'st
    hence safe
Does pay thy labor richly: go.   *Exit Mardian.*
                        Off, pluck off:
The sevenfold shield of Ajax° cannot keep
The battery° from my heart. O, cleave, my sides!
40   Heart, once be stronger than thy continent,°

19–20 *Packed cards . . . triumph* stacked the cards to favor herself
and Caesar, and so treacherously played her hand as to allow Caesar
to trump my glory   23 *sword* i.e., soldiership, masculinity   29 *unto
thy hand* already for you   33 *rend'red* surrendered   38 *sevenfold
shield of Ajax* (made of brass and lined with seven layers of oxhide)
39 *battery* bombardment   40 *thy continent* what holds you in

Crack thy frail case! Apace, Eros, apace.
No more a soldier. Bruisèd pieces,° go;
You have been nobly borne. —From me awhile.

Exit Eros.

I will o'ertake thee, Cleopatra, and
Weep for my pardon. So it must be, for now   *45*
All length° is torture: since the torch is out,
Lie down, and stray no farther. Now all labor
Mars what it does; yea, very force entangles
Itself with strength.° Seal then,° and all is done.
Eros! —I come, my queen. —Eros! —Stay for me.   *50*
Where souls do couch on flowers, we'll hand in hand,
And with our sprightly° port° make the ghosts gaze:
Dido and her Aeneas° shall want troops,°
And all the haunt be ours. —Come, Eros, Eros!

Enter Eros.

Eros. What would my lord?

Antony.   Since Cleopatra died,   *55*
I have lived in such dishonor that the gods
Detest my baseness. I, that with my sword
Quartered° the world and o'er green Neptune's back
With ships made cities, condemn myself to lack°
The courage of a woman; less noble mind   *60*
Than she which by her death our Caesar tells
"I am conqueror of myself." Thou art sworn, Eros,
That, when the exigent° should come, which now
Is come indeed, when I should see behind me
Th' inevitable prosecution° of   *65*
Disgrace and horror, that on my command
Thou then wouldst kill me. Do't, the time is come.

---

42 *pieces* armor   46 *length* length of life   48–49 *very force . . . strength* (the image probably is of a creature caught more tightly in a net by the very violence of its struggles)   49 *Seal then* finish then (i.e., the final act of sealing a document, especially a will)   52 *sprightly* (1) high-hearted, gay (2) ghostly   52 *port* bearing   53 *Dido . . . Aeneas* (the legendary lovers are brought together, though in Vergil, Dido repulses forever the faithless Aeneas)   53 *want troops* lack retinue   58 *Quartered* (1) covered with troops (2) carved up   59 *to lack* for lacking   63 *exigent* need   65 *inevitable prosecution* unescapable pursuit

Thou strik'st not me, 'tis Caesar thou defeat'st.
Put color in thy cheek.

Eros.   The gods withhold me!
Shall I do that which all the Parthian darts,
Though enemy, lost aim and could not?

Antony.   Eros,
Wouldst thou be windowed in great Rome and see
Thy master thus: with pleached° arms, bending down
His corrigible° neck, his face subdued
To penetrative shame,° whilst the wheeled seat
Of fortunate Caesar, drawn before him, branded
His baseness that ensued?°

Eros.   I would not see't.

Antony. Come then; for with a wound I must be cured.
Draw that thy honest sword, which thou hast worn
Most useful for thy country.

Eros.   O, sir, pardon me.

Antony. When I did make thee free, swor'st thou not
then
To do this when I bade thee? Do it at once,
Or thy precedent° services are all
But accidents unpurposed. Draw, and come.

Eros. Turn from me then that noble countenance
Wherein the worship of the whole world lies.

Antony. Lo thee!°   [*Turns from him.*]

Eros. My sword is drawn.

Antony.   Then let it do at once
The thing why thou hast drawn it.

Eros.   My dear master,

73 *pleached* folded (twisted behind?)   74 *corrigible* submissive
74–75 *subdued/To penetrative shame* filled with the humiliation of
deepest shame   76–77 *branded . . . ensued* made as hideously clear
as the mark branded on a criminal or animal the abject nature of
the man who followed   83 *precedent* former   87 *Lo thee* there you
are, then

My captain, and my emperor, let me say,　90
Before I strike this bloody stroke, farewell.

Antony. 'Tis said, man, and farewell.

Eros. Farewell, great chief. Shall I strike now?

Antony.　　　　　　　　　　　Now, Eros.

Eros. Why, there then! Thus I do escape the sorrow
Of Antony's death.　　　　　　*Kills himself.*

Antony.　　　　　Thrice-nobler than myself,　95
Thou teachest me, O valiant Eros, what
I should, and thou couldst not. My queen and Eros
Have by their brave instruction got upon me
A nobleness in record.° But I will be
A bridegroom in my death, and run into't　100
As to a lover's bed. Come then; and, Eros,
Thy master dies thy scholar. To do thus
　　　　　　　　　　　[Falls on his sword.]
I learned of thee. How? Not dead? Not dead?
The guard, ho! O, dispatch me!

Enter [Decretas and] a [Company of the] Guard.

First Guard.　　　　　　　What's the noise?

Antony. I have done my work ill, friends. O, make an
　end　　　　　　　　　　　　　　105
Of what I have begun.

Second Guard.　　　　The star is fall'n.

First Guard. And time is at his period.°

All.　　　　　　　　　　Alas, and woe!

Antony. Let him that loves me strike me dead.

First Guard.　　　　　　　　Not I.

Second Guard. Nor I.

Third Guard. Nor anyone.　　*Exeunt [Guard].* 110

Decretas. Thy death and fortunes bid thy followers fly.

98–99 *got . . . record* beaten me in achieving a noble place in the
story　107 *period* end

This sword but shown to Caesar, with this tidings,
Shall enter° me with him.

Enter Diomedes.

Diomedes. Where's Antony?

Decretas.   There, Diomed, there.

Diomedes.   Lives he?
115   Wilt thou not answer, man?   [*Exit Decretas.*]

Antony. Art thou there, Diomed? Draw thy sword, and give me
    Sufficing strokes for death.

Diomedes.   Most absolute lord,
    My mistress Cleopatra sent me to thee.

Antony. When did she send thee?

Diomedes.   Now, my lord.

Antony.   Where is she?

Diomedes. Locked in her monument. She had a
120   prophesying fear
    Of what hath come to pass; for when she saw
    (Which never shall be found) you did suspect
    She had disposed° with Caesar, and that your rage
    Would not be purged,° she sent you word she was
        dead;
125   But, fearing since how it might work, hath sent
    Me to proclaim the truth, and I am come,
    I dread, too late.

Antony. Too late, good Diomed. Call my guard, I
        prithee.

Diomedes. What ho! The Emperor's guard! The guard,
        what ho!
130   Come, your lord calls!

Enter four or five of the Guard of Antony.

Antony. Bear me, good friends, where Cleopatra bides;

113 *enter* recommend   123 *disposed* settled   things   124 *purged*
cured

'Tis the last service that I shall command you.

First Guard. Woe, woe are we, sir, you may not live
　　to wear
　All your true followers out.°

All.　　　　　　　　　　　Most heavy day!

Antony. Nay, good my fellows, do not please sharp
　　fate　　　　　　　　　　　　　　　　　　　 *135*
　To grace it with your sorrows. Bid that welcome
　Which comes to punish us, and we punish it,
　Seeming to bear it lightly. Take me up:
　I have led you oft; carry me now, good friends,
　And have my thanks for all.　　　　　　　　 *140*

　　　　　　Exit [*the Guard,*] *bearing Antony.*

[Scene XV. *Alexandria. The monument.*]

Enter Cleopatra and her Maids aloft,° *with
Charmian and Iras.*

Cleopatra. O, Charmian, I will never go from hence.

Charmian. Be comforted, dear madam.

Cleopatra.　　　　　　　　　No, I will not.
　All strange and terrible events are welcome,
　But comforts we despise. Our size of sorrow,
　Proportioned to our cause, must be as great　　 *5*
　As that which makes it.

　　　　　　Enter Diomed [*below*].

　　　　　　　　　How now? Is he dead?

Diomedes. His death 's upon him, but not dead.

133–34 *live . . . out* outlive all your faithful men　IV.xv.s.d. *aloft*
(presumably on the upper stage at the back of the main stage)

Look out o' th' other side your monument;
His guard have brought him thither.

Enter, [below,] Antony, and the Guard [bearing
him].

Cleopatra.   O sun,
    Burn the great sphere thou mov'st in: darkling°
10   stand
    The varying shore o' th' world! O Antony,
    Antony, Antony! Help, Charmian, help, Iras, help:
    Help, friends below, let's draw him hither.°

Antony.   Peace!
    Not Caesar's valor hath o'erthrown Antony,
15   But Antony's hath triumphed on itself.

Cleopatra. So it should be, that none but Antony
    Should conquer Antony, but woe 'tis so!

Antony. I am dying, Egypt, dying; only
    I here importune° death awhile, until
20   Of many thousand kisses the poor last
    I lay upon thy lips.

Cleopatra.   I dare not,° dear;
    Dear my lord, pardon: I dare not,
    Lest I be taken. Not th' imperious show
    Of the full-fortuned Caesar ever shall
25   Be brooched with me,° if knife, drugs, serpents have
    Edge, sting, or operation. I am safe:
    Your wife Octavia, with her modest eyes
    And still conclusion,° shall acquire no honor
    Demuring° upon me. But come, come, Antony—
30   Help me, my women—we must draw thee up:
    Assist, good friends.

Antony.   O, quick, or I am gone.

10 *darkling* in darkness   12–13 *Help . . . hither* (Shakespeare appears to have made a false start, afterwards left uncanceled, in lines 12–13, or even to line 29; Cleopatra's plan for getting Antony in is passed over, then repeated, in a curious way; and Antony's "I am dying" is also repeated)   19 *importune* beg   21 *dare not* i.e., dare not descend, or open the gates   25 *Be brooched with me* have me as its ornament   28 *still conclusion* (1) silent judgment (2) impassive finality   29 *Demuring* looking soberly

Cleopatra. Here's sport indeed! How heavy weighs my
    lord!
  Our strength is all gone into heaviness,°
  That makes the weight. Had I great Juno's power,
  The strong-winged Mercury should fetch thee up   *33*
  And set thee by Jove's side. Yet come a little,
  Wishers were ever fools. O, come, come, come.
            They heave Antony aloft to Cleopatra.
  And welcome, welcome! Die when thou hast lived,
  Quicken° with kissing. Had my lips that power,
  Thus would I wear them out.

All.   A heavy sight!   *40*

Antony. I am dying, Egypt, dying.
  Give me some wine, and let me speak a little.

Cleopatra. No, let me speak, and let me rail so high
  That the false housewife° Fortune break her wheel,°
  Provoked by my offense.°

Antony.   One word, sweet queen.   *45*
  Of Caesar seek your honor, with your safety. O!

Cleopatra. They do not go together.

Antony.   Gentle, hear me:
  None about Caesar trust but Proculeius.

Cleopatra. My resolution and my hands I'll trust,
  None about Caesar.
                                   50

Antony. The miserable change now at my end
  Lament nor sorrow at, but please your thoughts
  In feeding them with those my former fortunes,
  Wherein I lived; the greatest prince o' th' world,
  The noblest; and do now not basely die,   *55*
  Not cowardly put off my helmet to
  My countryman; a Roman, by a Roman

---

33 *heaviness* (1) weight (2) sorrow 39 *Quicken* come to life
44 *false housewife* treacherous hussy, strumpet 44 *wheel* (1) spin-
ning wheel (the especial property of a "housewife") (2) wheel of
Fortune, whose turns govern the affairs of men 45 *offense* insults

Valiantly vanquished. Now my spirit is going,
I can no more.

Cleopatra.   Noblest of men, woo't die?
60 Hast thou no care of me? Shall I abide
In this dull world, which in thy absence is
No better than a sty? O, see, my women,

                              [*Antony dies.*]

The crown o' th' earth doth melt. My lord!
O, withered is the garland° of the war,
65 The soldier's pole° is fall'n: young boys and girls
Are level now with men. The odds° is gone,
And there is nothing left remarkable°
Beneath the visiting moon.   [*Faints.*]

Charmian.   O, quietness, lady!

Iras. She's dead too, our sovereign.

Charmian.   Lady!

Iras.   Madam!

70 Charmian. O madam, madam, madam!

Iras. Royal Egypt! Empress!

Charmian.   Peace, peace, Iras!

Cleopatra. No more but e'en a woman, and commanded
By such poor passion as the maid that milks
And does the meanest chares.° It were for me
75 To throw my scepter at the injurious gods,
To tell them that this world did equal theirs
Till they had stol'n our jewel. All's but naught.
Patience is sottish,° and impatience does
Become a dog that's mad: then is it sin
80 To rush into the secret house of death
Ere death dare come to us? How do you, women?
What, what, good cheer! Why, how now, Charmian?
My noble girls! Ah, women, women, look,

64 *garland* flower, crown   65 *pole* (1) standard (2) polestar (3)
Maypole (suggested by "garland")   66 *odds* measure, distinctive
value   67 *remarkable* wonderful   74 *chares* chores   78 *sottish*
dully stupid

Our lamp is spent, it's out. Good sirs,° take heart:
We'll bury him; and then, what's brave, what's noble,   85
Let's do't after the high Roman fashion,
And make death proud to take us. Come, away.
This case of that huge spirit now is cold.
Ah, women, women! Come; we have no friend
But resolution, and the briefest° end.   90

                    Exeunt, bearing off Antony's body.

84 *sirs* (used of women, as of men)   90 *briefest* swiftest

[ACT V

Scene I. *Alexandria. Caesar's camp.*]

Enter Caesar, Agrippa, Dolabella, Maecenas,
[Gallus, Proculeius,] with his Council of War.

Caesar. Go to him, Dolabella, bid him yield:
 Being so frustrate, tell him, he mocks
 The pauses that he makes.°

Dolabella.   Caesar, I shall.   [*Exit.*]

 Enter Decretas, with the sword of Antony.

Caesar. Wherefore is that? And what art thou that
  dar'st
 Appear thus° to us?

5 *Decretas.*   I am called Decretas.
 Mark Antony I served, who best was worthy
 Best to be served. Whilst he stood up and spoke,
 He was my master, and I wore my life
 To spend upon his haters. If thou please
10 To take me to thee, as I was to him
 I'll be to Caesar; if thou pleasest not,
 I yield thee up my life.

Caesar.   What is't thou say'st?

V.i.2–3 *Being so . . . he makes* tell him that, since he is truly defeated,
these delays are a mere mockery   5 *thus* i.e., holding a naked sword

Decretas. I say, O Caesar, Antony is dead.

Caesar. The breaking° of so great a thing should make
  A greater crack.° The round world   15
  Should have shook lions into civil° streets
  And citizens to their dens. The death of Antony
  Is not a single doom; in the name lay
  A moiety° of the world.

Decretas.   He is dead, Caesar,
  Not by a public minister of justice   20
  Nor by a hirèd knife; but that self° hand
  Which writ his honor in the acts it did
  Hath, with the courage which the heart did lend it,
  Splitted the heart. This is his sword,
  I robbed his wound of it: behold it stained   25
  With his most noble blood.

Caesar.   [*Weeping*] Look you, sad friends.
  The gods rebuke me, but it is tidings
  To wash the eyes of kings.

Agrippa.   And strange it is
  That nature must compel us to lament
  Our most persisted° deeds.

Maecenas.   His taints and honors   30
  Waged equal with° him.

Agrippa.   A rarer spirit never
  Did steer humanity; but you gods will give us
  Some faults to make us men. Caesar is touched.

Maecenas. When such a spacious mirror's set before
  him,
  He needs must see himself.

14 *breaking* (1) destruction (2) disclosure, report 15 *crack* (1)
breach (2) explosive sound 16 *civil* city 19 *moiety* half 21 *self*
selfsame 30 *persisted* persisted in 31 *Waged equal with* were
equally matched in

35 *Caesar*.   O Antony,
    I have followed° thee to this. But we do launch°
    Diseases in our bodies. I must perforce
    Have shown to thee such a declining day
    Or look on thine: we could not stall° together
40 In the whole world. But yet let me lament
    With tears as sovereign° as the blood of hearts
    That thou, my brother, my competitor
    In top of all design,° my mate in empire,
    Friend and companion in the front of war,
45 The arm of mine own body, and the heart
    Where mine his° thoughts did kindle—that our
        stars,
    Unreconciliable, should divide
    Our equalness to this. Hear me, good friends—

                Enter an Egyptian.

    But I will tell you at some meeter season.
50 The business of this man looks out of him;
    We'll hear him what he says. Whence are you?

Egyptian. A poor Egyptian yet.° The Queen my
        mistress,
    Confined in all she has, her monument,
    Of thy intents desires instruction,
55 That she preparèdly may frame herself
    To th' way she's forced to.

Caesar.   Bid her have good heart:
    She soon shall know of us, by some of ours,
    How honorable and how kindly we
    Determine for her. For Caesar cannot live
    To be ungentle.

60 *Egyptian*.   So the gods preserve thee!   *Exit*.

Caesar. Come hither, Proculeius. Go and say
    We purpose her no shame: give her what comforts
    The quality of her passion° shall require,

36 *followed* pursued 36 *launch* lance 39 *stall* dwell 41 *sovereign*
potent 42–43 *my competitor . . . design* my partner in noblest
enterprise 46 *his* its 52 *yet* still (though Egypt will soon be
Roman) 63 *passion* strong emotion (here, grief)

Lest, in her greatness, by some mortal stroke
She do defeat us. For her life in Rome
Would be eternal in our triumph.° Go,   65
And with your speediest bring us what she says
And how you find of her.

Proculeius.   Caesar, I shall.
                              Exit Proculeius.

Caesar. Gallus, go you along. [*Exit Gallus.*] Where's
    Dolabella,
    To second Proculeius?

All.   Dolabella!   70

Caesar. Let him alone, for I remember now
    How he's employed. He shall in time be ready.
    Go with me to my tent, where you shall see
    How hardly° I was drawn into this war,
    How calm and gentle I proceeded still   75
    In all my writings. Go with me, and see
    What I can show in this.
                              Exeunt.

[Scene II. *Alexandria. The monument.*]

Enter Cleopatra, Charmian, Iras, and Mardian.

Cleopatra. My desolation does begin to make
    A better life. 'Tis paltry to be Caesar:
    Not being Fortune, he's but Fortune's knave,°
    A minister of her will. And it is great
    To do that thing that ends all other deeds,   5
    Which shackles accidents and bolts up change;

65–66 *For her . . . our triumph* alive, in Rome, walking in my triumphal procession, she would manifest my power to the end of
time   74 *hardly* reluctantly   V.ii.3 *knave* servant

Which sleeps, and never palates° more the dung,
The beggar's nurse and Caesar's.°

Enter, [to the gates of the monument,] Proculeius,
[Gallus, and Soldiers].

Proculeius. Caesar sends greeting to the Queen of
        Egypt,
10   And bids thee study on what fair demands
        Thou mean'st to have him grant thee.

Cleopatra.   What's thy name?

Proculeius. My name is Proculeius.

Cleopatra.   Antony
        Did tell me of you, bade me trust you, but
        I do not greatly care to be deceived,°
15   That have no use for trusting. If your master
        Would have a queen his beggar, you must tell him
        That majesty, to keep decorum, must
        No less beg than a kingdom: if he please
        To give me conquered Egypt for my son,
20   He gives me so much of mine own as I
        Will kneel to him with thanks.

Proculeius.   Be of good cheer:
        Y' are fall'n into a princely hand, fear nothing.
        Make your full reference freely° to my lord,
        Who is so full of grace that it flows over
25   On all that need. Let me report to him
        Your sweet dependency, and you shall find
        A conqueror that will pray in aid for kindness,°
        Where he for grace is kneeled to.

Cleopatra.   Pray you, tell him
        I am his fortune's vassal, and I send him
30   The greatness he has got. I hourly learn
        A doctrine of obedience, and would gladly
        Look him i' th' face.

7 *palates* tastes   7–8 *the dung . . . Caesar's* the dungy earth, whose
fruits are the source of life to beggar and to emperor   14 *to be
deceived* whether or not I am deceived   23 *Make . . . freely* hand
your affairs fully   27 *pray in aid for kindness* beg you to assist him
to be kind to you

Proculeius.   This I'll report, dear lady.
Have comfort, for I know your plight is pitied
Of him that caused it.

       [Enter Gallus and Soldiers behind.]°

You see how easily she may be surprised.   *35*
              [They seize Cleopatra.]
Guard her till Caesar come.

Iras. Royal Queen!

Charmian. O, Cleopatra! Thou art taken, Queen.

Cleopatra. Quick, quick, good hands!
              [Draws a dagger.]

Proculeius.   Hold, worthy lady, hold!
              [Disarms her.]
Do not yourself such wrong, who are in this   *40*
Relieved,° but not betrayed.

Cleopatra.   What, of death too,
That rids our dogs of languish?°

Proculeius.   Cleopatra,
Do not abuse my master's bounty by
Th' undoing of yourself: let the world see
His nobleness well acted, which your death   *45*
Will never let come forth.°

Cleopatra.   Where art thou, death?
Come hither, come! Come, come, and take a queen
Worth many babes and beggars!

Proculeius.   O, temperance, lady!

Cleopatra. Sir, I will eat no meat, I'll not drink, sir—
If idle talk will once be necessary—
I'll not sleep neither. This mortal house I'll ruin,   *50*
Do Caesar what he can. Know, sir, that I
Will not wait pinioned° at your master's court

34 s.d. (the Folio gives no stage direction here; it was presumably
left to the stage performance to decide on the procedure by which
the Romans capture the tomb) 41 *Relieved* rescued 42 *languish*
lingering illness 46 *let come forth* allow to be revealed 53 *pin-
ioned* with clipped wings

Nor once be chastised with the sober eye
55   Of dull Octavia. Shall they hoist me up
And show me to the shouting varletry°
Of censuring Rome? Rather a ditch in Egypt
Be gentle grave unto me! Rather on Nilus' mud
Lay me stark nak'd and let the waterflies
60   Blow° me into abhorring! Rather make
My country's high pyramides° my gibbet
And hang me up in chains!

Proculeius.   You do extend
These thoughts of horror further than you shall
Find cause in Caesar.

Enter Dolabella.

Dolabella.   Proculeius,
65   What thou hast done, thy master Caesar knows,
And he hath sent for thee. For the Queen,
I'll take her to my guard.

Proculeius.   So, Dolabella,
It shall content me best: be gentle to her.
[*To Cleopatra*] To Caesar I will speak what you
    shall please,
If you'll employ me to him.

70   *Cleopatra.*   Say, I would die.
Exit Proculeius [with Soldiers].

Dolabella. Most noble Empress, you have heard of me.

Cleopatra. I cannot tell.

Dolabella.   Assuredly you know me.

Cleopatra. No matter, sir, what I have heard or known.
You laugh when boys or women tell their dreams;
Is't not your trick?°

75   *Dolabella.*   I understand not, madam.

Cleopatra. I dreamt there was an Emperor Antony.

56 *varletry* mob   60 *Blow* swell   61 *pyramides* (four syllables,
accented on second)   75 *trick* way

   O, such another sleep, that I might see
   But such another man.

Dolabella.   If it might please ye—

Cleopatra. His face was as the heav'ns, and therein
   stuck
   A sun and moon, which kept their course and lighted   *80*
   The little *O,* th' earth.

Dolabella.   Most sovereign creature—

Cleopatra. His legs bestrid the ocean: his reared arm
   Crested the world: his voice was propertied
   As all the tunèd spheres,° and that to friends;
   But when he meant to quail° and shake the orb,   *85*
   He was as rattling thunder. For his bounty,
   There was no winter in't: an autumn 'twas
   That grew the more by reaping. His delights
   Were dolphinlike, they showed his back above
   The element they lived in. In his livery°   *90*
   Walked crowns and crownets:° realms and islands
     were
   As plates° dropped from his pocket.

Dolabella.   Cleopatra—

Cleopatra. Think you there was or might be such a man
   As this I dreamt of?

Dolabella.   Gentle madam, no.

Cleopatra. You lie, up to the hearing of the gods.
   But if there be nor ever were one such,
   It's past the size of dreaming;° nature wants stuff
   To vie strange forms with fancy, yet t' imagine   *95*

83–84 *propertied . . . spheres* musical as the spheres (referring to
the belief in the music of the spheres, made by the harmonious blend
of each planet's "note" and normally too fine for human ears to
catch)   85 *quail* make quail   90 *livery* (1) service (2) possession,
guardianship (legal term)   91 *crowns and crownets* i.e., kings and
princes   92 *plates* silver coins   96–97 *But if . . . dreaming* but
suppose you were right, and no such man exists, and never did exist,
how can I have imagined such a man, for no mere dreaming fantasy
could make something so great

An Antony were nature's piece 'gainst fancy,
Condemning shadows quite.°

100 *Dolabella.*   Hear me, good madam.
Your loss is as yourself, great; and you bear it
As answering to the weight. Would I might never
O'ertake pursued success, but I do° feel,
By the rebound of yours, a grief that smites
My very heart at root.

105 *Cleopatra.*   I thank you, sir.
Know you what Caesar means to do with me?

Dolabella. I am loath to tell you what I would you
knew.

Cleopatra. Nay, pray you, sir.

Dolabella.   Though he be honorable——

Cleopatra. He'll lead me, then, in triumph?

110 *Dolabella.* Madam, he will. I know't.

> *Flourish. Enter Proculeius, Caesar, Gallus,*
> *Maecenas, and others of his Train.*

All. Make way there! Caesar!

Caesar. Which is the Queen of Egypt?

Dolabella. It is the Emperor, madam.
                                    Cleopatra kneels.

Caesar. Arise! You shall not kneel:
I pray you rise; rise, Egypt.

115 *Cleopatra.*   Sir, the gods
Will have it thus. My master and my lord
I must obey.

Caesar.   Take to you no hard thoughts.
The record of what injuries you did us,

97–100 *nature . . . quite* reality lacks the material to compete with
imagination in the creation of strange forms, yet the creation of an
Antony would be a masterpiece of conception on the part of reality,
surpassing and discrediting all the illusions of imagination   103 *but
I do* if I do not

Though written in our flesh, we shall remember
As things but done by chance.

Cleopatra.   Sole sir o' th' world,   120
I cannot project° mine own cause so well
To make it clear,° but do confess I have
Been laden with like frailties which before
Have often shamed our sex.

Caesar.   Cleopatra, know,
We will extenuate rather than enforce.°   125
If you apply° yourself to our intents,
Which towards you are most gentle, you shall find
A benefit in this change; but if you seek
To lay on me a cruelty by taking
Antony's course, you shall bereave yourself   130
Of my good purposes, and put your children
To that destruction which I'll guard them from
If thereon you rely. I'll take my leave.

Cleopatra. And may, through all the world: 'tis yours,
    and we,
Your scutcheons° and your signs of conquest, shall   135
Hang in what place you please. Here, my good lord.
                    [*Hands him a paper.*]

Caesar. You shall advise me in all for Cleopatra.

Cleopatra. This is the brief° of money, plate, and
    jewels
I am possessed of. 'Tis exactly valued,
Not petty things admitted. [*Calling*] Where's
    Seleucus?
                                                               140

[*Enter Seleucus.*]

Seleucus. Here, madam.

Cleopatra. This is my treasurer; let him speak, my lord,
    Upon his peril, that I have reserved
    To myself nothing. Speak the truth, Seleucus.

121 *project* set forth (accented on first syllable)   122 *clear* innocent
125 *enforce* emphasize   126 *apply* conform   135 *scutcheons* armo-
rial bearings (alluding to the captured shields displayed by a conqueror)   138 *brief* summary

145 *Seleucus*. Madam,
    I had rather seel° my lips than to my peril
    Speak that which is not.

Cleopatra.   What have I kept back?

Seleucus. Enough to purchase what you have made
    known.

Caesar. Nay, blush not, Cleopatra, I approve
    Your wisdom in the deed.

150 *Cleopatra*.   See, Caesar: O, behold,
    How pomp is followed! Mine° will now be yours,
    And should we shift estates, yours would be mine.
    The ingratitude of this Seleucus does
    Even make me wild. O slave, of no more trust
155   Than love that's hired! What, goest thou back? Thou
    shalt
    Go back, I warrant thee; but I'll catch thine eyes,
    Though they had wings. Slave, soulless villain, dog!
    O rarely° base!

Caesar.   Good Queen, let us entreat you.

Cleopatra. O Caesar, what a wounding shame is this,
160   That thou vouchsafing here to visit me,
    Doing the honor of thy lordliness
    To one so meek, that mine own servant should
    Parcel° the sum of my disgraces by
    Addition of his envy.° Say, good Caesar,
165   That I some lady° trifles have reserved,
    Immoment° toys, things of such dignity
    As we greet modern° friends withal; and say
    Some nobler token I have kept apart
    For Livia° and Octavia, to induce
170   Their mediation——must I be unfolded
    With° one that I have bred? The gods! it smites me

---

146 *seel* sew up   151 *Mine* i.e., my followers   158 *rarely* exception-
ally   163 *Parcel* piece out   164 *envy* malice   165 *lady* lady's   166
Immoment unimportant   167 *modern* ordinary   169 *Livia* Caesar's
wife   170–71 *unfolded/With* exposed by

Beneath the fall I have. [*To Seleucus*] Prithee go
  hence,
Or I shall show the cinders° of my spirits
Through th' ashes of my chance.° Wert thou a man,
Thou wouldst have mercy on me.

Caesar.   Forbear, Seleucus. *175*
                                [*Exit Seleucus.*]

Cleopatra. Be it known that we, the greatest, are mis-
  thought°
For things that others do, and when we fall,
We answer others' merits in our name,°
Are therefore to be pitied.

Caesar.   Cleopatra,
Not what you have reserved, nor what acknowledged, *180*
Put we i' th' roll of conquest: still be't yours,
Bestow it at your pleasure, and believe
Caesar's no merchant, to make prize° with you
Of things that merchants sold. Therefore be cheered,
Make not your thoughts your prisons: no, dear
  Queen,   *185*
For we intend so to dispose you as
Yourself shall give us counsel. Feed and sleep:
Our care and pity is so much upon you
That we remain your friend; and so adieu.

Cleopatra. My master, and my lord!

Caesar.   Not so. Adieu. *190*
      Flourish. Exeunt Caesar and his Train.

Cleopatra. He words me, girls, he words me, that I
  should not
Be noble to myself! But hark thee, Charmian.
                  [*Whispers to Charmian.*]

Iras. Finish, good lady, the bright day is done,
And we are for the dark.

---

173 *cinders* burning coals 174 *chance* fortune 176 *misthought*
misjudged 178 *We . . . name* (1) we have to be responsible for
faults committed in our name (*merits* = deserts, acts deserving punishment) (2) our name is used to validate the actions of others
183 *make prize* haggle

Cleopatra.   Hie thee again:
195 I have spoke already, and it is provided;
     Go put it to the haste.

Charmian.   Madam, I will.

                  Enter Dolabella.

Dolabella. Where is the Queen?

Charmian.   Behold, sir.   [*Exit.*]

Cleopatra.   Dolabella!

Dolabella. Madam, as thereto sworn, by your command
     (Which my love makes religion to obey)
200 I tell you this: Caesar through Syria
     Intends his journey, and within three days
     You with your children will he send before.
     Make your best use of this. I have performed
     Your pleasure, and my promise.

Cleopatra.   Dolabella,
     I shall remain your debtor.

205 *Dolabella.*   I, your servant.
     Adieu, good Queen; I must attend on Caesar.

Cleopatra. Farewell, and thanks.   *Exit* [*Dolabella*].
                  Now, Iras, what think'st thou?
     Thou, an Egyptian puppet,° shall be shown
     In Rome as well as I: mechanic slaves°
210 With greasy aprons, rules, and hammers shall
     Uplift us to the view. In their thick breaths,
     Rank of gross diet,° shall we be enclouded,
     And forced to drink their vapor.

Iras.   The gods forbid!

Cleopatra. Nay, 'tis most certain, Iras. Saucy lictors°
21.   Will catch at us like strumpets, and scald° rhymers
     Ballad us out o' tune. The quick comedians

208 *puppet* (she envisages Iras as a doll manipulated by the pup-
peteer, Octavius—i.e., a figure posed on a float following Caesar in
the triumphal procession)   209 *mechanic slaves* vulgar workmen
212 *Rank of gross diet* stinking of bad food   214 *Saucy lictors* in-
solent officers   215 *scald* scurvy

Extemporally will stage us, and present
Our Alexandrian revels: Antony
Shall be brought drunken forth, and I shall see
Some squeaking Cleopatra boy my greatness°　　220
I' th' posture of a whore.

Iras.　　　　　　　　　O, the good gods!

Cleopatra. Nay, that's certain.

Iras. I'll never see't! For I am sure mine nails
Are stronger than mine eyes.

Cleopatra.　　　　　　　Why, that's the way
To fool their preparation, and to conquer　　225
Their most absurd intents.

Enter Charmian.

　　　　　　　　　Now, Charmian!
Show me, my women, like a queen: go fetch
My best attires. I am again for Cydnus,
To meet Mark Antony. Sirrah° Iras, go.
Now, noble Charmian, we'll dispatch indeed,　　230
And when thou hast done this chare,° I'll give thee
leave
To play till doomsday. —Bring our crown and all.
　　　　　　　　[*Exit Iras.*] *A noise within.*
Wherefore's this noise?

Enter a Guardsman.

Guardsman.　　　　　　Here is a rural fellow
That will not be denied your Highness' presence:
He brings you figs.　　235

Cleopatra. Let him come in.　　*Exit Guardsman.*
　　　　　　　　What poor an° instrument
May do a noble deed! He brings me liberty.
My resolution's placed,° and I have nothing

---

220 *boy my greatness* reduce my greatness to the crude imitation
that a boy can manage (in England women's parts were acted by
boys or young men)　229 *Sirrah* (an address to inferiors, used
equally of men or women)　231 *chare* chore　236 *What poor an*
what a poor　238 *placed* fixed

Of woman in me: now from head to foot
240 I am marble-constant: now the fleeting moon°
No planet is of mine.

Enter Guardsman and Clown° [*with basket*].

Guardsman.   This is the man.

Cleopatra. Avoid,° and leave him.   *Exit Guardsman.*
Hast thou the pretty worm of Nilus° there,
That kills and pains not?

245 *Clown.* Truly I have him; but I would not be the party
that should desire you to touch him, for his biting is
immortal:° those that do die of it do seldom or never
recover.

Cleopatra. Remember'st thou any that have died on't?

250 *Clown.* Very many, men and women too. I heard of°
one of them no longer than yesterday; a very honest°
woman, but something given to lie, as a woman
should not do but in the way of honesty; how she
died of the biting of it, what pain she felt; truly, she
255 makes a very good report o' th' worm; but he that
will believe all that they say shall never be saved
by half that they do; but this is most falliable, the
worm's an odd worm.

Cleopatra. Get thee hence, farewell.

260 *Clown.* I wish you all joy of the worm.
                    [*Sets down his basket.*]

Cleopatra. Farewell.

Clown. You must think this, look you, that the worm
will do his kind.°

Cleopatra. Ay, ay, farewell.

240 *fleeting moon* (a symbol of fickleness, especially in women; and
Cleopatra's special symbol, as being Isis or moon goddess)   241 s.d.
Clown rustic   242 *Avoid* depart   243 *worm of Nilus* serpent of
Nile, i.e., asp or small viper   247 *immortal* (his blunder for "mortal")   250 *heard of* heard from   251 *honest* (1) chaste (2) truthful
(similar innuendoes fill the speech, with puns on "lie" and "die")
263 *do his kind* act according to his nature

Clown. Look you, the worm is not to be trusted but in 265
the keeping of wise people: for indeed there is no
goodness in the worm.

Cleopatra. Take thou no care; it shall be heeded.

Clown. Very good. Give it nothing, I pray you, for it
is not worth the feeding. 270

Cleopatra. Will it eat me?

Clown. You must not think I am so simple but I know
the devil himself will not eat a woman. I know that
a woman is a dish for the gods, if the devil dress°
her not. But truly, these same whoreson devils do 275
the gods great harm in their women; for in every
ten that they make, the devils mar five.

Cleopatra. Well, get thee gone, farewell.

Clown. Yes, forsooth. I wish you joy o' th' worm. *Exit.*

[*Enter Iras with a robe, crown, etc.*]

Cleopatra. Give me my robe, put on my crown, I have 280
Immortal longings° in me. Now no more
The juice of Egypt's grape shall moist this lip.
Yare,° yare, good Iras; quick: methinks I hear
Antony call: I see him rouse himself
To praise my noble act. I hear him mock 285
The luck of Caesar, which the gods give men
To excuse their after wrath.°   Husband, I come:
Now to that name my courage prove my title!
I am fire, and air; my other elements
I give to baser life.° So, have you done? 290
Come then, and take the last warmth of my lips.
Farewell, kind Charmian, Iras, long farewell.
                [*Kisses them. Iras falls and dies.*]

274 *dress* (1) prepare (i.e., of food)   (2) clothe, equip   281 *Immortal longings* (1) the desires of a goddess (2) longings for im-
mortality   283 *Yare* quickly   287 *their after wrath* the retributive
punishments heaped by the gods on those who have been too proud
of their good fortune   289–90 *I am fire . . . life* (man was believed
to be made up of four elements, two higher—fire and air—and two
lower or baser—earth and water)

Have I the aspic° in my lips? Dost fall?
If thou and nature can so gently part,
295   The stroke of death is as a lover's pinch,
Which hurts, and is desired. Dost thou lie still?
If thus thou vanishest, thou tell'st the world
It is not worth leave-taking.

Charmian. Dissolve, thick cloud, and rain, that I may
  say
The gods themselves do weep.

300 *Cleopatra.*   This proves me base:
If she first meet the curlèd° Antony,
He'll make demand of her, and spend that kiss
Which is my heaven to have. Come, thou mortal
  wretch,°
      [To an asp, which she applies to her breast.]
With thy sharp teeth this knot intrinsicate°
305   Of life at once untie. Poor venomous fool,
Be angry, and dispatch.° O, couldst thou speak,
That I might hear thee call great Caesar ass
Unpolicied!°

Charmian.   O eastern star!°

Cleopatra.   Peace, peace!
Dost thou not see my baby at my breast,
That sucks the nurse asleep?

310 *Charmian.*   O, break! O, break!

Cleopatra. As sweet as balm, as soft as air, as gentle—
O, Antony! Nay, I will take thee too:
      [Applies another asp to her arm.]
What° should I stay—   *Dies.°*

---

293 *aspic* asp   301 *curlèd* freshly barbered   303 *thou mortal wretch* you deadly little object (*wretch,* like *fool* in line 305, is often an affectionate term, used especially of children)   304 *intrinsicate* intricate   306 *dispatch* quickly end it   308 *Unpolicied* lacking statecraft   308 *eastern star* morning star, Venus   313 *What* why   313 s.d. *Dies* (modern actresses prefer to die upright, seated regally, but Caesar's penultimate and final speeches suggest that Cleopatra dies —as in Plutarch—"upon a bed")

Charmian. In this wild world? So, fare thee well.
  Now boast thee, death, in thy possession lies   *315*
  A lass unparalleled. Downy windows, close;
  And golden Phoebus° never be beheld
  Of eyes again so royal! Your crown's awry;
  I'll mend it, and then play—

      Enter the Guard, rustling in.

First Guard. Where's the Queen?

Charmian.   Speak softly, wake her not. *320*

First Guard. Caesar hath sent—

Charmian.   Too slow a messenger.
                     [Applies an asp.]
  O, come apace, dispatch; I partly feel thee.

First Guard. Approach, ho! All's not well: Caesar's
  beguiled.

Second Guard. There's Dolabella sent from Caesar;
  call him.

First Guard. What work is here! Charmian, is this well
  done?   *325*

Charmian. It is well done, and fitting for a princess
  Descended of so many royal kings.
  Ah, soldier!   *Charmian dies.*

      Enter Dolabella.

Dolabella. How goes it here?   *330*

Second Guard.   All dead.

Dolabella.   Caesar, thy thoughts
  Touch their effects° in this: thyself art coming
  To see performed the dreaded act which thou
  So sought'st to hinder.

    Enter Caesar and all his Train, marching.

All.   A way there, a way for Caesar!

---

317 *Phoebus* sun god   330 *Touch their effects* meet with realization

Dolabella. O, sir, you are too sure an augurer:
That you did fear is done.

Caesar.   Bravest at the last,
335   She leveled at° our purposes, and being royal,
Took her own way. The manner of their deaths?
I do not see them bleed.

Dolabella.   Who was last with them?

First Guard. A simple countryman, that brought her
figs.
This was his basket.

Caesar.   Poisoned, then.

First Guard.   O, Caesar,
340   This Charmian lived but now, she stood and spake;
I found her trimming up the diadem
On her dead mistress; tremblingly she stood,
And on the sudden dropped.

Caesar.   O, noble weakness!
If they had swallowed poison, 'twould appear
345   By external swelling; but she looks like sleep,
As she would catch another Antony
In her strong toil° of grace.

Dolabella.   Here, on her breast,
There is a vent° of blood, and something blown;°
The like is on her arm.

350 *First Guard.* This is an aspic's trail; and these fig leaves
Have slime upon them, such as th' aspic leaves
Upon the caves of Nile.

Caesar.   Most probable
That so she died: for her physician tells me
She hath pursued conclusions° infinite
355   Of easy ways to die. Take up her bed,
And bear her women from the monument.
She shall be buried by her Antony.

· 335 *leveled at* (1) guessed (2) fought against   347 *toil* snare   348
vent discharge   348 *blown* swollen   354 *conclusions* experiments

No grave upon the earth shall clip° in it
A pair so famous. High events as these
Strike° those that make them; and their story is   360
No less in pity, than his glory which
Brought them to be lamented. Our army shall
In solemn show attend this funeral,
And then to Rome. Come, Dolabella, see
High order in this great solemnity.   *Exeunt omnes.*   365

FINIS

358 *clip* clasp   360 *Strike* touch

Textual Note

Antony and Cleopatra was entered in the Stationers' Register in May, 1608. Though this procedure normally suggested that publication would follow shortly, the play remained, in fact, unprinted until 1623, when it appeared in the "Tragedies" section of the First Folio. This First Folio text of the play is therefore the single authoritative one, and all succeeding editions—including of course the present one—derive from it.

It is widely agreed that the Folio text of *Antony and Cleopatra* was almost certainly printed direct from Shakespeare's own manuscript, and not from a transcript or prompter's copy. The features of the Folio text that suggest a source in Shakespearean manuscript may be briefly summarized as follows. First, it contains unusual spellings and word usages, some of which seem to be peculiar to Shakespeare, and some of which were, at any rate, archaic by the time the Folio was printed. Secondly, many of the Folio misprints are of the kind (occurring also in other texts of the plays) that would seem to arise from the individual character of Shakespeare's own handwriting. Thirdly, it lacks all act and scene divisions, except for the opening "Actus Primus, Scoena Prima"; a lack which indicates copy prepared primarily for the theater. Fourthly, its stage directions are unusually full and detailed, and are often of the nature of an author's "notes on the text"; for example, "Alarum afar off, as at a sea fight." And lastly, the Folio text contains a passage in the first Monument scene

(IV.xv.12–29) that suggests the direct carrying over of the author's deletions and rewritings. (See relevant footnote to text.) None of this is absolutely conclusive, but taken together the evidence leaves little doubt that the Folio text was printed direct from Shakespeare's manuscript.

As a text, it is relatively good: it contains many slips but few real difficulties. Its major flaw is the occurrence of very frequent mislineation. This has been silently adjusted in the present edition, as the "correct" lineation is either clear, or, where doubtful, immaterial. The present edition also adds a list of dramatis personae, which is lacking in the Folio; and it adds act and scene divisions, and indications of locality, except for the Folio's opening "Actus Primus, Scoena Prima" which is here translated. It also supplements the existing stage directions. All such additions and supplementations are indicated by square brackets. The positions of a few stage directions have been slightly altered; speech prefixes and other abbreviations are expanded, punctuation and spelling are modernized. The spelling of proper names is regularized: for example, "Cleopatra" is given, though in F "Cleopater" also appears; again, "Decretas" is given though in F "Decretus" also appears; "Canidius" is given for F's "Camidius," "Camidias," and "Camindius"; and so forth. (In a few instances, where the change is more marked, the reading is listed below.) All other departures from the Folio text are listed below, and utilize earlier editorial emendations; the adopted reading is given in italics, and then the original reading in roman. As in the footnotes to the text, a line number followed by "s.d." indicates the stage direction which follows the given line, or which interrupts it.

I.i.39 *On* One   \50 *whose* who

I.ii.4 *charge* change   40 *fertile* foretell   63 *Alexas* [F treats "Alexas" as a speech prefix and gives him the rest of the speech here given to Charmian]   81 *Saw* Saue   113 [F adds s.d.: Enter another Messenger]   114 *ho, the news!* how the newes?   115 *First*

Attendant 1 Mes　116 *Second Attendant* 2 Mes　119 *Messenger*
3 Mes　131 *Ho now, Enobarbus!* How now Enobarbus.　138 *occasion* an occasion　181 *leave* loue　186 *Hath* Haue　195 *hair*
heire

I.iii.25 *first* fitst　43 *services* Seruicles　82 *by my sword* by Sword

I.iv.3 *Our* One　8 *Vouchsafed* vouchsafe　9 *abstract* abstracts
44 *deared* fear'd　46 *lackeying* lacking　56 *wassails* Vassailes
58 *Pansa* Pausa　75 *we* me

I.v.34 s.d. *Antony* Caesar　50 *dumbed* dumbe　61 *man* mans

II.i.16,18,38 [F's speech prefix here, as for all speeches in the scene
other than those of Pompey and Varrius, is "*Mene*." But the context clearly indicates that Menas as well as Menecrates speaks in
the scene]　21 *waned* wand　41 *warred* wan'd

II.ii.125 *not so* not, say　126 *reproof* proofe　176 s.d. *Exit* Exit
omnes. Manet　210 *glow* gloue　212 *gentlewomen* Gentlewoman
229 *heard* hard　238 *pow'r breathe* powr breath

II.iii.23 *afeard* a feare　31 *away* alway

II.v.12 *Tawny-finned* Tawny fine　43 *is* 'tis

II.vi.s.d. *Agrippa, with* Agrippa, Menas with　19 *is* his　52 *jailer*
laylor　58 *composition* composion　66 *meanings* meaning　69 *more
of* more

II.vii.1 *their* th' their　4 *high-colored* high Conlord　12 *lief* liue
36 *pyramises* Pyramisis　94 *then* then he　102 *grows* grow
113 *bear* beate　126 *Splits* Spleet's　130 *father's* Father　131–
35 *Take heed . . . sound out* [F gives all to Enobarbus, mistaking
(?) speech prefix "*Menas*" for vocative]

III.i.5 *Silius* Romaine [so throughout scene]　8 *whither* whether

III.ii.10 *Agrippa* Ant　16 *figures* Figure　59 *wept* weepe

III.iv.9 *took't* look't　24 *yours* your　30 *Your* You　38 *has* he's

III.v.14 *world, thou hast* would thou hadst　16 *the one the other*
the other

III.vi.13 *he there* hither　13 *kings of kings* King of Kings
74 *Comagene* Comageat

III.vii.4 *it is* it it　5 *Is't* If　23 *Toryne* Troine　35 *muleters* Mili-
ters　51 *Actium* Action　69 *led* leade　72 *Canidius* Ven

III.x.s.d. *Enobarbus* Enobarbus and Scarus　14 *June* Inne　27 *he*
his

III.xi.19 *that* them　44 *He is* Hee's　47 *seize* cease　51 *whither*
whether　58 *tow* stowe　59 *Thy* The

III.xiii.10 *merèd* meered　55 *Caesar* Caesars　56 *embraced* embrace　74 *deputation* disputation　104 *errand* arrant　162 *smite*

smile 165 *discandying* discandering 168 *sits* sets 199 *preys on* prayes in 201 s.d. *Exit* Exeunt

IV.ii.1 *Domitius* Domitian

IV.iii.7 *Third Soldier* 1

IV.iv.5–8 *Nay, I'll help . . . must be* [F gives all to Cleopatra, mistaking (?) speech prefix "Anthony" for vocative, and misplacing (?) it after "help too"] 8 *Sooth, la* Sooth-law 13 *daff't* daft 24 *Captain* Alex

IV.v.1,3,6 *Soldier* Eros

IV.viii.2 *gests* guests 23 *favoring* sauoring

IV.xii.4 *augurers* Auguries 21 *spanieled* pannelled

IV.xiv.4 *towered* toward 10 *dislimns* dislimes 19 *Caesar* Caesars 104 *ho!* how?

IV.xv.72 *e'en* in 90 s.d. *off* of

V.i.s.d. *Maecenas* Menas 28,31 *Agrippa* Dol 59 *live* leaue

V.ii.56 *varletry* Varlotarie 81 *little O, th' earth* little o' th' earth 87 *autumn 'twas* Anthony it was 104 *smites* suites 216 *Ballad* Ballads 216 *o' tune* a Tune 228 *Cydnus* Cidrus 318 *awry* away 319 s.d. *rustling in* rustling in and Dolabella

The Source of *Antony and Cleopatra*

The principal source of *Antony and Cleopatra* is the "Life of Marcus Antonius," in Sir Thomas North's translation of Plutarch's *Lives of the Noble Grecians and Romans* (published 1579). Shakespeare seems to have known parts, at least, of North's Plutarch for some ten years before he wrote *Antony and Cleopatra;* and he had already used the early part of the "Life of Marcus Antonius" when gathering materials for *Julius Caesar,* seven or so years before. The use Shakespeare makes of this "Life" for *Antony and Cleopatra,* however, is far more thorough, more extensive, and more interesting. Considerable insight into Shakespeare's artistry and method of working may be gained from a comparison of the source with the play: so much does Shakespeare take from Plutarch, and so radically does he transform it. From Plutarch's whole conception of Antony, down to the last few words of his Charmion, Shakespeare borrows heavily and directly, humanizing and deepening all that he borrows; and the process is illuminating. For this reason, all the space available here will be given to the selections from Plutarch. A reader interested in the other works which contributed to the play (to a much smaller degree, but still interestingly) will find a discussion of them in Professor Kenneth Muir's valuable study, *Shakespeare's Sources* (London, 1957), Vol. I, "Comedies and Tragedies," pp. 201–19.

Shakespeare's handling of his main source may be briefly outlined as follows. Plutarch's life of Antony is full, leisurely, and detailed: the excerpts given here represent only about a quarter of the whole. Shakespeare takes from Plutarch all the major events of Antony's later life, with one exception: the long and unsuccessful campaign against the Parthians; he also makes use of events that take place before the opening of the play, such as Antony's first meeting with Cleopatra and what ensues from it. In addition, he borrows—sometimes to an exceptional degree—from Plutarch's vivid, pithy, and dignified narration of speeches and events. In each case, the rehandling is instructive.

Two examples of the first kind of borrowing must suffice here. First, the situation at the opening of the play. Plutarch recounts how Antony, while with Cleopatra in Alexandria, hears news both of Fulvia's and Lucius' wars against Caesar, their defeat and expulsion from Italy, and of Labienus' victories in Asia; Antony prepares to meet the Parthians but is recalled to Italy by letters from his wife, and on the journey hears of her death. At a later point, after his marriage to Octavia, the threat from Sextus Pompeius arises. All this Shakespeare compacts into the news brought, with an effect of rapidly mounting disaster, to Antony in Cleopatra's court, violently challenging his former mood of serene and triumphant exhilaration and necessitating his immediate departure. Thus, in the first two scenes of the play, Shakespeare uses Plutarch's materials cogently and with strong effect, establishing thereby the major conflict of the play. For a second example: his handling of the events succeeding Actium. Shakespeare abbreviates and rearranges, so that the defeat's importance and finality (and Cleopatra's blame in it) are accentuated; the desertion of Domitius (a minor character in Plutarch, whom Shakespeare converts into the far more important Enobarbus) is moved from before Actium to after it, accentuating Antony's isolation in defeat, and the deserter dies not of illness but of a broken heart; and the one successful sally against Caesar, Shakespeare places after, instead of before, Antony's farewell to his servants and the departure of Hercules—thus making the isolated Antony's last exhilaration of victory the more ironic and pathetic, and yet paradoxically heroic. In each of these examples, Shakespeare is not merely compacting and rearranging for dramatic purposes; he is making great tragedy out of good history.

The same may be said of some of the passages where the verbal echoes and reminiscences are strongest. For example, Enobarbus' famous "The barge she sat in, like a burnished throne . . ." is extremely close to Plutarch's beautiful description of Cleopatra at Cydnus. But where Plutarch is describing a rich and exquisite scene, Shakespeare is creating—by small additions and alterations—the extraordinary power of Cleopatra that draws the people, the winds, and the water longingly after her. By giving the speech of reminiscence to the tough and common-sense Enobarbus, and touching it with his humor and "Roman" sanity, Shakespeare heightens, by contrast, the hyperbolical praise of Cleopatra; and, more, he brings alive the conflicting values of the play. Antony is about to marry Octavia; Enobarbus' speech revives the full and fatal power of Cleopatra, at her first meeting with Antony. Both the re-creation of the speech and its placing in the play throw the greatest light on Shakespeare's artistic intentions.

The selections that follow offer a wealth of such comparisons, revealing both Shakespeare's large-scale handling of his materials and his transformation of work that is, in its own right, not without excellence and interest.

PLUTARCH

From "Life of Marcus Antonius," in *The Lives of the Noble Grecians and Romans*

He had a noble presence, and showed a countenance of one of a noble house: he had a goodly thick beard, a broad forehead, crook-nosed, and there appeared such a manly look in his countenance as is commonly seen in Hercules' pictures, stamped or graven in metal. Now it had been a speech of old time that the family of the Antonii were descended from one Anton, the son of Hercules, whereof the family took name. This opinion did Antonius seek to confirm in all his doings, not only resembling him in the likeness of his body, as we have said before, but also in the wearing of his garments. For when he would openly show himself abroad before many people, he would always wear his cassock girt down low upon his hips, with a great sword hanging by his side, and upon that some ill-favored cloak. Furthermore, things that seem intolerable in other men, as to boast commonly, to jest with one or other, to drink like a good fellow with everybody, to sit with the soldiers when they dine, and to eat and drink with them soldierlike, it is incredible what wonderful love it won him

Spelling and punctuation have been modernized. Large excisions are made from Plutarch's account of Antony's life before the meeting with Cleopatra; after this point, omissions are briefly summarized between square brackets. The reader who wishes to read Plutarch's words (in North's translation) rather than the editor's occasional summaries, can find them conveniently in *Shakespeare's Plutarch*, ed. Walter W. Skeat (London, 1875), and in *Shakespeare's Plutarch*, ed. C. F. Tucker Brooke (London, 1909).

amongst them. And furthermore, being given to love, that made him the more desired, and by that means he brought many to love him. For he would further every man's love, and also would not be angry that men should merrily tell him of those he loved. But besides all this, that which most procured his rising and advancement was his liberality, who gave all to the soldiers and kept nothing for himself; and when he was grown to great credit, then was his authority and power also very great, the which notwithstanding himself did overthrow by a thousand other faults he had.

. . . Antonius being thus inclined, the last and extremist mischief of all other (to wit, the love of Cleopatra) lighted on him, who did waken and stir up many vices yet hidden in him, and were never seen to any; and if any spark of goodness or hope of rising were left him, Cleopatra quenched it straight and made it worse than before. The manner how he fell in love with her was this. Antonius, going to make war with the Parthians, sent to command Cleopatra to appear personally before him, when he came into Cilicia, to answer unto such accusations as were laid against her, being this: that she had aided Cassius and Brutus in their war against him. The messenger sent unto Cleopatra to make this summons unto her was called Dellius, who when he had throughly considered her beauty, the excellent grace and sweetness of her tongue, he nothing mistrusted that Antonius would do any hurt to so noble a lady, but rather assured himself that within few days she should be in great favor with him. Thereupon he did her great honor and persuaded her to come into Cilicia as honorably furnished as she could possible, and bade her not to be afraid at all of Antonius, for he was a more courteous lord than any that she had ever seen. Cleopatra, on the other side, believing Dellius' words, and guessing by the former access and credit she had with Julius Caesar and Cneius Pompey (the son of Pompey the Great) only for her beauty, she began to have good hope that she might more easily win Antonius. For Caesar and Pompey knew her when she was but a young thing, and knew not then what the world meant; but now she went to Antonius at the age when a woman's beauty is at the prime, and she also of best judgment. So, she furnished herself with a world of gifts, store of gold and silver, and of riches and other sumptuous ornaments as is credible enough she might bring from so great a house, and from so wealthy and rich a realm as Egypt was. But yet she carried nothing with her wherein she trusted more than in herself, and in the charms and enchantment of her passing beauty and grace. Therefore when she was sent unto by divers letters, both from Antonius himself and also from his friends, she made so light of it and mocked Antonius so much that she disdained to set forward otherwise, but to take her barge in the river of Cydnus, the poop whereof was of gold, the sails of purple, and the oars of silver, which kept stroke in rowing after the sound of the music of flutes, hautboys, citherns, viols, and such other instruments as they played upon in the barge. And now for the person of herself: she was laid under a pavilion of cloth of gold of tissue, appareled and attired like the goddess Venus commonly drawn in picture; and hard by her, on either hand of her, pretty fair boys appareled as painters do set forth god Cupid, with little fans in their hands, with the which they fanned wind upon her. Her ladies and gentlewomen also, the fairest of them were appareled like the nymphs Nereides (which are the mermaids of the waters) and like the Graces, some steering the helm, others tending the tackle and ropes of the barge, out of the which there came a wonderful passing sweet savor of perfumes that perfumed the wharf's side, pestered with innumerable multitudes of people. Some of them followed the barge all alongst the river's side; others also ran out of the city to see her coming in. So that in the end, there ran such multitudes of people one after another to see her that Antonius was left post alone in the market place in his imperial seat to give audience, and there went a rumor in the people's mouths that the goddess Venus was come to play with the god Bacchus for the general good of all Asia. When Cleopatra landed, Antonius sent to invite her to supper to him. But she sent him word again, he should do better rather to come and sup with her. Antonius, therefore, to show himself courteous unto her at her arrival, was contented to obey her, and went to supper to her, where he found such passing sumptuous fare that no tongue can express it. But amongst all other things, he most wondered at the infinite number of lights and torches hanged on the top of the house, giving light in every place, so artificially set and ordered by devices, some round, some square, that it was the rarest thing to behold that eye could discern, or that ever books could mention. The next night, Antonius feasting her contended to pass her in magnificence and fineness, but she overcame him in both. So that he himself began to scorn the gross service of his house, in respect of Cleopatra's sumptuousness and fineness. And, when Cleopatra found Antonius' jests and slents to be but gross and soldierlike in plain manner, she gave it him finely and without fear taunted him throughly. Now her beauty (as it is reported) was not so passing, as unmatchable of other women, nor yet such as upon present view did enamor men with her; but so sweet was her company and conversation that a man could not possibly but be taken. And besides her beauty, the good grace she had to talk and discourse, her courteous nature that tempered her words and deeds, was a spur that pricked to the quick. Furthermore, besides all these, her voice and words were marvelous pleasant, for her tongue was an instrument of music to divers sports and pastimes, the which she easily turned to any language that pleased her. She spake unto few barbarous people by interpreter, but made them answer herself, or at least the most part of them: as the Ethiopians, the Arabians, the Troglodytes, the Hebrews, the Syrians, the Medes, and the Parthians, and to many others also, whose languages she had learned. Whereas divers of her progenitors, the kings of Egypt, could scarce learn the Egyptian tongue only, and many of them forgot to speak the Macedonian. Now Antonius was so ravished with the love of Cleopatra that though his wife Fulvia had great wars, and much ado with Caesar for his affairs, and that the army of the Parthians (the which the king's lieutenants had given to the only leading of Labienus) was now assembled in Mesopotamia ready to invade Syria, yet, as though all this had nothing touched him, he yielded himself to go with Cleopatra into Alexandria, where he spent and lost in childish sports (as a man might say) and idle pastimes the most precious thing a man can spend, as Antiphon saith, and that is, time.

. . . For she, were it in sport or in matter of earnest, still devised new delights to have Antonius at commandment, never leaving him night nor day, nor once letting him go out of her sight. For she would play at dice with him, drink with him, and hunt commonly with him, and also be with him when he went to any exercise or activity of body. And sometime also, when he would go up and down the city disguised like a slave in the night, and would peer into poor men's windows and their shops, and scold and brawl with them within the house, Cleopatra would be also in a chambermaid's array, and amble up and down the streets with him, so that oftentimes Antonius bare away both mocks and blows. Now, though most men misliked this manner, yet the Alexandrians were commonly glad of this jollity, and liked it well, saying very gallantly and wisely that Antonius showed them a comical face, to wit, a merry countenance; and the Romans a tragical face, to say, a grim look. But to reckon up all the foolish sports they made, reveling in this sort, it were too fond a part of me, and therefore I will only tell you one among the rest. On a time he went to angle for fish, and when he could take none he was as angry as could be, because Cleopatra stood by. Wherefore he secretly commanded the fishermen that when he cast in his line they should straight dive under the water and put a fish on his hook which they had taken before; and so snatched up his angling rod and brought up fish twice or thrice. Cleopatra found it straight, yet she seemed not to see it, but wondered at his excellent fishing; but, when she was alone by herself among her own people, she told them how it was and bade them the next morning to be on the water to see the fishing. A number of people came to the haven and got into the fisher boats to see this fishing. Antonius then threw in his line, and

Cleopatra straight commanded one of her men to dive underwater before Antonius' men, and to put some old salt fish upon his bait, like unto those that are brought out of the country of Pont. When he had hung the fish on his hook, Antonius, thinking he had taken a fish indeed, snatched up his line presently. Then they all fell a-laughing. Cleopatra laughing also, said unto him: "Leave us (my lord) Egyptians (which dwell in the country of Pharus and Canobus) your angling rod: this is not thy profession; thou must hunt after conquering of realms and countries." Now Antonius, delighting in these fond and childish pastimes, very ill news were brought him from two places. The first from Rome, that his brother Lucius and Fulvia his wife fell out first between themselves and afterwards fell to open war with Caesar, and had brought all to nought that they were both driven to fly out of Italy. The second news, as bad as the first: that Labienus conquered all Asia with the army of the Parthians, from the river of Euphrates and from Syria, unto the countries of Lydia and Ionia. Then began Antonius with much ado a little to rouse himself, as if he had been wakened out of a deep sleep, and as a man may say, coming out of a great drunkenness. So, first of all he bent himself against the Parthians and went as far as the country of Phoenicia; but there he received lamentable letters from his wife Fulvia. Whereupon he straight returned towards Italy with two hundred sail; and as he went, took up his friends by the way that fled out of Italy to come to him. By them he was informed that his wife Fulvia was the only cause of this war, who, being of a peevish, crooked, and troublesome nature, had purposely raised this uproar in Italy, in hope thereby to withdraw him from Cleopatra. But by good fortune his wife Fulvia, going to meet with Antonius, sickened by the way and died in the city of Sicyon; and therefore Octavius Caesar and he were the easilier made friends together. For when Antonius landed in Italy, and that men saw Caesar asked nothing of him, and that Antonius on the other side laid all the fault and burden on his wife Fulvia, the friends of both parties would not suffer them to unrip any old matters and to prove or defend who had the wrong or right and who was the first procurer of this war, fearing to make matters worse between them; but they made them friends together and divided the Empire of Rome between them, making the sea Ionium the bounds of their division. For they gave all the provinces eastward unto Antonius, and the countries westward unto Caesar: and left Africk unto Lepidus, and made a law that they three one after another should make their friends consuls, when they would not be themselves. This seemed to be a sound counsel, but yet it was to be confirmed with a straiter bond, which fortune offered thus. There was Octavia, the eldest sister of Caesar, not by one mother, for she came of Ancharia, and Caesar himself afterwards of Accia. It is reported that he dearly loved his sister Octavia, for indeed she was a noble lady and left the widow of her first husband Caius Marcellus, who died not long before; and it seemed also that Antonius had been widower ever since the death of his wife Fulvia. For he denied not that he kept Cleopatra, but so did he not confess that he had her as his wife; and so with reason he did defend the love he bare unto this Egyptian Cleopatra. Thereupon every man did set forward this marriage, hoping thereby that this Lady Octavia, having an excellent grace, wisdom, and honesty, joined unto so rare a beauty, that when she were with Antonius (he loving her as so worthy a lady deserveth) she should be a good mean to keep good love and amity betwixt her brother and him. So, when Caesar and he had made the match between them, they both went to Rome about this marriage, although it was against the law that a widow should be married within ten months after her husband's death. Howbeit the Senate dispensed with the law, and so the marriage proceeded accordingly. Sextus Pompeius at that time kept in Sicilia and so made many an inroad into Italy with a great number of pinnaces and other pirates' ships, of the which were captains two notable pirates, Menas and Menecrates, who so scoured all the sea thereabouts that none durst peep out with a sail. Furthermore, Sextus Pompeius had dealt very friendly with Antonius, for he had courteously received his mother, when she fled out of Italy with Fulvia; and therefore they thought good to make peace with him. So they met all three together by the mount of Misenum, upon a hill that runneth far into the sea, Pompey having his ships riding hard by at anchor, and Antonius and Caesar their armies upon the shore side, directly over against him. Now, after they had agreed that Sextus Pompeius should have Sicile and Sardinia, with this condition, that he should rid the sea of all thieves and pirates and make it safe for passengers and withal that he should send a certain [amount] of wheat to Rome, one of them did feast another and drew cuts who should begin. It was Pompeius' chance to invite them first. Whereupon Antonius asked him: "And where shall we sup?" "There," said Pompey and showed him his admiral galley which had six banks of oars: "That," said he, "is my father's house they have left me." He spake it to taunt Antonius, because he had his father's house, that was Pompey the Great. So he cast anchors enow into the sea to make his galley fast, and then built a bridge of wood to convey them to his galley from the head of Mount Misenum, and there he welcomed them and made them great cheer. Now in the midst of the feast, when they fell to be merry with Antonius' love unto Cleopatra, Menas the pirate came to Pompey and, whispering in his ear, said unto him: "Shall I cut the cables of the anchors and make thee lord not only of Sicile and Sardinia, but of the whole Empire of Rome besides?" Pompey, having paused awhile upon it, at length answered him: "Thou shouldst have done it, and never have told it me, but now we must content us with that we have. As for myself, I was never taught to break my faith nor to be counted a traitor." The other two also did likewise feast him in their camp, and then he returned into Sicile. Antonius, after this agreement made, sent Ventidius before into Asia to stay the Parthians and to keep them they should come no further; and he himself in the meantime, to gratify Caesar, was contented to be chosen Julius Caesar's priest and sacrificer, and so they jointly together dispatched all great matters concerning the state of the Empire. But in all other manner of sports and exercises, wherein they passed the time away the one with the other, Antonius was ever inferior unto Caesar and always lost, which grieved him much. With Antonius there was a soothsayer or astronomer of Egypt that could cast a figure and judge of men's nativities, to tell them what should happen to them. He, either to please Cleopatra or else for that he found it so by his art, told Antonius plainly that his fortune (which of itself was excellent good and very great) was altogether blemished and obscured by Caesar's fortune; and therefore he counseled him utterly to leave his company and to get him as far from him as he could. "For thy Demon," said he, "that is to say, the good angel and spirit that keepeth thee, is afraid of his, and being courageous and high when he is alone, becometh fearful and timorous when he cometh near unto the other." Howsoever it was, the events ensuing proved the Egyptian's words true. For it is said that as often as they two drew cuts for pastime, who should have anything, or whether they played at dice, Antonius always lost. Oftentimes, when they were disposed to see cockfight, or quails that were taught to fight one with another, Caesar's cocks or quails did ever overcome. The which spited Antonius in his mind, although he made no outward show of it, and therefore he believed the Egyptian the better. In fine, he recommended the affairs of his house unto Caesar and went out of Italy with Octavia his wife, whom he carried into Greece after he had had a daughter by her. So Antonius lying all the winter at Athens, news came unto him of the victories of Ventidius, who had overcome the Parthians in battle, in the which also were slain Labienus and Pharnabates, the chiefest captain King Orodes had. For these good news he feasted all Athens and kept open house for all the Grecians, and many games of price were played at Athens, of the which he himself would be judge. . . .

In the meantime, Ventidius once again overcame Pacorus (Orodes' son, King of Parthia) in a battle fought in the country of Cyrrestica, he being come again with a great army to invade Syria, at which battle was slain a great number of the Parthians and among them Pacorus the King's own son slain. This noble exploit, as famous as ever any was, was a full revenge to the Romans of the shame and loss they had received before by the death of Marcus Crassus, and he made the Parthians fly and glad to keep themselves within the confines and territories of Mesopotamia and Media, after they had thrice together been overcome in several battles. Howbeit Ventidius durst not undertake to follow them any further, fearing lest he should have gotten Antonius' displeasure by it. . . . Ventidius was the only man that ever triumphed of the Parthians until this present day, a mean man born and of no noble house nor family, who only came to that he attained unto through Antonius' friendship, the which delivered him happy occasion to achieve to great matters. And yet, to say truly, he did so well quit himself in all his enterprises that he confirmed that which was spoken of Antonius and Caesar, to wit, that they were alway more fortunate when they made war by their lieutenants, than by themselves. For Sossius, one of Antonius' lieutenants in Syria, did notable good service, and Canidius, whom he had also left his lieutenant in the borders of Armenia, did conquer it all.

[Hostility develops again between Antony and Octavius, but Octavia makes peace between them. After a brief interval Antony rejoins Cleopatra and heaps honors on her and their children. His long unsuccessful campaign against the Parthians follows. Octavia prepares to rejoin Antony, encouraged by Octavius, who hopes to find grounds for war if she is rebuffed by her husband; and she is rebuffed. The patience and charity of her behavior on her return angers all Rome against Antony, an anger increased by his gifts of lands to Cleopatra's children. Octavius declares war against Cleopatra. Antony and Octavius prepare for war; Cleopatra persuades Antony to let her accompany him.]

Now Antonius was made so subject to a woman's will that though he was a great deal the stronger by land, yet for Cleopatra's sake he would needs have this battle tried by sea, though he saw before his eyes, that, for lack of watermen, his captains did press by force all sorts of men out of Greece that they could take up in the field, as travelers, muleteers, reapers, harvest men, and young boys, and yet could they not sufficiently furnish his galleys so that the most part of them were empty, and could scant row, because they lacked watermen enow. But on the contrary side Caesar's ships were not built for pomp, high and great, only for a sight and bravery, but they were light of yarage, armed and furnished with watermen as many as they needed, and had them all in readiness in the havens of Tarentum and Brundusium. So Octavius Caesar sent unto Antonius, to will him to delay no more time, but to come on with his army into Italy, and that for his own part he would give him safe harbor, to land without any trouble, and that he would withdraw his army from the sea as far as one horse could run, until he had put his army ashore and had lodged his men. Antonius on the other side bravely sent him word again and challenged the combat of him man to man, though he were the elder, and that if he refused him so, he would then fight a battle with him in the fields of Pharsalia, as Julius Caesar and Pompey had done before. Now whilst Antonius rode at anchor, lying idly in the harbor at the head of Actium, in the place where the city of Nicopolis standeth at this present, Caesar had quickly passed the sea Ionium and taken a place called Toryne, before Antonius understood that he had taken ship. Then began his men to be afraid, because his army by land was left behind. But Cleopatra making light of it, "And what danger, I pray you," said she, "if Caesar keep at Toryne?" The next morning by break of day, his enemies coming with full force of oars in battle against him, Antonius was afraid that if they came to join they would take and carry away his ships, that had no men of war in them. So he armed all his watermen and set them in order of battle upon the forecastle of their ships, and then lift up all his ranks of oars towards the elements, as well of the one side as the other, with the prows against the enemies, at the entry and mouth of the gulf which beginneth at the point of Actium, and so kept them in order of battle, as if they had been armed and furnished with watermen and soldiers. Thus Octavius Caesar, being finely deceived by this stratagem, retired presently, and therewithal Antonius very wisely and suddenly did cut him off from fresh water. For, understanding that the places where Octavius Caesar landed had very little store of water, and yet very bad, he shut them in with strong ditches and trenches he cast, to keep them from sallying out at their pleasure, and so to go seek water further off. Furthermore, he dealt very friendly and courteously with Domitius, and against Cleopatra's mind. For, he being sick of an ague when he went and took a little boat to go to Caesar's camp, Antonius was very sorry for it, but yet he sent after him all his carriage, train, and men; and the same Domitius, as though he gave him to understand that he repented his open treason, he died immediately after. There were certain kings also that forsook him, and turned on Caesar's side: as Amyntas and Deïotarus. Furthermore his fleet and navy that was unfortunate in all things, and unready for service, compelled him to change his mind and to hazard battle by land. And Canidius also, who had charge of his army by land, when time came to follow Antonius' determination, he turned him clean contrary and counseled him to send Cleopatra back again, and himself to retire into Macedon, to fight there on the mainland. And furthermore told him, that Dicomes King of the Getae promised him to aid him with a great power, and that it should be no shame nor dishonor to him to let Caesar have the sea (because himself and his men both had been well practiced and exercised in battles by sea, in the war of Sicilia against Sextus Pompeius), but rather that he should do against all reason, he having so great skill and experience of battles by land as he had, if he should not employ the force and valiantness of so many lusty armed footmen as he had ready, but would weaken his army by dividing them into ships. But now, notwithstanding all these good persuasions, Cleopatra forced him to put all to the hazard of battle by sea, considering with herself how she might fly and provide for her safety, not to help him to win the victory, but to fly more easily after the battle lost. Betwixt Antonius' camp and his fleet of ships there was a great high point of firm land that ran a good way into the sea, the which Antonius often used for a walk, without mistrust of fear or danger. One of Caesar's men perceived it, and told his master that he would laugh an [i.e., if] they could take up Antonius in the midst of his walk. Thereupon Caesar sent some of his men to lie in ambush for him, and they missed not much of taking of him, for they took him that came before him, because they discovered too soon, and so Antonius scaped very hardly. So, when Antonius had determined to fight by sea, he set all the other ships afire but threescore ships of Egypt, and reserved only but the best and greatest galleys, from three banks unto ten banks of oars. In them he put two-and-twenty thousand fighting men, with two thousand darters and slingers. Now, as he was setting his men in order of battle, there was a captain and a valiant man that had served Antonius in many battles and conflicts and had all his body hacked and cut, who, as Antonius passed by him, cried out unto him and said: "O noble Emperor, how cometh it to pass that you trust to these vile brittle ships? What, do you mistrust these wounds of mine and this sword? Let the Egyptians and Phoenicians fight by sea, and set us on the mainland, where we use to conquer or to be slain on our feet." Antonius passed by him and said never a word, but only beckoned to him with his hand and head, as though he willed him to be of good courage, although indeed he had no great courage himself.

[An account of the battle follows.]

. . . Howbeit the battle was yet of even hand, and the victory doubtful, being indifferent to both, when suddenly they saw the threescore ships of Cleopatra busy about their yard masts and hoising sail to fly. So they fled through the midst of them that were in fight, for they had been placed behind the great ships, and did marvelously disorder the other ships. For the enemies themselves wondered much to see them sail in that sort, with full sail towards Peloponnesus. There Antonius showed plainly that he had not only lost the courage and heart of an emperor, but also of a valiant man, and that he was not his own man (proving that true which an old man spake in mirth, that the soul of a lover lived in another body, and not in his own); he was so carried away with the vain love of this woman, as if he had been glued unto her and that she could not have removed without moving of him also. For when he saw Cleopatra's ship under sail, he forgot, forsook, and betrayed them that fought for him and embarked upon a galley with five banks of oars, to follow her that had already begun to overthrow him and would in the end be his utter destruction. When she knew this galley afar off, she lift up a sign in the poop of her ship, and so Antonius coming to it was plucked up where Cleopatra was; howbeit he saw her not at his first coming, nor she him, but went and sate down alone in the prow of his ship, and said never a word, clapping his head between both his hands. . . .

Now for himself, he determined to cross over into Africk and took one of his carracks or hulks loaden with gold and silver and other rich carriage and gave it unto his friends, commanding them to depart and to seek to save themselves. They answered him weeping, that they would neither do it nor yet forsake him. Then Antonius very courteously and lovingly did comfort them and prayed them to depart; and wrote unto Theophilus, Governor of Corinth, that he would see them safe, and help to hide them in some secret place, until they had made their way and peace with Caesar. . . .

Many plainly saw Antonius fly, and yet could hardly believe it that he, that had nineteen legions whole by land and twelve thousand horsemen upon the seaside, would so have forsaken them and have fled so cowardly, as if he had not oftentimes proved both the one and the other fortune, and that he had not been throughly acquainted with the diverse changes and fortunes of battles. And yet his soldiers still wished for him and ever hoped that he would come by some means or other unto them. Furthermore, they showed themselves so valiant and faithful unto him that after they certainly knew he was fled, they kept themselves whole together seven days. In the end Canidius, Antonius' lieutenant, flying by night and forsaking his camp, when they saw themselves thus destitute of their heads and leaders, they yielded themselves unto the stronger.

[Antony retires hopeless to the isle of Pharos; but on hearing that his army is totally lost and the last of his allies have deserted to Caesar, he at length takes up again his life of revelry with Cleopatra, who begins to experiment to find a painless method of suicide.]

This notwithstanding, they sent ambassadors unto Octavius Caesar in Asia, Cleopatra requesting the realm of Egypt for her children, and Antonius praying that he might be suffered to live at Athens like a private man if Caesar would not let him remain in Egypt. And, because they had no other men of estimation about them, for that some were fled and those that remained, they did not greatly trust them, they were enforced to send Euphronius, the schoolmaster of their children. For Alexas Laodicean, who was brought into Antonius' house and favor by means of Timagenes, and afterwards was in greater credit with him than any other Grecian (for that he had alway been one of Cleopatra's ministers to win Antonius and to overthrow all his good determinations to use his wife Octavia well) him Antonius had sent unto Herodes King of Jewry, hoping still to keep him his friend, that he should not revolt from him. But he remained there and betrayed Antonius. For where he should have kept Herodes from revolting from him, he persuaded him to turn to Caesar; and trusting King Herodes, he presumed to come in Caesar's presence. Howbeit Herodes did him no pleasure, for he was presently taken prisoner and sent in chains to his own country and there by Caesar's commandment put to death. Thus was Alexas in Antonius' lifetime put to death for betraying of him. Furthermore, Caesar would not grant unto Antonius' requests; but for Cleopatra, he made her answer that he would deny her nothing reasonable, so that she would either put Antonius to death or drive him out of her country. Therewithal he sent Thyreus one of his men unto her, a very wise and discreet man, who, bringing letters of credit from a young lord unto a noble lady, and that besides greatly liked her beauty, might easily by his eloquence have persuaded her. He was longer in talk with her than any man else was, and the Queen herself also did him great honor, insomuch as he made Antonius jealous of him.

Whereupon Antonius caused him to be taken and well-favoredly whipped, and so sent him unto Caesar, and bade him tell him that he made him angry with him, because he showed himself proud and disdainful towards him, and now specially when he was easy to be angered, by reason of his present misery. "To be short, if this mislike thee," said he, "thou hast Hipparchus one of my enfranchised bondmen with thee; hang him if thou wilt, or whip him at thy pleasure, that we may cry quittance." From thenceforth Cleopatra, to clear herself of the suspicion he had of her, she made more of him than ever she did. For first of all, where she did solemnize the day of her birth very meanly and sparingly, fit for her present misfortune, she now in contrary manner did keep it with such solemnity that she exceeded all measure of sumptuousness and magnificence, so that the guests that were bidden to the feasts, and came poor, went away rich.

[After the winter, Caesar advances upon Antony and Cleopatra; she withdraws her treasures into her tombs and monuments.]

So Caesar came, and pitched his camp hard by the city, in the place where they run and manage their horses. Antonius made a sally upon him and fought very valiantly, so that he drave Caesar's horsemen back, fighting with his men even into their camp. Then he came again to the palace, greatly boasting of this victory, and sweetly kissed Cleopatra, armed as he was when he came from the fight, recommending one of his men of arms unto her, that had valiantly fought in this skirmish. Cleopatra to reward his manliness gave him an armor and headpiece of clean gold; howbeit the man-at-arms, when he received this rich gift, stale away by night and went to Caesar. Antonius sent again to challenge Caesar to fight with him hand to hand. Caesar answered him that he had many other ways to die than so. Then Antonius, seeing there was no way more honorable for him to die than fighting valiantly, he determined to set up his rest, both by sea and land. So, being at supper (as it is reported), he commanded his officers and household servants that waited on him at his board, that they should fill his cups full and make as much of him as they could: "For," said he, "you know not whether you shall do so much for me tomorrow or not, or whether you shall serve another master, and it may be you shall see me no more, but a dead body." This notwithstanding, perceiving that his friends and men fell a-weeping to hear him say so, to salve that he had spoken, he added this more unto it, that he would not lead them to battle, where he thought not rather safely to return with victory than valiantly to die with honor. Furthermore, the selfsame night within little of midnight, when all the city was quiet, full of fear and sorrow, thinking what would be the issue and end of this war, it is said that suddenly they heard a marvelous sweet harmony of sundry sorts of instruments of music, with the cry of a multitude of people, as they had been dancing and had sung as they use in Bacchus' feasts, with movings and turnings after the manner of the satyrs; and it seemed that this dance went through the city unto the gate that opened to the enemies, and that all the troop that made this noise they heard went out of the city at that gate. Now, such as in reason sought the depth of the interpretation of this wonder, thought that it was the god unto whom Antonius bare singular devotion to counterfeit and resemble him, that did forsake them. The next morning by break of day, he went to set those few footmen he had in order upon the hills adjoining unto the city; and there he stood to behold his galleys which departed from the haven and rowed against the galleys of his enemies, and so stood still, looking what exploits his soldiers in them would do. But when by force of rowing they were come near unto them, they first saluted Caesar's men, and then Caesar's men resaluted them also, and of two armies made but one, and then did all together row toward the city. When Antonius saw that his men did forsake him and yielded unto Caesar, and that his footmen were broken and overthrown, he then fled into the city, crying out that Cleopatra had betrayed him unto them, with whom he had made war for her sake. Then she, being afraid of his fury, fled into the tomb which she had caused to be made, and there locked the doors unto her and shut all the springs of the locks with great bolts, and in the meantime sent unto Antonius to tell him that she was dead. Antonius, believing it, said unto himself: "What dost thou look for further, Antonius, sith spiteful fortune hath taken from thee the only joy thou hadst, for whom thou yet reservedst thy life?" When he had said these words, he went into a chamber and unarmed himself, and being naked said thus: "O Cleopatra, it grieveth me not that I have lost thy company, for I will not be long from thee; but I am sorry that, having been so great a captain and emperor, I am indeed condemned to be judged of less courage and noble mind than a woman." Now he had a man of his called Eros, whom he loved and trusted much, and whom he had long before caused to swear unto him that he should kill him when he did command him; and then he willed him to keep his promise. His man drawing his sword lift it up as though he had meant to have stricken his master, but turning his head at one side he thrust his sword into himself and fell down dead at his master's foot. Then said Antonius, "O noble Eros, I thank thee for this, and it is valiantly done of thee, to show me what I should do to myself, which thou couldst not do for me." Therewithal he took his sword and thrust it into his belly and so fell down upon a little bed. The wound he had killed him not presently, for the blood stinted a little when he was laid; and when he came somewhat to himself again, he prayed them that were about him to dispatch him. But they all fled out of the chamber and left him crying out and tormenting himself, until at last there came a secretary unto him called Diomedes, who was commanded to bring him into the tomb or monument where Cleopatra was. When he heard that she was alive, he very earnestly prayed his men to carry his body thither, and so he was carried in his men's arms into the entry of the monument. Notwithstanding, Cleopatra would not open the gates, but came to the high windows and cast out certain chains and ropes, in the which Antonius was trussed; and Cleopatra her own self, with two women only, which she had suffered to come with her into these monuments, triced Antonius up. They that were present to behold it said they saw so pitiful a sight. For they plucked up poor Antonius all bloody as he was, and drawing on with pangs of death, who holding up his hand to Cleopatra raised up himself as well as he could. It was a hard thing for these women to do, to lift him up; but Cleopatra stooping down with her head, putting to all her strength to her uttermost power, did lift him up with much ado and never let go her hold, with the help of the women beneath that bade her be of good courage and were as sorry to see her labor so as she herself. So when she had gotten him in after that sort and laid him on a bed, she rent her garments upon him, clapping her breast and scratching her face and stomach. Then she dried up his blood that had berayed his face and called him her lord, her husband, and emperor, forgetting her own misery and calamity for the pity and compassion she took of him. Antonius made her cease her lamenting and called for wine, either because he was athirst or else for that he thought thereby to hasten his death. When he had drunk, he earnestly prayed her and persuaded her that she would seek to save her life, if she could possible, without reproach and dishonor, and that chiefly she should trust Proculeius above any man else about Caesar. And, as for himself, that she should not lament nor sorrow for the miserable change of his fortune at the end of his days, but rather that she should think him the more fortunate for the former triumphs and honors he had received, considering that while he lived he was the noblest and greatest prince of the world, and that now he was overcome not cowardly, but valiantly, a Roman by another Roman. As Antonius gave the last gasp, Proculeius came that was sent from Caesar. For after Antonius had thrust his sword in himself, as they carried him into the tombs and monuments of Cleopatra, one of his guard called Dercetaeus took his sword with the which he had stricken himself, and hid it; then he secretly stale away and brought Octavius Caesar the first news of his death and showed him his sword that was bloodied. Caesar hearing these news straight withdrew himself into a secret place of his tent and there burst out with tears, lamenting his hard and miserable fortune that had been his friend and brother-in-law, his equal in the Empire and companion with him in sundry great exploits and battles. Then he called for all his friends and showed them the letters Antonius had written to him and his answers also sent him again during their quarrel and strife, and how fiercely and proudly the other answered him to all just and reasonable matters he wrote unto him. After this, he sent Proculeius and commanded him to do what he could possible to get Cleopatra alive, fearing lest otherwise all the treasure would be lost; and furthermore, he thought that if he could take Cleopatra and bring her alive to Rome, she would marvelously beautify and set out his triumph. But Cleopatra would never put herself into Proculeius' hands, although they spake together. For Proculeius came to the gates that were very thick and strong and surely barred, but yet there were some cranews through the which her voice might be heard, and so they without understood that Cleopatra demanded the kingdom of Egypt for her sons, and that Proculeius answered her that she should be of good cheer and not be afraid to refer all unto Caesar. After he had viewed the place very well, he came and reported her answer unto Caesar, who immediately sent Gallus to speak once again with her and bade him purposely hold her with talk whilst Proculeius did set up a ladder against that high window by the which Antonius was triced up, and came down into the monument with two of his men, hard by the gate where Cleopatra stood to hear what Gallus said unto her. One of her women which was shut in her monuments with her saw Proculeius by chance as he came down and shrieked out: "O poor Cleopatra, thou art taken." Then, when she saw Proculeius behind her as she came from the gate, she thought to have stabbed herself in with a short dagger she ware of purpose by her side. But Proculeius came suddenly upon her, and taking her by both the hands said unto her: "Cleopatra, first thou shalt do thyself great wrong, and secondly unto Caesar, to deprive him of the occasion and opportunity openly to show his bounty and mercy, and to give his enemies cause to accuse the most courteous and noble prince that ever was, and to appeach him as though he were a cruel and merciless man that were not to be trusted." So even as he spake the word, he took her dagger from her and shook her clothes for fear of any poison hidden about her. Afterwards Caesar sent one of his enfranchised men called Epaphroditus, whom he straightly charged to look well unto her and to beware in any case that she made not herself away, and, for the rest, to use her with all the courtesy possible.

[Cleopatra, after burying Antony royally, gives way to intense grief.]

Shortly after, Caesar came himself in person to see her and to comfort her. Cleopatra being laid upon a little low bed in poor estate, when she saw Caesar come into her chamber she suddenly rose up, naked in her smock, and fell down at his feet marvelously disfigured, both for that she had plucked her hair from her head, as also for that she had martyred all her face with her nails, and besides, her voice was small and trembling, her eyes sunk into her head with continual blubbering, and moreover they might see the most part of her stomach torn in sunder. To be short, her body was not much better than her mind; yet her good grace and comeliness and the force of her beauty was not altogether defaced. But notwithstanding this ugly and pitiful state of hers, yet she showed herself within by her outward looks and countenance. When Caesar had made her lie down again and sate by her bed's side, Cleopatra began to clear and excuse herself for that she had done, laying all to the fear she had of Antonius; Caesar, in contrary manner, reproved her in every point. Then she suddenly altered her speech and prayed him to pardon her, as though she were afraid to die and desirous to live. At length, she gave him a brief and memorial of all the ready money and treasure she had. But by chance there stood Seleucus by, one of her treasurers, who to seem a good servant came straight to Caesar to disprove Cleopatra that she had not set in all, but kept many things back of purpose. Cleopatra was in such a rage with him that she flew upon him and took him by the hair of the head and boxed him well-favoredly. Caesar fell a-laughing and parted the fray. "Alas," said she, "O Caesar, is not this a great shame and reproach, that thou having vouchsafed to take the pains to come unto me, and hast done me this honor, poor wretch and caitiff creature, brought into this pitiful and miserable estate, and that mine own servants should come now to accuse me, though it may be that I have reserved some jewels and trifles meet for women, but not for me (poor soul) to set out myself withal, but meaning to give some pretty present and gifts unto Octavia and Livia, that they making means and intercession for me to thee, thou mightest yet extend thy favor and mercy upon me?" Caesar was glad to hear her say so, persuading himself thereby that she had yet a desire to save her life. So he made her answer that he did not only give her that to dispose of at her pleasure which she had kept back, but further promised to use her more honorably and bountifully than she would think fit; and so he took his leave of her, supposing he had deceived her, but indeed he was deceived himself. There was a young gentleman Cornelius Dolabella that was one of Caesar's very great familiars, and besides did bear no evil will unto Cleopatra. He sent her word secretly as she had requested him, that Caesar determined to take his journey through Syria, and that within three days he would send her away before with her children. When this was told Cleopatra, she requested Caesar that it would please him to suffer her to offer the last oblations of the dead unto the soul of Antonius. This being granted her, she was carried to the place where his tomb was, and there falling down on her knees, embracing the tomb with her women, the tears running down her cheeks, she began to speak in this sort: "O my dear Lord Antonius, not long sithence I buried thee here, being a freewoman; and now I offer unto thee the funeral sprinklings and oblations, being a captive and prisoner, and yet I am forbidden and kept from tearing and murdering this captive body of mine with blows, which they carefully guard and keep, only to triumph of thee; look therefore henceforth for no other honors, offerings, nor sacrifices from me, for these are the last which Cleopatra can give thee, sith now they carry her away. Whilst we lived together, nothing could sever our companies; but now at our death I fear me they will make us change our countries. For as thou, being a Roman, hast been buried in Egypt, even so wretched creature I, an

Egyptian, shall be buried in Italy, which shall be all the good that I have received by thy country. If therefore the gods where thou art now have any power and authority, sith our gods here have forsaken us, suffer not thy true friend and lover to be carried away alive, that in me they triumph of thee, but receive me with thee, and let me be buried in one self tomb with thee. For though my griefs and miseries be infinite, yet none hath grieved me more, nor that I could less bear withal than this small time which I have been driven to live alone without thee." Then, having ended these doleful plaints and crowned the tomb with garlands and sundry nosegays and marvelous lovingly embraced the same, she commanded they should prepare her bath, and when she had bathed and washed herself she fell to her meat and was sumptuously served. Now whilst she was at dinner, there came a countryman and brought her a basket. The soldiers that warded at the gates asked him straight what he had in his basket. He opened the basket and took out the leaves that covered the figs and showed them that they were figs he brought. They all of them marveled to see so goodly figs. The countryman laughed to hear them and bade them take some if they would. They believed he told them truly, and so bade him carry them in. After Cleopatra had dined, she sent a certain table written and sealed unto Caesar and commanded them all to go out of the tombs where she was, but the two women; then she shut the doors to her. Caesar, when he received this table and began to read her lamentation and petition, requesting him that he would let her be buried with Antonius, found straight what she meant and thought to have gone thither himself; howbeit he sent one before in all haste that might be, to see what it was. Her death was very sudden. For those whom Caesar sent unto her ran thither in all haste possible and found the soldiers standing at the gate, mistrusting nothing nor understanding of her death. But when they had opened the doors, they found Cleopatra stark dead, laid upon a bed of gold, attired and arrayed in her royal robes, and one of her two women, which was called Iras, dead at her feet, and her other woman called Charmion half dead and trembling, trimming the diadem which Cleopatra ware upon her dead. One of the soldiers, seeing her, angrily said unto her: "Is that well done, Charmion?" "Very well," said she again, "and meet for a princess descended from the race of so many noble kings." She said no more, but fell down dead hard by the bed. Some report that this aspic was brought unto her in the basket with figs, and that she had commanded them to hide it under the fig leaves, that when she should think to take out the figs, the aspic should bite her before she should see her; howbeit that, when she would have taken away the leaves for the figs, she perceived it and said, "Art thou here then?" And so, her arm being naked, she put it to the aspic to be bitten. Other say again, she kept it in a box, and that she did prick and thrust it with a spindle of gold, so that the aspic being angered withal, leapt out with great fury and bit her in the arm. Howbeit few can tell the truth. For they report also that she had hidden poison in a hollow razor which she carried in the hair of her head: and yet was there no mark seen of her body, or any sign discerned that she was poisoned, neither also did they find this serpent in her tomb. But it was reported only that there were seen certain fresh steps or tracks where it had gone, on the tomb side toward the sea and specially by the door's side. Some say also that they found two little pretty bitings in her arm, scant to be discerned, the which it seemeth Caesar himself gave credit unto, because in his triumph he carried Cleopatra's image, with an aspic biting of her arm. And thus goeth the report of her death. Now Caesar, though he was marvelous sorry for the death of Cleopatra, yet he wondered at her noble mind and courage and therefore commanded she should be nobly buried and laid by Antonius, and willed also that her two women should have honorable burial.

Commentaries

SAMUEL JOHNSON

from *The Plays of William Shakespeare*

This play keeps curiosity always busy, and the passions always interested. The continual hurry of the action, the variety of incidents, and the quick succession of one personage to another, call the mind forward without intermission from the first act to the last. But the power of delighting is derived principally from the frequent changes of the scene; for, except the feminine arts, some of which are too low, which distinguish *Cleopatra*, no character is very strongly discriminated. *Upton,* who did not easily miss what he desired to find, has discovered that the language of *Antony* is, with great skill and learning, made pompous and superb, according to his real practice. But I think his diction not distinguishable from that of others: the most tumid speech in the play is that which *Caesar* makes to *Octavia.*

The events, of which the principal are described according to history, are produced without any art of connection or care of disposition. [1765]

A. C. BRADLEY

Shakespeare's "Antony and Cleopatra"

Coleridge's one page of general criticism on *Antony and Cleopatra* contains some notable remarks. "Of all Shakespeare's historical plays," he writes, *"Antony and Cleopatra* is by far the most wonderful. There is not one in which he has followed history so minutely, and yet there are few in which he impresses the notion of angelic strength so much—perhaps none in which he impresses it more strongly. This is greatly owing to the manner in which the fiery force is sustained throughout." In a later sentence he refers to the play as "this astonishing drama." In another he describes the style: *"feliciter audax* is the motto for its style comparatively with that of Shakespeare's other works." And he translates this motto in the phrase "happy valiancy of style."

Coleridge's assertion that in *Antony and Cleopatra* Shakespeare followed history more minutely than in any other play might well be disputed; and his statement about the style of this drama requires some qualification in view of the results of later criticism as to the order of Shakespeare's works. The style is less individual than he imag-

1 As this lecture was composed after the publication of my *Shakespearean Tragedy,* I ignored in it, as far as possible, such aspects of the play as were noticed in that book, to the Index of which I may refer the reader.

From *Oxford Lectures on Poetry* by A. C. Bradley. London: Macmillan and Co., Ltd., 1909. Reprinted by permission of Macmillan and Co., Ltd., and St Martin's Press, Inc.

ined. On the whole it is common to the six or seven dramas subsequent to *Macbeth,* though in *Antony and Cleopatra,* probably the earliest of them, its development is not yet complete. And we must add that this style has certain special defects, unmentioned by Coleridge, as well as the quality which he points out in it. But it is true that here that quality is almost continuously present; and in the phrase by which he describes it, as in his other phrases, he has signalized once for all some of the most salient features of the drama.

It is curious to notice, for example, alike in books and in conversation, how often the first epithets used in reference to *Antony and Cleopatra* are "wonderful" and "astonishing." And the main source of the feeling thus expressed seems to be the "angelic strength" or "fiery force" of which Coleridge wrote. The first of these two phrases is, I think, the more entirely happy. Except perhaps towards the close, one is not so conscious of fiery force as in certain other tragedies; but one is astonished at the apparent ease with which extraordinary effects are produced, the ease, if I may paraphrase Coleridge, of an angel moving with a wave of the hand that heavy matter which men find so intractable. We feel this sovereign ease in contemplating Shakespeare's picture of the world—a vast canvas, crowded with figures, glowing with color and a superb animation, reminding one spectator of Paul Veronese and another of Rubens. We feel it again when we observe (as we can even without consulting Plutarch) the nature of the material; how bulky it was, and, in some respects, how undramatic; and how the artist, though he could not treat history like legend or fiction, seems to push whole masses aside, and to shift and refashion the remainder, almost with the air of an architect playing (at times rather carelessly) with a child's bricks.

Something similar is felt even in the portrait of Cleopatra. Marvelous as it is, the drawing of it suggests not so much the passionate concentration or fiery force of *Macbeth,* as that sense of effortless and exultant mastery which we feel in the portraits of Mercutio and Falstaff. And surely it is a total mistake to find in this portrait any trace of the distempered mood which disturbs our pleasure in

Troilus and Cressida. If the sonnets about the dark lady were, as need not be doubted, in some degree autobiographical, Shakespeare may well have used his personal experience both when he drew Cressida and when he drew Cleopatra. And, if he did, the story in the later play was the nearer to his own; for Antony might well have said what Troilus could never say,

> When my love swears that she is made of truth,
> I do believe her, though I know she lies.

But in the later play, not only is the poet's vision unclouded, but his whole nature, emotional as well as intellectual, is free. The subject no more embitters or seduces him than the ambition of Macbeth. So that here too we feel the angelic strength of which Coleridge speaks. If we quarreled with the phrase at all, it would be because we fancied we could trace in Shakespeare's attitude something of the irony of superiority; and this may not altogether suit our conception of an angel.

I have still another sentence to quote from Coleridge: "The highest praise, or rather form of praise, of this play which I can offer in my own mind, is the doubt which the perusal always occasions in me, whether the *Antony and Cleopatra* is not, in all exhibitions of a giant power in its strength and vigor of maturity, a formidable rival of *Macbeth, Lear, Hamlet,* and *Othello.*" Now, unless the clause here about the "giant power" may be taken to restrict the rivalry to the quality of angelic strength, Coleridge's doubt seems to show a lapse in critical judgment. To regard this tragedy as a rival of the famous four, whether on the stage or in the study, is surely an error. The world certainly has not so regarded it; and, though the world's reasons for its verdicts on works of art may be worth little, its mere verdict is worth much. Here, it seems to me, that verdict must be accepted. One may notice that, in calling *Antony and Cleopatra* wonderful or astonishing, we appear to be thinking first of the artist and his activity, while in the case of the four famous tragedies it is the product of this activity, the thing presented, that first engrosses us. I know that I am stating this difference too sharply, but I believe that it is often felt; and, if this is so, the fact is significant. It implies that, although *Antony and Cleopatra* may be for us as wonderful an achievement as the greatest of Shakespeare's plays, it has not an equal value. Besides, in the attempt to rank it with them there is involved something more, and more important, than an error in valuation. There is a failure to discriminate the peculiar marks of *Antony and Cleopatra* itself, marks which, whether or no it be the equal of the earlier tragedies, make it decidedly different. If I speak first of some of these differences it is because they thus contribute to the individuality of the play, and because they seem often not to be distinctly apprehended in criticism.

I

Why, let us begin by asking, is *Antony and Cleopatra,* though so wonderful an achievement, a play rarely acted? For a tragedy, it is not painful. Though unfit for children, it cannot be called indecent; some slight omissions, and such a flattening of the heroine's part as might confidently be expected, would leave it perfectly presentable. It is, no doubt, in the third and fourth acts, very defective in construction. Even on the Elizabethan stage, where scene followed scene without a pause, this must have been felt; and in our theaters it would be felt much more. There, in fact, these two and forty scenes could not possibly be acted as they stand. But defective construction would not distress the bulk of an audience, if the matter presented were that of *Hamlet* or *Othello,* of *Lear* or *Macbeth.* The matter, then, must lack something which is present in those tragedies; and it is mainly owing to this difference in substance that *Antony and Cleopatra* has never attained their popularity either on the stage or off it.

Most of Shakespeare's tragedies are dramatic, in a special sense of the word as well as in its general sense, from beginning to end. The story is not merely exciting and impressive from the movement of conflicting forces towards a terrible issue, but from time to time there come situations and events which, even apart from their bearing on this issue, appeal most powerfully to the dramatic feelings— scenes of action or passion which agitate the audience with alarm, horror, painful expectation, or absorbing sympathies and antipathies. Think of the street fights in *Romeo and Juliet,* the killing of Mercutio and Tybalt, the rapture of the lovers, and their despair when Romeo is banished. Think of the ghost scenes in the first act of *Hamlet,* the passion of the early soliloquies, the scene between Hamlet and Ophelia, the play scene, the sparing of the King at prayer, the killing of Polonius. Is not *Hamlet,* if you choose so to regard it, the best melodrama in the world? Think at your leisure of *Othello, Lear,* and *Macbeth* from the same point of view; but consider here and now even the two tragedies which, as dealing with Roman history, are companions of *Antony and Cleopatra.* Recall in *Julius Caesar* the first suggestion of the murder, the preparation for it in a "tempest dropping fire," the murder itself, the speech of Antony over the corpse, and the tumult of the furious crowd; in *Coriolanus* the bloody battles on the stage, the scene in which the hero attains the consulship, the scene of rage in which he is banished. And remember that in each of these seven tragedies the matter referred to is contained in the first three acts.

In the first three acts of our play what is there resembling this? Almost nothing. People converse, discuss, accuse one another, excuse themselves, mock, describe, drink together, arrange a marriage, meet and part; but they do not kill, do not even tremble or weep. We see hardly one violent movement; until the battle of Actium is over we witness scarcely any vehement passion; and that battle, as it is a naval action, we do not see. Even later, Enobarbus, when he dies, simply dies; he does not kill himself.[2] We hear wonderful talk; but it is not talk, like that of Macbeth and Lady Macbeth, or that of Othello and Iago, at which we hold our breath. The scenes that we remember first are those that portray Cleopatra; Cleopatra coquetting, tormenting, beguiling her lover to stay; Cleopatra left with her women and longing for him; Cleopatra receiving the news of his marriage; Cleopatra questioning the messenger

2 See Note A.

about Octavia's personal appearance. But this is to say that the scenes we remember first are the least indispensable to the plot. One at least is not essential to it at all. And this, the astonishing scene where she storms at the messenger, strikes him, and draws her dagger on him, is the one passage in the first half of the drama that contains either an explosion of passion or an exciting bodily action. Nor is this all. The first half of the play, though it forebodes tragedy, is not decisively tragic in tone. Certainly the Cleopatra scenes are not so. We read them, and we should witness them, in delighted wonder and even with amusement. The only scene that can vie with them, that of the revel on Pompey's ship, though full of menace, is in great part humorous. Enobarbus, in this part of the play, is always humorous. Even later, when the tragic tone is deepening, the whipping of Thyreus [i.e., Thidias], in spite of Antony's rage, moves mirth. A play of which all this can truly be said may well be as masterly as *Othello* or *Macbeth,* and more delightful; but, in the greater part of its course, it cannot possibly excite the same emotions. It makes no attempt to do so; and to regard it as though it made this attempt is to miss its specific character and the intention of its author.

That character depends only in part on Shakespeare's fidelity to his historical authority, a fidelity which, I may remark, is often greatly exaggerated. For Shakespeare did not merely present the story of ten years as though it occupied perhaps one-fifth of that time, nor did he merely invent freely, but in critical places he effected startling changes in the order and combination of events. Still it may be said that, dealing with a history so famous, he could not well make the first half of his play very exciting, moving, or tragic. And this is true so far as mere situations and events are concerned. But, if he had chosen, he might easily have heightened the tone and tension in another way. He might have made the story of Antony's attempt to break his bondage, and the story of his relapse, extremely exciting, by portraying with all his force the severity of the struggle and the magnitude of the fatal step.

And the structure of the play might seem at first to

suggest this intention. At the opening, Antony is shown almost in the beginning of his infatuation; for Cleopatra is not sure of her power over him, exerts all her fascination to detain him, and plays the part of the innocent victim who has yielded to passion and must now expect to be deserted by her seducer. Alarmed and ashamed at the news of the results of his inaction, he rouses himself, tears himself away, and speeds to Italy. His very coming is enough to frighten Pompey into peace. He reconciles himself with Octavius, and, by his marriage with the good and beautiful Octavia, seems to have knit a bond of lasting amity with her brother, and to have guarded himself against the passion that threatened him with ruin. At this point his power, the world's peace, and his own peace, appear to be secured; his fortune has mounted to its apex. But soon (very much sooner than in Plutarch's story) comes the downward turn or counterstroke. New causes of offense arise between the brothers-in-law. To remove them Octavia leaves her husband in Athens and hurries to Rome. Immediately Antony returns to Cleopatra and, surrendering himself at once and wholly to her enchantment, is quickly driven to his doom.

Now Shakespeare, I say, with his matchless power of depicting an inward struggle, might have made this story, even where it could not furnish him with thrilling incidents, the source of powerful tragic emotions; and, in doing so, he would have departed from his authority merely in his conception of the hero's character. But he does no such thing till the catastrophe is near. Antony breaks away from Cleopatra without any strenuous conflict. No serious doubt of his return is permitted to agitate us. We are almost assured of it through the impression made on us by Octavius, through occasional glimpses into Antony's mind, through the absence of any doubt in Enobarbus, through scenes in Alexandria which display Cleopatra and display her irresistible. And, finally, the downward turn itself, the fatal step of Antony's return, is shown without the slightest emphasis. Nay, it is not shown, it is only reported; and not a line portrays any inward struggle preceding it. On this side also, then, the drama makes no attempt to rival the other tragedies; and it was essential to its own peculiar character and its most transcendent effects that this attempt should not be made, but that Antony's passion should be represented as a force which he could hardly even desire to resist. By the very scheme of the work, therefore, tragic impressions of any great volume or depth were reserved for the last stage of the conflict; while the main interest, down to the battle of Actium, was directed to matters exceedingly interesting and even, in the wider sense, dramatic, but not overtly either terrible or piteous: on the one hand, to the political aspect of the story; on the other, to the personal causes which helped to make the issue inevitable.

II

The political situation and its development are simple. The story is taken up almost where it was left, years before, in *Julius Caesar*. There Brutus and Cassius, to prevent the rule of one man, assassinate Caesar. Their purpose is condemned to failure, not merely because they make mistakes, but because that political necessity which Napoleon identified with destiny requires the rule of one man. They spill Caesar's blood, but his spirit walks abroad and turns their swords against their own breasts; and the world is left divided among three men, his friends and his heir. Here *Antony and Cleopatra* takes up the tale; and its business, from this point of view, is to show the reduction of these three to one. That Lepidus will not be this one was clear already in *Julius Caesar;* it must be Octavius or Antony. Both ambitious, they are also men of such opposite tempers that they would scarcely long agree even if they wished to, and even if destiny were not stronger than they. As it is, one of them has fixed his eyes on the end, sacrifices everything for it, uses everything as a means to it. The other, though far the greater soldier and worshiped by his followers, has no such singleness of aim; nor yet is power, however desirable to him, the most desirable thing in the world. At the beginning he is risking it for love; at the end he has lost his half of the world, and lost his life, and Octavius rules alone. Whether Shakespeare had this clearly in his mind is a question neither answerable nor important; this is what came out of his mind.

Shakespeare, I think, took little interest in the character of Octavius, and he has not made it wholly clear. It is not distinct in Plutarch's "Life of Antony"; and I have not found traces that the poet studied closely the "Life of Octavius" included in North's volume. To Shakespeare he is one of those men, like Bolingbroke and Ulysses, who have plenty of "judgment" and not much "blood." Victory in the world, according to the poet, almost always goes to such men; and he makes us respect, fear, and dislike them. His Octavius is very formidable. His cold determination half paralyzes Antony; it is so even in *Julius Caesar*. In *Antony and Cleopatra* Octavius is more than once in the wrong; but he never admits it; he silently pushes his rival a step backward; and, when he ceases to fear, he shows contempt. He neither enjoys war nor is great in it; at first, therefore, he is anxious about the power of Pompey and stands in need of Antony. As soon as Antony's presence has served his turn, and he has patched up a union with him and seen him safely off to Athens, he destroys first Pompey and next Lepidus. Then, dexterously using Antony's faithlessness to Octavia and excesses in the East in order to put himself in the right, he makes for his victim with admirable celerity while he is still drunk with the joy of reunion with Cleopatra. For his ends Octavius is perfectly efficient, but he is so partly from his limitations. One phrase of his is exceedingly characteristic. When Antony in rage and desperation challenges him to single combat, Octavius calls him "the old ruffian." There is a horrid aptness in the phrase, but it disgusts us. It is shameful in this boy, as hard and smooth as polished steel, to feel at such a time nothing of the greatness of his victim and the tragedy of his victim's fall. Though the challenge of Antony is absurd, we would give much to see them sword to sword. And when Cleopatra by her death cheats the conqueror of his prize, we feel unmixed delight.

The doubtful point in the character is this. Plutarch says that Octavius was reported to love his sister dearly; and

Shakespeare's Octavius several times expresses such love. When, then, he proposed the marriage with Antony (for of course it was he who spoke through Agrippa), was he honest, or was he laying a trap and, in doing so, sacrificing his sister? Did he hope the marriage would really unite him with his brother-in-law; or did he merely mean it to be a source of future differences; or did he calculate that, whether it secured peace or dissension, it would in either case bring him great advantage? Shakespeare, who was quite as intelligent as his readers, must have asked himself some such question; but he may not have cared to answer it even to himself; and, in any case, he has left the actor (at least the actor in days later than his own) to choose an answer. If I were forced to choose, I should take the view that Octavius was, at any rate, not wholly honest; partly because I think it best suits Shakespeare's usual way of conceiving a character of the kind; partly because Plutarch construed in this manner Octavius's behavior in regard to his sister at a later time, and this hint might naturally influence the poet's way of imagining his earlier action.[3]

Though the character of Octavius is neither attractive nor wholly clear, his figure is invested with a certain tragic dignity, because he is felt to be the Man of Destiny, the agent of forces against which the intentions of an individual would avail nothing. He is represented as having himself some feeling of this sort. His lament over Antony, his grief that their stars were irreconcilable, may well be genuine, though we should be surer if it were uttered in soliloquy. His austere words to Octavia again probably speak his true mind:

---

[3] "Now whilest Antonius was busie in this preparation, Octavia his wife, whom he had left at Rome, would needs take sea to come unto him. Her brother Octauius Cæsar was willing vnto it, not for his respect at all (as most authors do report) as for that he might haue an honest colour to make warre with Antonius if he did misuse her, and not esteeme of her as she ought to be."—*Life of Antony* (North's Translation), sect. 29. The view I take does not, of course, imply that Octavius had no love for his sister.

> Be you not troubled with the time, which drives
> O'er your content these strong necessities;
> But let determined things to destiny
> Hold unbewailed their way.

In any case the feeling of fate comes through to us. It is aided by slight touches of supernatural effect; first in the Soothsayer's warning to Antony that his genius or angel is overpowered whenever he is near Octavius; then in the strangely effective scene where Antony's soldiers, in the night before his last battle, hear music in the air or under the earth:

> 'Tis the god Hercules, whom Antony loved,
> Now leaves him.

And to the influence of this feeling in giving impressiveness to the story is added that of the immense scale and world-wide issue of the conflict. Even the distances traversed by fleets and armies enhance this effect.

And yet there seems to be something halfhearted in Shakespeare's appeal here, something even ironical in his presentation of this conflict. Its external magnitude, like Antony's magnificence in lavishing realms and gathering the kings of the East in his support, fails to uplift or dilate the imagination. The struggle in Lear's little island seems to us to have an infinitely wider scope. It is here that we are sometimes reminded of *Troilus and Cressida* and the cold and disenchanting light that is there cast on the Trojan War. The spectacle which he portrays leaves Shakespeare quite undazzled; he even makes it appear inwardly small. The lordship of the world, we ask ourselves, what is it worth, and in what spirit do these "world-sharers" contend for it? They are no champions of their country like Henry V. The conqueror knows not even the glory of battle. Their aims, for all we see, are as personal as if they were captains of banditti; and they are followed merely from self-interest or private attachment. The scene on Pompey's galley is full of this irony. One "third part of the world" is carried drunk to bed. In the midst of this mock boon companionship the pirate whispers to his leader to cut first the cable of his ship and then the throats of the two other emperors; and at the moment we should not greatly care if Pompey took the advice. Later, a short scene, totally useless to the plot and purely satiric in its purport, is slipped in to show how Ventidius fears to pursue his Parthian conquests because it is not safe for Antony's lieutenant to outdo his master.[4] A painful sense of hollowness oppresses us. We know too well what must happen in a world so splendid, so false, and so petty. We turn for relief from the political game to those who are sure to lose it; to those who love some human being better than a prize, to Eros and Charmian and Iras; to Enobarbus, whom the world corrupts, but who has a heart that can break with shame; to the lovers, who seem to us to find in death something better than their victor's life.

This presentation of the outward conflict has two results. First, it blunts our feeling of the greatness of Antony's fall from prosperity. Indeed this feeling, which we might expect to be unusually acute, is hardly so; it is less acute, for example, than the like feeling in the case of Richard II, who loses so much smaller a realm. Our deeper sympathies are focused rather on Antony's heart, on the inward fall to which the enchantment of passion leads him, and the inward recovery which succeeds it. And the second result is this. The greatness of Antony and Cleopatra in their fall is so much heightened by contrast with the world they lose and the conqueror who wins it that the positive element in the final tragic impression, the element of reconciliation, is strongly emphasized. The peculiar effect of the drama depends partly, as we have seen, on the absence of decidedly tragic scenes and events in its first half; but it depends quite as much on this emphasis. In any Shakespearean tragedy we watch some elect spirit colliding, partly through its error and defect, with a superhuman power which bears it down; and yet we feel that this spirit, even in the error and defect, rises by its greatness into ideal union with the power that overwhelms it. In some tragedies this latter feeling is relatively weak. In *Antony and Cleopatra* it is unusually strong; stronger, with some readers at

4 See Note B.

least, than the fear and grief and pity with which they con-
template the tragic error and the advance of doom.

III

The two aspects of the tragedy are presented together
in the opening scene. Here is the first. In Cleopatra's palace
one friend of Antony is describing to another, just arrived
from Rome, the dotage of their great general; and, as the
lovers enter, he exclaims:

> Look, where they come:
> Take but good note, and you shall see in him
> The triple pillar of the world transformed
> Into a strumpet's fool: behold and see.

With the next words the other aspect appears:

Cleopatra. If it be love indeed, tell me how much.

Antony. There's beggary in the love that can be reckoned.

Cleopatra. I'll set a bourne how far to be beloved.

Antony. Then must thou needs find out new heaven, new
earth.

And directly after, when he is provoked by reminders of
the news from Rome:

> Let Rome in Tiber melt, and the wide arch
> Of the ranged empire fall! Here is my space.
> Kingdoms are clay: our dungy earth alike
> Feeds beast as man: the nobleness of life
> Is to do thus.

Here is the tragic excess, but with it the tragic greatness,
the capacity of finding in something the infinite, and of
pursuing it into the jaws of death.

The two aspects are shown here with the exaggera-
tion proper in dramatic characters. Neither the phrase "a
strumpet's fool," nor the assertion "the nobleness of life
is to do thus," answers to the total effect of the play. But

the truths they exaggerate are equally essential; and the commoner mistake in criticism is to understate the second. It is plain that the love of Antony and Cleopatra is destructive; that in some way it clashes with the nature of things; that, while they are sitting in their paradise like gods, its walls move inward and crush them at last to death. This is no invention of moralizing critics; it is in the play; and anyone familiar with Shakespeare would expect beforehand to find it there. But then to forget because of it the other side, to deny the name of love to this ruinous passion, to speak as though the lovers had utterly missed the good of life, is to mutilate the tragedy and to ignore a great part of its effect upon us. For we sympathize with them in their passion; we feel in it the infinity there is in man; even while we acquiesce in their defeat we are exulting in their victory; and when they have vanished we say,

> the odds is gone,
> And there is nothing left remarkable
> Beneath the visiting moon.

Though we hear nothing from Shakespeare of the cruelty of Plutarch's Antony, or of the misery caused by his boundless profusion, we do not feel the hero of the tragedy to be a man of the noblest type, like Brutus, Hamlet, or Othello. He seeks power merely for himself, and uses it for his own pleasure. He is in some respects unscrupulous; and, while it would be unjust to regard his marriage exactly as if it were one in private life, we resent his treatment of Octavia, whose character Shakespeare was obliged to leave a mere sketch, lest our feeling for the hero and heroine should be too much chilled. Yet, for all this, we sympathize warmly with Antony, are greatly drawn to him, and are inclined to regard him as a noble nature half spoiled by his time.

It is a large, open, generous, expansive nature, quite free from envy, capable of great magnanimity, even of entire devotion. Antony is unreserved, naturally straightforward, we may almost say simple. He can admit faults, accept advice and even reproof, take a jest against himself with good humor. He is courteous (to Lepidus, for example, whom Octavius treats with cold contempt); and, though he can be exceedingly dignified, he seems to prefer a blunt though sympathetic plainness, which is one cause of the attachment of his soldiers. He has none of the faults of the brooder, the sentimentalist, or the man of principle; his nature tends to splendid action and lusty enjoyment. But he is neither a mere soldier nor a mere sensualist. He has imagination, the temper of an artist who revels in abundant and rejoicing appetites, feasts his senses on the glow and richness of life, flings himself into its mirth and revelry, yet feels the poetry in all this, and is able also to put it by and be more than content with the hardships of adventure. Such a man could never have sought a crown by a murder like Macbeth's, or, like Brutus, have killed on principle the man who loved him, or have lost the world for a Cressida.

Beside this strain of poetry he has a keen intellect, a swift perception of the lie of things, and much quickness in shaping a course to suit them. In *Julius Caesar* he shows this after the assassination, when he appears as a dexterous politician as well as a warmhearted friend. He admires what is fine and can fully appreciate the nobility of Brutus; but he is sure that Brutus's ideas are moonshine, that (as he says in our play) Brutus is mad; and, since his mighty friend, who was incomparably the finest thing in the world, has perished, he sees no reason why the inheritance should not be his own. Full of sorrow, he yet uses his sorrow like an artist to work on others and greets his success with the glee of a successful adventurer. In the earlier play he proves himself a master of eloquence, and especially of pathos; and he does so again in the later. With a few words about his fall he draws tears from his followers and even from the caustic humorist Enobarbus. Like Richard II, he sees his own fall with the eyes of a poet, but a poet much greater than the young Shakespeare, who could never have written Antony's marvelous speech about the sunset clouds. But we listen to Antony, as we do not to Richard, with entire sympathy, partly because he is never unmanly, partly because he himself is sympathetic and longs for sympathy.

The first of living soldiers, an able politician, a most persuasive orator, Antony nevertheless was not born to rule the world. He enjoys being a great man, but he has not the love of rule for rule's sake. Power for him is chiefly a means to pleasure. The pleasure he wants is so huge that he needs a huge power; but half the world, even a third of it, would suffice. He will not pocket wrongs, but he shows not the slightest wish to get rid of his fellow triumvirs and reign alone. He never minded being subordinate to Julius Caesar. By women he is not only attracted but governed; from the effect of Cleopatra's taunts we can see that he had been governed by Fulvia. Nor has he either the patience or the steadfastness of a born ruler. He contends fitfully and is prone to take the step that is easiest at the moment. This is the reason why he consents to marry Octavia. It seems the shortest way out of an awkward situation. He does not intend even to try to be true to her. He will not think of the distant consequences.

A man who loved power as much as thousands of insignificant people love it, would have made a sterner struggle than Antony's against his enchantment. He can hardly be said to struggle at all. He brings himself to leave Cleopatra only because he knows he will return. In every moment of his absence, whether he wake or sleep, a siren music in his blood is singing him back to her; and to this music, however he may be occupied, the soul within his soul leans and listens. The joy of life had always culminated for him in the love of women: he could say "no" to none of them: of Octavia herself he speaks like a poet. When he meets Cleopatra he finds his Absolute. She satisfies, nay glorifies, his whole being. She intoxicates his senses. Her wiles, her taunts, her furies and meltings, her laughter and tears, bewitch him all alike. She loves what he loves, and she surpasses him. She can drink him to his bed, outjest his practical jokes, outact the best actress who ever amused him, outdazzle his own magnificence. She is his playfellow, and yet a great queen. Angling in the river, playing billiards, flourishing the sword he used at Philippi, hopping forty paces in a public street, she remains an enchantress. Her spirit is made of wind and flame, and the

poet in him worships her no less than the man. He is under
no illusion about her, knows all her faults, sees through
her wiles, believes her capable of betraying him. It makes
no difference. She is his heart's desire made perfect. To
love her is what he was born for. What have the gods in
heaven to say against it? To imagine heaven is to imagine
her; to die is to rejoin her. To deny that this is love is the
madness of morality. He gives her every atom of his heart.

She destroys him. Shakespeare, availing himself of the
historic fact, portrays, on Antony's return to her, the sud-
denness and the depth of his descent. In spite of his own
knowledge, the protests of his captains, the entreaties even
of a private soldier, he fights by sea simply and solely because she wishes it. Then in mid-battle, when she flies, he
deserts navy and army and his faithful thousands and follows her. "I never saw an action of such shame," cries
Scarus; and we feel the dishonor of the hero keenly. Then
Shakespeare begins to raise him again. First, his own overwhelming sense of shame redeems him. Next, we watch
the rage of the dying lion. Then the mere sally before the
final defeat—a sally dismissed by Plutarch in three lines—
is magnified into a battle, in which Antony displays to us,
and himself feels for the last time, the glory of his soldiership. And, throughout, the magnanimity and gentleness
which shine through his desperation endear him to us. How
beautiful is his affection for his followers and even for his
servants, and the devotion they return! How noble his reception of the news that Enobarbus has deserted him! How ·
touchingly significant the refusal of Eros either to kill him
or survive him! How pathetic and even sublime the com-
pleteness of his love for Cleopatra! His anger is born and
dies in an hour. One tear, one kiss, outweighs his ruin. He
believes she has sold him to his enemy, yet he kills himself
because he hears that she is dead. When, dying, he learns
that she has deceived him once more, no thought of reproach crosses his mind: he simply asks to be carried to
her. He knows well that she is not capable of dying because he dies, but that does not sting him; when, in his
last agony, he calls for wine that he may gain a moment's

strength to speak, it is to advise her for the days to come. Shakespeare borrowed from Plutarch the final speech of Antony. It is fine, but it is not miraculous. The miraculous speeches belong only to his own hero:

> I am dying, Egypt, dying; only
> I here importune death awhile, until
> Of many thousand kisses the poor last
> I lay upon thy lips;

or the first words he utters when he hears of Cleopatra's death:

> Unarm, Eros: the long day's task is done,
> And we must sleep.

If he meant the task of statesman and warrior, that is not what his words mean to us. They remind us of words more familiar and less great—

> No rest but the grave for the pilgrim of love.

And he is more than love's pilgrim; he is love's martyr.

IV

To reserve a fragment of an hour for Cleopatra, if it were not palpably absurd, would seem an insult. If only one could hear her own remarks upon it! But I had to choose between this absurdity and the plan of giving her the whole hour; and to that plan there was one fatal objection. She has been described (by Ten Brink) as a courtesan of genius. So brief a description must needs be incomplete, and Cleopatra never forgets, nor, if we read aright, do we forget, that she is a great queen. Still the phrase is excellent; only a public lecture is no occasion for the full analysis and illustration of the character it describes.

Shakespeare has paid Cleopatra a unique compliment. The hero dies in the fourth act, and the whole of the fifth is devoted to the heroine.[5] In that act she becomes un-questionably a tragic character, but, it appears to me, not till then. This, no doubt, is a heresy; but as I cannot help holding it, and as it is connected with the remarks already made on the first half of the play, I will state it more fully. Cleopatra stands in a group with Hamlet and Falstaff. We might join with them Iago if he were not decidedly their inferior in one particular quality. They are inexhaustible. You feel that, if they were alive and you spent your whole life with them, their infinite variety could never be staled by custom; they would continue every day to surprise, perplex, and delight you. Shake-speare has bestowed on each of them, though they differ so much, his own originality, his genius. He has given it most fully to Hamlet, to whom none of the chambers of experience is shut, and perhaps more of it to Cleo-patra than to Falstaff. Nevertheless, if we ask whether Cleopatra, in the first four acts, is a tragic figure like Hamlet, we surely cannot answer "yes." Naturally it does not follow that she is a comic figure like Falstaff. This would be absurd; for, even if she were ridiculous like Falstaff, she is not ridiculous to herself; she is no humorist. And yet there is a certain likeness. She shares a weakness with Falstaff—vanity; and when she displays it, as she does quite naïvely (for instance, in the second interview with the Messenger), she does become comic. Again, though like Falstaff she is irresistible and carries us away no less than the people around her, we are secretly aware, in the midst of our delight, that her em-pire is built on sand. And finally, as his love for the Prince gives dignity and pathos to Falstaff in his over-throw, so what raises Cleopatra at last into pure tragedy is, in part, that which some critics have denied her, her love for Antony.

Many unpleasant things can be said of Cleopatra; and the more that are said, the more wonderful she appears. The exercise of sexual attraction is the element of her life; and she has developed nature into a consummate

---

[5] The point of this remark is unaffected by the fact that the play is not divided into acts and scenes in the folios.

art. When she cannot exert it on the present lover she imagines its effects on him in absence. Longing for the living, she remembers with pride and joy the dead; and the past which the furious Antony holds up to her as a picture of shame is, for her, glory. She cannot see an ambassador, scarcely even a messenger, without desiring to bewitch him. Her mind is saturated with this element. If she is dark, it is because the sun himself has been amorous of her. Even when death is close at hand she imagines his touch as a lover's. She embraces him that she may overtake Iras and gain Antony's first kiss in the other world.

She lives for feeling. Her feelings are, so to speak, sacred, and pain must not come near her. She has tried numberless experiments to discover the easiest way to die. Her body is exquisitely sensitive, and her emotions marvelously swift. They are really so; but she exaggerates them so much, and exhibits them so continually for effect, that some readers fancy them merely feigned. They are all-important, and everybody must attend to them. She announces to her women that she is pale, or sick and sullen; they must lead her to her chamber but must not speak to her. She is as strong and supple as a leopard, can drink down a master of revelry, can raise her lover's helpless heavy body from the ground into her tower with the aid only of two women; yet, when he is sitting apart sunk in shame, she must be supported into his presence, she cannot stand, her head droops, she will die (it is the opinion of Eros) unless he comforts her. When she hears of his marriage and has discharged her rage, she bids her women bear her away; she faints; at least she would faint, but that she remembers various questions she wants put to the Messenger about Octavia. Enobarbus has seen her die twenty times upon far poorer moment than the news that Antony is going to Rome.

Some of her feelings are violent, and, unless for a purpose, she does not dream of restraining them; her sighs and tears are winds and waters, storms and tempests. At times, as when she threatens to give Charmian bloody teeth, or hales the luckless Messenger up and down by

the hair, strikes him, and draws her knife on him, she
resembles (if I dare say it) Doll Tearsheet sublimated.
She is a mother; but the threat of Octavius to destroy her
children if she takes her own life passes by her like the
wind (a point where Shakespeare contradicts Plutarch).
She ruins a great man, but shows no sense of the tragedy
of his ruin. The anguish of spirit that appears in his language to his servants is beyond her; she has to ask Enobarbus what he means. Can we feel sure that she would
not have sacrificed him if she could have saved herself
by doing so? It is not even certain that she did not attempt it. Antony himself believes that she did—that the
fleet went over to Octavius by her orders. That she and
her people deny the charge proves nothing. The best
we can say is that, if it were true, Shakespeare would
have made that clear. She is willing also to survive her
lover. Her first thought, to follow him after the high
Roman fashion, is too great for her. She would live on
if she could, and would cheat her victor too of the best
part of her fortune. The thing that drives her to die is
the certainty that she will be carried to Rome to grace
his triumph. That alone decides her.[6]

The marvelous thing is that the knowledge of all this
makes hardly more difference to us than it did to Antony.
It seems to us perfectly natural, nay, in a sense perfectly
right, that her lover should be her slave; that her women
should adore her and die with her; that Enobarbus, who
foresaw what must happen, and who opposes her wishes
and braves her anger, should talk of her with rapture
and feel no bitterness against her; that Dolabella, after a
minute's conversation, should betray to her his master's
intention and enable her to frustrate it. And when Octavius shows himself proof against her fascination, instead of admiring him we turn from him with disgust
and think him a disgrace to his species. Why? It is not
that we consider him bound to fall in love with her. Enobarbus did not; Dolabella did not; we ourselves do not.
The feeling she inspires was felt then, and is felt now,
by women no less than men, and would have been shared

6 See Note C.

by Octavia herself. Doubtless she wrought magic on the
senses, but she had not extraordinary beauty, like Helen's,
such beauty as seems divine.[7] Plutarch says so. The man
who wrote the sonnets to the dark lady would have known
it for himself. He goes out of his way to add to her age,
and tells us of her wrinkles and the waning of her lip.
But Enobarbus, in his very mockery, calls her a wonderful piece of work. Dolabella interrupts her with the cry,
"Most sovereign creature," and we echo it. And yet Octavius, face to face with her and listening to her voice,
can think only how best to trap her and drag her to public
dishonor in the streets of Rome. We forgive him only
for his words when he sees her dead:

> She looks like sleep,
> As she would catch another Antony
> In her strong toil of grace.

And the words, I confess, sound to me more like Shakespeare's than his.

That which makes her wonderful and sovereign laughs
at definition, but she herself came nearest naming it when,
in the final speech (a passage surpassed in poetry, if at
all, only by the final speech of Othello), she cries,

> I am fire and air; my other elements
> I give to baser life.

The fire and air which at death break from union with
those other elements, transfigured them during her life,
and still convert into engines of enchantment the very
things for which she is condemned. I can refer only to
one. She loves Antony. We should marvel at her less and
love her more if she loved him more—loved him well
enough to follow him at once to death; but it is to blunder
strangely to doubt that she loved him, or that her glorious
description of him (though it was also meant to work on
Dolabella) came from her heart. Only the spirit of fire
and air within her refuses to be trammeled or extin-

[7] See Note D.

guished; burns its way through the obstacles of fortune
and even through the resistance of her love and grief;
and would lead her undaunted to fresh life and the conquest of new worlds. It is this which makes her "strong
toil of grace" unbreakable; speaks in her brows' bent and
every tone and movement; glorifies the arts and the rages
which in another would merely disgust or amuse us; and,
in the final scenes of her life, flames into such brilliance
that we watch her entranced as she struggles for freedom,
and thrilled with triumph as, conquered, she puts her
conqueror to scorn and goes to meet her lover in the
splendor that crowned and robed her long ago, when her
barge burnt on the water like a burnished throne, and
she floated to Cydnus on the enamoured stream to take
him captive forever.[8]

Why is it that, although we close the book in a triumph
which is more than reconciliation, this is mingled, as we
look back on the story, with a sadness so peculiar, almost
the sadness of disenchantment? Is it that, when the glow
has faded, Cleopatra's ecstasy comes to appear, I would
not say factitious, but an effort strained and prodigious
as well as glorious, not, like Othello's last speech, the final
expression of character, of thoughts and emotions which
have dominated a whole life? Perhaps this is so, but there
is something more, something that sounds paradoxical:
we are saddened by the very fact that the catastrophe
saddens us so little; it pains us that we should feel so
much triumph and pleasure. In *Romeo and Juliet, Hamlet, Othello,* though in a sense we accept the deaths of
hero and heroine, we feel a keen sorrow. We look back,
think how noble or beautiful they were, wish that fate
had opposed to them a weaker enemy, dream possibly
of the life they might then have led. Here we can hardly
do this. With all our admiration and sympathy for the
lovers we do not wish them to gain the world. It is better
for the world's sake, and not less for their own, that they

---

[8] Of the "good" heroines, Imogen is the one who has most of this
spirit of fire and air; and this (in union, of course, with other qualities)
is perhaps the ultimate reason why for so many readers she is, what Mr.
Swinburne calls her, "the woman above all Shakespeare's women."

should fail and die. At the very first they came before us, unlike those others, unlike Coriolanus and even Macbeth, in a glory already tarnished, half-ruined by their past. Indeed one source of strange and most unusual effect in their story is that this marvelous passion comes to adepts in the experience and art of passion, who might be expected to have worn its charm away. Its splendor dazzles us; but, when the splendor vanishes, we do not mourn, as we mourn for the love of Romeo or Othello, that a thing so bright and good should die. And the fact that we mourn so little saddens us.

A comparison of Shakespearean tragedies seems to prove that the tragic emotions are stirred in the fullest possible measure only when such beauty or nobility of character is displayed as commands unreserved admiration or love; or when, in default of this, the forces which move the agents, and the conflict which results from these forces, attain a terrifying and overwhelming power. The four most famous tragedies satisfy one or both of these conditions; *Antony and Cleopatra,* though a great tragedy, satisfies neither of them completely. But to say this is not to criticize it. It does not attempt to satisfy these conditions and then fail in the attempt. It attempts something different and succeeds as triumphantly as *Othello* itself. In doing so it gives us what no other tragedy can give, and it leaves us, no less than any other, lost in astonishment at the powers which created it.

1905

NOTE A

We are to understand, surely, that Enobarbus dies of "thought" (melancholy or grief), and has no need to seek a "swifter mean." Cf. IV.vi.34 *seq.,* with the death scene and his address there to the moon as the "sovereign mistress of true melancholy" (IV.ix). Cf. also III.xiii, where, to Cleopatra's question after Actium, "What shall we do, Enobarbus?" he answers, "Think, and die."

The character of Enobarbus is practically an invention of Shakespeare's. The death scene, I may add, is one of the many passages which prove that he often wrote what pleased his imagination but would lose half its effect in the theater. The darkness and moonlight could not be represented on a public stage in his time.

NOTE B

The scene is the first of the third act. Here Ventidius says:

> Caesar and Antony have ever won
> More in their officer than person : Sossius,
> One of my place in Syria, his lieutenant,
> For quick accumulation of renown,
> Which he achieved by the minute, lost his favor.

Plutarch (North, sec. 19) says that "Sossius, one of Antonius' lieutenants in Syria, did notable good service," but I cannot find in him the further statement that Sossius lost Antony's favor. I presume it is Shakespeare's invention, but I call attention to it on the bare chance that it may be found elsewhere than in Plutarch, when it would point to Shakespeare's use of a second authority.

NOTE C

Since this lecture was published (*Quarterly Review,* April, 1906) two notable editions of *Antony and Cleopatra* have been produced. Nothing recently written on Shakespeare, I venture to say, shows more thorough scholarship or better judgment than Mr. Case's edition in the Arden series; and Dr. Furness has added to the immense debt which students of Shakespeare owe to him, and (if that is possible) to the admiration and respect with which they regard him, by the appearance of *Antony and Cleopatra* in his New Variorum edition.

On one question about Cleopatra both editors, Mr. Case more tentatively and Dr. Furness very decidedly, dissent from the interpretation given in the last pages of my lecture. The question is how we are to understand the fact that, although on Antony's death Cleopatra expresses her intention of following him, she does not carry out this intention until she has satisfied herself that Octavius means to carry her to Rome to grace his triumph. Though I do not profess to feel certain that my interpretation is right, it still seems to me a good deal the most probable, and therefore I have not altered what I wrote. But my object here is not to defend my view or to criticize other views, but merely to call attention to the discussion of the subject in Mr. Case's Introduction and Dr. Furness's Preface.

NOTE D

Shakespeare, it seems clear, imagined Cleopatra as a gypsy. And this, I would suggest, may be the explanation of a word which has caused much difficulty. Antony, when "all is lost," exclaims (IV.xii.25):

> O this false soul of Egypt! this grave charm—
> Whose eye beck'd forth my wars, and call'd them home,
> Whose bosom was my crownet, my chief end—

> Like a right gypsy, hath, at fast and loose,
> Beguil'd me to the very heart of loss.

Pope changed "grave" in the first line into "gay." Others conjecture "great" and "grand." Steevens says that "grave" means "deadly," and that the word "is often used by Chapman" thus; and one of his two quotations supports this statement; but certainly in Shakespeare the word does not elsewhere bear this sense. It could mean "majestic," as Johnson takes it here. But why should it not have its usual meaning? Cleopatra, we know, was a being of "infinite variety," and her eyes may sometimes have had, like those of some gypsies, a mysterious gravity or solemnity which would exert a spell more potent than her gaiety. Their color, presumably, was what is called "black"; but surely they were not, like those of Tennyson's Cleopatra, "*bold* black eyes." Readers interested in seeing what criticism is capable of may like to know that it has been proposed to read, for the first line of the quotation above, "O this false fowl of Egypt! haggard charmer." [Though I have not canceled this note I have modified some phrases in it, as I have not much confidence in my suggestion, and am inclined to think that Steevens was right.]

JOHN F. DANBY

"Antony and Cleopatra": A Shakespearian
Adjustment

At each stage in his development Shakespeare displays a surprising capacity for renewal. Let us assume that *Antony and Cleopatra* comes after *King Lear*, that it goes with *Coriolanus,* and that both it and *Coriolanus* immediately precede the so-called "last period." Between *Antony and Cleopatra* and the plays that have gone before there is no obvious connection in theme or technique. At the same time, only Plutarch links it with *Coriolanus*. Nothing in it would normally prepare us for *Cymbeline* or *The Winter's Tale* to follow. This apparent isolation is one of the main obstacles to a correct focus on the play. There seems to be a break in the internal continuity of the Shakespearian series—a continuity of series which stretches, I think, from *Henry VI* to *King Lear* at least, and which could possibly be extended to include *Timon*: though here again there is something of a lesion, and special factors, external to the "inner biography" of Shakespeare as a playwright, might have to be invoked to explain all that is happening. *Timon,* however, it might be granted, is the aftermath of *King Lear*. Can the same be said about *Antony and Cleopatra?*

From *Poets on Fortune's Hill* by John F. Danby. London: Faber and Faber, Ltd., 1952. Reprinted by permission of Faber and Faber, Ltd.

I

To describe the swiftness of *Antony and Cleopatra* we need to draw on the imagery of the cinema. There is more cinematic movement, more panning, tracking, and playing with the camera, more mixing of shots than in any other of Shakespeare's tragedies. At the same time the technique is always under deliberate, almost cool, control. *Antony and Cleopatra* has none of the haphazardies of *Pericles* nor any of the plot-imposed vagaries of the last period. The technique is inwardly related to the meaning Shakespeare has to express. What is indicated is not enervation or indifference, but rather what Coleridge recognized as "giant power," an "angelic strength."

The swift traverse of time and space has often been commented upon. There is also the mixing. Egypt is called up vividly in Rome by Enobarbus's descriptions. Rome is always felt as a real presence in Egypt. On the frontiers of Empire Ventidius discusses what repercussions his victories will have on the people at staff headquarters. Equally the present is interpenetrated by the past. Antony's past, particularly, is always powerfully put before us:

> Antony,
> Leave thy lascivious wassails. When thou once
> Wast beaten from Modena, where thou slew'st
> Hirtius and Pansa, consuls, at thy heels
> Did famine follow, whom thou fought'st against
> Though daintily brought up, with patience more
> Than savages could suffer; thou didst drink
> The stale of horses, and the gilded puddle
> Which beasts would cough at; thy palate then did deign
> The roughest berry on the rudest hedge;
> Yea, like the stag, when snow the pasture sheets,
> The barks of trees thou browsed. On the Alps

It is reported thou didst eat strange flesh,
Which some did die to look on.   (I.iv.55–68)

So, too, is Cleopatra's:

I found you as a morsel cold upon
Dead Caesar's trenchar; nay, you were a fragment
Of Cneius Pompey's; besides what hotter hours,
Unregister'd in vulgar fame, you have
Luxuriously pick'd out.   (III.xiii.116–20)

The hinterland of the quarrels that alternately divide and
bring together again the triumvirate is constantly being
suggested, troubles, truces, and maneuvers that go back
(like Cleopatra's love affairs) to Julius Caesar's days. In
no other of his plays is Shakespeare at such pains to suggest the stream of time past and its steady course through
the present. In the public world of Roman affairs this is
especially so. In the other world of Cleopatra the same
suggestion of perspective always frames what is said and
done. Is Antony merely the last of a long succession of
such lovers? Or is this affair singular and unique as all
love affairs claim to be? Not enough weight has been
given in recent assessments of the play to the ambiguity
which invests everything in Egypt equally with all things
in Rome. Yet this ambiguity is central to Shakespeare's
experience in the play. If it is wrong to see the "mutual
pair" as a strumpet and her fool, it is also wrong to see
them as a Phoenix and a Turtle.

In addition to the swiftness and the variety of the im-
pacts, and the interpenetration of the parts of time and
space as they mix in the speech of the people immediately
before us, there is also the added burden which Shakespeare's "giant power" of compelling presentation imposes.
The effects are at once those of a rapid impressionism
and a careful lapidary enrichment. Each figure, however
minor, has its moment when it comes up into the brilliant
foreground light—the Soothsayer with his "infinite book
of secrecy," the Old Man wishing "much joy o' the
worm," Enobarbus describing the barge on the Nile,

Lepidus asking "What manner o' thing is your crocodile?" Ventidius giving once for all the field officer's view of the higher-ups, the Eunuch and the game of billiards, Dolabella, Octavia, even Fulvia whom we never see: the canvas seems covered with Constable's snow.

Another feature of Shakespeare's technique which makes for the impression of uniqueness might be pointed to here. Shakespeare seems to be innovating also in methods of character portrayal. Some of the stage conventions, as described by Miss Bradbrook, do not seem to apply. Which, for example, are we to believe—what Caesar says about Antony after he is dead, or what he says about him, and his conduct towards him, while he is alive? What was Fulvia's "character," about whom we have such conflicting reports? Throughout the play we are forced by Shakespeare himself not to take comment at its face value. Judgments are more personal here than elsewhere. Goneril and Regan discussing their father's condition are reliable judges. Caesar, Antony, Enobarbus, the soldiers Demetrius and Philo, are not—or not to the same extent. Judgment knits itself back into character as it might do in Ibsen, and character issues from a mutable and ambiguous flux of things. Antony's momentary *anagnorisis* can be generalized to cover the whole play:

> Sometimes we see a cloud that's dragonish;
> A vapor sometimes like a bear or lion,
> A tower'd citadel, a pendant rock,
> A forked mountain, or blue promontory,
> With trees upon't, that nod unto the world
> And mock our eyes with air: thou hast seen these signs;
> They are black vespers pageants . . .
> That which is now a horse, even with a thought
> The rack dislimns, and makes it indistinct
> As water is in water . . .
> My good knave, Eros, now thy captain is
> Even such a body: here I am Antony,
> Yet cannot hold this visible shape, my knave.

> (IV.xiv.2–14)

There is something deliquescent in the reality behind
the play. It is a deliquescence to the full display of which
each judgment, each aspect pointed to, and each character, is necessary, always provided that no single one of
these is taken as final. The proportion of comment and
judgment on the central characters is higher in *Antony
and Cleopatra* than anywhere else in Shakespeare. This
further underlines its uniqueness and the difficulties of
coming by an adequate final assessment. Antony and
Cleopatra are presented in three ways. There is what is
said about them; there is what they say themselves; there
is what they do. Each of these might correspond to a
different "level" of response. Each is in tension against
the others. Each makes its continuous and insistent claim
on the spectator for judgment in his own right. The pig-
ments vividly opposed to each other on the canvas have
to mix in the spectator's eye.

Underlying, however, the bewildering oscillations of
scene, the overlapping and pleating of different times and
places, the co-presence of opposed judgments, the innumerable opportunities for radical choice to intervene, there
is, I think, a deliberate logic. It is this which gives the
play its compact unity of effect and makes its movement
a sign of angelic strength rather than a symptom of fe-
brility. It is the logic of a peculiarly Shakespearian dialectic. Opposites are juxtaposed, mingled, married; then
from the very union which seems to promise strength
dissolution flows. It is the process of this dialectic—the
central process of the play—which we must trace if we
wish to arrive anywhere near Shakespeare's meaning.

II

The first scene opens with Philo's comment on the
"dotage" of his general:

> those his goodly eyes
> That o'er the files and musters of the war
> Have glow'd like plated Mars: now bend, now turn
> The office and devotion of their view

Upon a tawny front; his captain's heart,
Which in the scuffles of great fights hath burst
The buckles on his breast, reneges all temper,
And is become the bellows and the fan
To cool a gypsy's lust.   (I.i.2–10)

Nothing more has time to be said. Antony and Cleopatra
themselves appear. Their first words express the essence
of romantic love, a tacit contradiction of all that Philo
seems to have just suggested:

Cleopatra. If it be love indeed, tell me how much.

Antony. There's beggary in the love that can be reckoned.

Cleopatra. I'll set a bourn how far to be belov'd.

Antony. Then must thou needs find out new heaven, new
    earth.   (I.i.14–17)

Again immediately, an attendant announces the arrival
of news from Rome. The atmosphere of the Egyptian
court changes. We see the opposite effects of the intrusion
on the two it most concerns. Antony will not hear the
messengers. Cleopatra insists that he shall. Antony is
taunted with a wicked caricature of what the news might
be, and of the relation in which he stands to Rome. Yet
the version is sufficiently like to make Antony blush—
from anger, or shame, or both:

                    Your dismission
Is come from Caesar; therefore hear it, Antony,
Where's Fulvia's process? Caesar's would I say? both?
Call in the messengers. As I am Egypt's queen,
Thou blushest, Antony, and that blood of thine
Is Caesar's homager; else so thy cheek pays shame
When shrill-tongued Fulvia scolds.   (I.i.26–32)

Antony's reaction is to pitch his romantic vows higher
still, asserting his independence of Rome in terms that
should leave no doubt as to where he stands:

> Let Rome in Tiber melt, and the wide arch
> Of the rang'd empire fall! Here is my space.
> Kingdoms are clay; our dungy earth alike
> Feeds beast as man: the nobleness of life
> Is to do thus; when such a mutual pair
> And such a twain can do't, in which I bind
> On pain of punishment, the world to weet
> We stand up peerless.   (I.i.33—40)

This again has all the ring of absolute and heroic self-committal. Cleopatra's reply, however, is typical both of herself and of the ambivalence that runs through everything in the play:

> Excellent falsehood!
> Why did he marry Fulvia and not love her?
> I'll seem the fool I am not; Antony
> Will be himself.   (I.i.40—43)

Her first words might be oxymoron or plain disbelief. The next call up the vista of Antony's past, with its broken pledges and unconscious insincerities—if they were no more. Her last words are highly ambiguous and turn the whole situation upside-down: she is the helpless creature willfully blinding and deceiving herself, Antony is the self-contained and calculating manipulator of her weaknesses. In replying, Antony is like the man innocent of jujutsu who thinks he is pushing when really he is being pulled:

> But stirr'd by Cleopatra.
> Now, for the love of Love and her soft hours,
> Let's not confound the time with conference harsh . . .
> . . . What sport tonight?   (I.i.43—47)

Shakespeare gives the operative lines a subtle falsity of note that could equally indicate hearty play acting, slightly awkward self-consciousness, or willful evasion. Cleopatra's answer is realist and comes with a new urgency:

> Hear the ambassadors.   (I.i.48)

It drives Antony also to something we can recognize as more fully himself—something that is perceptive and tinged with the masterful as well as the reckless:

> Fie, wrangling queen!
> Whom everything becomes, to chide, to laugh,
> To weep; whose every passion fully strives
> To make itself in thee fair and admir'd.
> No messenger, but thine; and all alone,
> Tonight we'll wander through the streets and note
> The qualities of people. Come, my queen;
> Last night you did desire it: speak not to us.
>
> (I.i.48–55)

This is not only Antony's view of Cleopatra's character, and a reliable account of what she is really like. It is also an expression of the deliquescent reality at the heart of the play which incarnates itself most completely in the persons of the hero and heroine. After Antony's speech, with this twofold authority it bears, the comment of the soldiers seems peculiarly limited and out of place:

Demetrius. Is Caesar with Antonius priz'd so slight?

Philo. Sir, sometimes when he is not Antony,
He comes too short of that great property
Which still should go with Antony.

Demetrius. I am full sorry
That he approves the common liar, who
Thus speaks of him at Rome; but I will hope
Of better deeds tomorrow.   (I.i.56–62)

It serves to remind us, however, of the world that stands around the lovers, the world of the faithful soldier who can only understand the soldierly, the world of "the common liar" that enjoys the unpleasant "truth," the world, too, of Rome and Caesar that is radically opposed to the world of Egypt and Cleopatra.

The first scene is only slightly more than sixty lines long. Yet it is sufficient to illustrate all the main features of the play we have pointed to, and extensive enough to set up the swinging ambivalence—the alternatives and ambiguities constantly proposed to choice—which will govern and control our whole reaction to the play. There is the speed and oscillation, the interpenetration of Rome and Egypt and of present and past. Above all there is the dialectic marriage of the contraries and their disso-lution through union. The jealousy of Cleopatra towards Fulvia, the outrage of Caesar to Antony's *amour propre* —these negative repulsions can serve to hold the mutual pair together as firmly as positive attractions. Antony and Cleopatra are opposed to the world that surrounds and isolates them. In this isolation their union seems absolute, infinite, and self-sufficient. Yet the war of the contraries pervades the love, too. In coming together they lapse, slide, and fall apart unceasingly.

The outstanding achievement of the first scene is the way in which it begins with the soldiers' condemnation and returns us at the end to the same thing—allowing for this side eighteen lines out of the sixty-two. Yet at the end we are no longer satisfied as to the adequacy of what Demetrius and Philo say. Not that what they say has been disproved by what we have seen of Antony and Cleopatra. They are and they remain a strumpet and her fool. To have any judgment at all is to choose, apparently, either the judgment of the soldiers at the beginning of the scene or the lovers' own self-assessment that immediately fol-lows it. (Coleridge chose the former; Dr. Sitwell and Mr. Wilson Knight take the latter.) To entertain either judg-ment, however, is not enough. The deliquescent truth is neither in them nor between them, but contains both. *Antony and Cleopatra* is Shakespeare's critique of judg-ment.

Scene i played out romantic love and lovers' quarrels on a lofty stage. It also gave the sharp local comment of the soldiery. Scene ii takes the theme of love belowstairs and changes key. It also gives the universal comment of the Soothsayer, with its suggestion that everything is al-ready decided, the tragedy is in the nature of things, now is already over, the future past, the present always:

> In nature's infinite book of secrecy
> A little can I read . . .
> I make not but foresee. . . . .
> You have seen and prov'd a fairer former fortune
> Than that which is to approach.   (I.ii.9–35)

In place of the "romance" of love, Charmian, Iras, and
Alexas give the "reality." The reality in this case is a
strong succession of rich, powerful, and adequate males:

Let me be married to three kings in a forenoon, and widow
them all; let me have a child at fifty to whom Herod of
Jewry may do homage; find me to marry with Octavius
Caesar, and companion me with my mistress.

It reads like a parody of Cleopatra's aspirations, just as
the women's bickering and teasing of Alexas mimics Cleopatra's handling of Antony:

Alexas—come, his fortune, his fortune. O! let him marry a
woman that cannot go, sweet Isis, I beseech thee; and let her
die too, and give him a worse; and let worse follow worse, till
the worst of all follow him laughing to his grave, fiftyfold a
cuckold!

This seems a nightmare version of Antony's fate—the
reflection in a distorting mirror of the thoughts and feelings that course through Antony after Cleopatra's desertion in the disastrous sea fight.

The group is interrupted in its fortune-telling by the
entry of Cleopatra. She is looking for Antony. Her remarks prepare us for the different mood about to establish
itself:

> Saw you my lord? . . .
> He was disposed to mirth; but on the sudden
> A Roman thought hath struck him.
>
>   (I.ii.81–84)

Antony is heard approaching. Cleopatra immediately goes
off. Now that he is coming she will refuse to see him.

When Antony appears he is surrounded by the messengers from Rome and immersed in Roman affairs. He
veers savagely to the point of view both of the soldiers in
the first scene and "the common liar" in Rome. Throughout the play this is what marks him off from Cleopatra
and makes him a more complex meeting ground for the
opposites than even she is herself. He can understand and
respond to the appeal of Rome as much as he can understand and respond to Egypt:

> Speak to me home, mince not the general tongue;
> Name Cleopatra as she's called in Rome;
> Rail thou in Fulvia's phrase; and taunt my faults
> With such full license as both truth and malice
> Have power to utter. O! then we bring forth weeds
> When our quick winds lie still; and our ills told us
> Is as our earing. Fare thee well awhile . . .
> These strongly Egyptian fetters I must break,
> Or lose myself in dotage.   (I.ii.106–18)

The second messenger brings news of Fulvia's death. It
is characteristic of the play that what is hated during life
should find favor once it is dead. Later in this scene that
is reported to be the case with Pompey in the popular
reaction to him:

>   our slippery people—
> Whose love is never link'd to the deserver
> Till his deserts are past—begin to throw
> Pompey the great and all his dignities
> Upon his son.   (I.ii.187–91)

This is what happens, too, in Antony's case when, once
he is dead, Octavius sings his praises. It also happens
when Cleopatra is thought to have committed suicide and
Antony flings from vituperation to acclamation almost
without pausing. It happens now with Fulvia. Antony
says:

> There's a great spirit gone! Thus did I desire it:
> What our contempts do often hurl from us

We wish it ours again; the present pleasure,
By revolution lowering, does become
The opposite of itself: she's good being gone.
The hand could pluck her back that shov'd her on.
I must from this enchanting queen break off.

(I.ii.123–29)

Typically, when he joins the general, Enobarbus summons all the counterarguments. To leave Egypt would be to kill Cleopatra. "She is cunning," Antony says, "past man's thought." "Alack, sir, no," Enobarbus rejoins,

her passions are made of nothing but the finest part of pure love. We cannot call her winds and waters sighs and tears; they are greater storms and tempests than almanacs can report; this cannot be cunning in her; if it be, she makes a shower of rain as well as Jove. (I.ii.148–53)

Even if we read Enobarbus's words as irony, the double irony that works by virtue of the constant ambivalence in the play still turns them back to something approaching the truth: and Cleopatra's real distress and anxiety over Antony's departure have already cut through the scene like a knife. The dingdong continues:

Antony. Would I had never seen her!

Enobarbus. O, sir! you had then left unseen a wonderful piece of work. . . .

Antony. Fulvia is dead.

Enobarbus. Sir?

Antony. Fulvia is dead.

Enobarbus. Fulvia?

Antony. Dead.

Enobarbus. Why, sir, give the gods a thankful sacrifice . . . this grief is crown'd with consolation; your old smock brings forth a new petticoat. (I.ii.154–71)

Antony, however, has made up his mind to go back to Rome.

Antony does go back to Rome—but not in the mood and not with the motives of thoroughgoing reformation in which he remains at the end of Scene ii. In Scene iii the alchemy of the Shakespearian process is further at work. It works to make Antony do the thing resolved upon but for reasons the very opposite of those which led him to the resolve. The scene of his departure is chosen for Cleopatra's most sincere avowal. Having tormented Antony beyond all bearing she suddenly breaks off with:

> Courteous lord, one word.
> Sir, you and I must part, but that's not it;
> Sir, you and I have loved, but there's not it;
> That you know well: something it is I would—
> O my oblivion is a very Antony
> And I am all forgotten.   (I.iii.86–91)

Antony's final words in the scene almost catch the very idiom of *The Phoenix and the Turtle:*

> Let us go. Come.
> Our separation so abides and flies,
> That thou, residing here, go'st yet with me,
> And I, hence fleeting, here remain with thee.
> Away!   (I.iii.101–05)

It is, so to speak, the honeymoon of the contraries—only possible while the lovers are apart.

III

The first three scenes show how pervasive is that quality in technique and vision which we have called the Shakespearian "dialectic." It comes out in single images, it can permeate whole speeches, it governs the build-up inside each scene, it explains the way one scene is related to another. The word "dialectic," of course, is unfortunately post-Hegelian. The thing we wish to point to, however, in using the word, is Shakespearian. In *Antony and Cleopatra* Shakespeare needs the opposites that merge, unite, and fall apart. They enable him to handle the reality he is writing about—the vast containing opposites of Rome and Egypt, the World and the Flesh.

Rome is the sphere of the political. Shakespeare uses the contraries (long before Blake) to give some sort of rational account of the irrationals there involved. The common people, for example, is "the common liar." Antony has already noted that its love is "never link'd to the deserver till his deserts are past." Caesar, too, has his own cold knowledge of the same fact:

> It hath been taught us from the primal state
> That he which is was wished until he were;
> And the ebb'd man, ne'er loved till ne'er worth love,
> Comes dear'd by being lack'd. This common body,
> Like to the vagabond flag upon the stream,
> Goes to and back, lackeying the varying tide,
> To rot itself with motion.   (I.iv.41–47)

The great men, however, behave exactly as they say the commons do, too. With Antony, Fulvia becomes dear'd by being lack'd. In Caesar's case it is the same. The threat of Pompey makes him suddenly appreciate the grandeur of Antony's leadership, courage, and endurance. The magnanimous praise of Antony in Act V is only possible because Antony by then is dead. The law is general: judgment is a kind of accommodation to the irrational on reason's part:

>   men's judgments are
> A parcel of their fortunes, and things outward
> Do draw the inward quality after them,
> To suffer all alike.   (III.xiii.31–34)

Even soldierly "honor" is rooted in the ambiguous. When Pompey's man mentions his treacherous scheme for disposing of all Pompey's rivals at one blow (the rivals are also Pompey's guests on board ship), Pompey exclaims:

          Ah, this thou should'st have done
And not have spoken on't. In me 'tis villainy;
In thee't had been good service. Thou must know
'Tis not my profit that does lead mine honor;
Mine honor it. Repent that e'er thy tongue
Hath so betray'd thine act; being done unknown,
I should have found it afterwards well done,
But must condemn it now.   (II.vii.75–82)

The law is general because it reflects the nature of the
terrene world—the tidal swing of the opposites on which
all things balance in a motion that rots them away.
    The self-destruction of things that rot with the motion
which their own nature and situation dictate is almost
obsessive with Shakespeare throughout the play. The political world is the manipulation of the common body they
despise by the great men whom the commons can never
love until they are safely rid of them. The pattern which
remains constant in all the possible groupings is that of
open conflict alternating with diseased truce, neither of
them satisfactory:

  Equality of two domestic powers
  Breeds scrupulous faction. The hated, grown to strength,
  Are newly grown to love. . . .
  And quietness, grown sick of rest, would purge
  By any desperate change.   (I.iii.47–54)

Compacts between the great men merely represent the
temporary sinking of lesser enmities in front of greater:

          lesser enmities give way to greater.
  Were't not that we stand up against them all
  'Twere pregnant they should square amongst themselves.
                                          (II.i.43–45)

Pompey's is a correct appreciation. It is because of him
that Octavius and Antony are reconciled. They will rivet
the alliance by means of Antony's marriage to Caesar's
sister. Enobarbus knows automatically that this union is
a certain way of making conflict ultimately inevitable:

you shall find the bond that seems to tie their friendship together will be the very strangler of their amity.

(II.vi.120–22)

Octavia is one of Shakespeare's minor triumphs in the play, beautifully placed in relation to the main figures and the tenor of their meaning. Her importance is apt to be overlooked unless her careful positioning is noted. Her presence gives a symmetrical form to the main relations of the play. Octavia is the opposite of Cleopatra as Antony is the opposite of Caesar. She is woman made the submissive tool of Roman policy where Cleopatra always strives to make the political subservient to her. (It is the thought of being led in triumph by Caesar as much as the thought of Antony's death which finally decides Cleopatra for suicide.) Where Caesar and Cleopatra are simple and opposite, Octavia—like Antony—is a focal point for the contraries. There is nothing in her as a "character study" to account for the effect her presence has. It is rather that she is transparent to the reality behind the play and one of its least mistakable mediators. On the occasions when she appears herself, or when mention is made of her, it is the interfluent life of this reality rather than the personality of its vehicle which fills the scene.

Her first entry is significant. It comes immediately after the triumvirate and Pompey have made their pact. We have just heard the following satiric account of Lepidus's behavior—and Lepidus, like Octavia, has to stand between the two demi-Atlases:

Agrippa. 'Tis a noble Lepidus.

Eno. A very fine one. O! how he loves Caesar.

Agrippa. Nay, but how dearly he adores Mark Antony.

Eno. Caesar? Why, he's the Jupiter of men!

Agrippa. What's Antony? the god of Jupiter.

Eno. Spake you of Caesar? How, the nonpareil!

Agrippa. O Antony! O thou Arabian bird!   (III.ii.6–12)

Then the triumvirate and Octavia come on. Octavia stirs Antony deeply. But the imagery in which his vision of her is clothed carries us past the person described to the "varying tide" by which everything in the play is moved:

> Her tongue will not obey her heart, nor can
> Her heart obey her tongue; the swan's-down feather
> That stands upon the swell of the full tide
> And neither way inclines.   (III.ii.47–50)

Octavia never escapes from her position midway between the contraries that maintain and split the world. With Antony away in Athens, her brother first falls on Pompey, then finds a pretext to destroy Lepidus. He is now ready to mount his attack on the last remaining rival, his "competitor in top of all design." Hearing of it, Octavia cries:

>   A more unhappy lady,
> If this division chance, ne'er stood between,
> Praying for both parts. . . .
> . . . Husband win, win brother,
> Prays and destroys the prayer; no midway
> 'Twixt these extremes at all.   (III.iv.12–20)

Octavia's is the alternative plight to Cleopatra's for womanhood in the play. The choice is merely between alternative methods of destruction—either at one's own hands or through the agency of the process. The "swan's-down feather," like the "vagabond flag," can only swing on the tide until it rots with motion.

Rome is the world of politics and policy. Its supreme term is Octavius Caesar himself. He, like Octavia, must be brought into relation with the pattern which he helps in part to define. Half his significance is lost if he is seen only as a "character." In Octavius's case we have aids external to the play which help towards a clear focus on what Shakespeare intends by him. He falls recognizably into Shakespeare's studies of the "politician"—the series that begins with Richard III and continues down through Edmund.

Octavius is a notable development in the figure which started as a machiavel pure and simple. Shakespeare now betrays no sign of alarm, no hint of revulsion or rejection, almost no trace of emotion in putting him into a story. He is taken completely for granted. He has arrived and he will stay. He is part of the structure of things. He is "Rome." In matters of politics and policy it is obvious that only the politicians count: and politics is one half of life. The politician is a perfectly normal person. Given all his own way he would doubtless bring—as Octavius is certain his triumphs eventually will bring—a "universal peace." To be normal like him, of course, and to enjoy the peace he offers, two conditions are necessary. First, one must sacrifice the other half of life; then, one must be prepared to make complete submission. By the time Shakespeare comes to depict Octavius he has refined away all the accidentals from the portrait—the diabolism, the rhetoric, the elaborate hypocrisy, the perverse glamor: everything but the essential deadliness and inescapability. Octavius marks an advance on Goneril and Regan. He shares their impatience with tavern and brothel. He has no share in the lust which entraps even them. We might almost doubt whether Octavius has any personal appetite at all, even the lust for power. His plan to lead Cleopatra in triumph has the appearance of a desire for personal satisfaction, but it is more likely that it fits into an impersonal wish on Caesar's part to subdue all things to Rome. Caesar, of course, is Rome—but a kind of impersonal embodiment. He is more like a cold and universal force than a warm-blooded man. He is the perfect commissar, invulnerable as no human being should be. Egypt has no part in his composition.

Caesar has the deceitfulness of the machiavel, but he plays his cards without any flourish. He can rely on his opponents to undo themselves: they are more complicated than he. He puts the deserters from Antony in the van of his own battle:

> Plant those that are revolted in the van,
> That Antony may seem to spend his fury
> Upon himself.   (IV.vi.9–11)

The strength and weakness of those ranged against him constitute Caesar's fifth column. The opposition will rot away or eat the sword it fights with.

It is in the last act that Egypt and Rome confront each other singly, the duplicity of Caesar pitted against the duplicity of Cleopatra. There is no doubt as to who shall survive the contest. The tension is maintained throughout the fifth act only by the doubt left in the spectator's mind right up to the end as to which way Cleopatra will jump: will she accept submission or will she take her own life? The whole play has prepared us for just this doubt. In a sense, whichever way the decision goes it is immaterial. The point of the play is not the decisions taken but the dubieties and ambivalences from which choice springs—the barren choice that only hastens its own negation. Rome, from the nature of things, can admit no compromise. Egypt, equally, can never submit to its contrary. So Cleopatra kills herself.

Cleopatra has been loved by recent commentators not wisely but too well. As Caesar impersonates the World, she, of course, incarnates the Flesh. Part of Shakespeare's sleight of hand in the play—his trickery with our normal standards and powers of judgment—is to construct an account of the human universe consisting of only these two terms. There is no suggestion that the dichotomy is resolvable: unless we are willing to take the delusions of either party as a resolution, the "universal peace" of Caesar, the Egypt-beyond-the-grave of Antony and Cleopatra in their autotoxic exaltations before they kill themselves.

Cleopatra is the Flesh, deciduous, opulent, and endlessly renewable:

> she did make defect perfection . . .
> Age cannot wither her, nor custom stale
> Her infinite variety; other women cloy

> The appetites they feed, but she makes hungry
> Where most she satisfies; for vilest things
> Become themselves in her, that the holy priests
> Bless her when she is riggish.   (II.ii.237–46)

The Flesh is also the female principle. Cleopatra is Eve, and Woman:

> No more but e'en a woman, and commanded
> By such poor passion as the maid that milks
> And does the meanest chares.   (IV.xv.72–74)

She is also Circe:

> Let witchcraft join with beauty, lust with both!
>   (II.i.22)

Shakespeare gives Cleopatra everything of which he is capable except his final and absolute approval. Cleopatra is not an Octavia, much less a Cordelia. The profusion of rich and hectic color that surrounds her is the color of the endless cycle of growth and decay, new greenery on old rottenness, the color of the passions, the wild flaring of life as it burns itself richly away to death so that love of life and greed for death become indistinguishable:

there is mettle in death which commits some loving act upon her, she hath such a celerity in dying.   (I.ii.144–46)

The strength of the case Shakespeare puts against her is undeniable. The soldiers, and Caesar, and Antony when the consciousness of Rome speaks through him, are right, as far as they go. The strength of the case for her is that it is only Rome that condemns her. And Egypt is a force as universal as Rome—as hot as the other is cold, as inevitably self-renewing as the other is inescapably deadly. And the only appeal that can be made in the play is from Egypt to Rome, from Rome to Egypt. And neither of these is final, because between them they have brought down Antony, the "man of men."

For the tragedy of *Antony and Cleopatra* is, above all, the tragedy of Antony. His human stature is greater than either Cleopatra's or Caesar's. Yet there is no sphere in which he can express himself except either Rome or Egypt, and to bestride both like a Colossus and keep his balance is impossible. The opposites play through Antony and play with him, and finally destroy him. To Caesar (while Antony is in Egypt, and alive) he is:

> A man who is the abstract of all faults
> That all men follow.   (I.iv.9–10)

To Cleopatra he appears instead a "heavenly mingle":

> Be'st thou sad or merry,
> The violence of either thee becomes,
> So it does no man else.   (I.v.59–61)

When she sees him returning safe from the battlefield she cries:

> O infinite virtue! Com'st thou smiling from
> The world's great snare uncaught?
>   (IV.viii.17–18)

After he is dead she remembers him as a kind of Mars:

> His face was as the heavens and therein stuck
> A sun and moon, which kept their course, and lighted
> This little O, the earth . . .
> His legs bestrid the ocean; his rear'd arm
> Crested the world; his voice was propertied
> As all the tuned spheres, and that to friends;
> But when he meant to quail and shake the orb,
> He was as rattling thunder. For his bounty,
> There was no winter in't, an autumn 'twas
> That grew the more by reaping; his delights
> Were dolphinlike, they show'd his back above
> The element they lived in; in his livery

Walk'd crowns and crownets, realms and islands were
As plates dropped from his pocket . . .
          . . . Nature wants stuff
To vie strange forms with fancy, yet t'imagine
An Antony were nature's piece 'gainst fancy,
Condemning shadows quite.   (V.ii.79–100)

This, of course, is again the past catching fire from the
urgent needs of the present, flaring in memory and imagination as it never did in actuality. Antony is nothing so
unambiguous as this. The most judicious account of him is
that of Lepidus when he is replying to Caesar's strictures:

          I must not think there are
Evils enow to darken all his goodness:
His faults in him seem as the spots of heaven,
More fiery by night's blackness; hereditary
Rather than purchased, what he cannot change
Than what he chooses.   (I.iv.10–15)

Here the ambiguities of the play's moral universe get their
completest expression: faults shine like stars, the heaven
is black, the stars are spots. Ambivalence need go no
further.

                              IV

   The earlier criticism of *Antony and Cleopatra* tended
to stress the downfall of the soldier in the middle-aged
infatuate. More recent criticism has seen the play as the
epiphany of the soldier in the lover, and the reassurance
of all concerned that death is not the end. In the view
that has been put forward here neither of these is right.
The meaning of *Antony and Cleopatra* is in the Shakespearian "dialectic"—in the deliquescent reality that expresses itself through the contraries.
   Antony and Cleopatra swims with glamor. Once we
lose sight of the controlling structure of the opposites

which holds the play together we are at the mercy of any random selection from its occasions. And occasions abound—moments, opinions, moods, speeches, characters, fragments of situation, forked mountains and blue promontories, imposed upon us with all the force of a "giant power." It is, then, eminently understandable that critics should succumb like Antony or hold aloof like Demetrius and Philo.

The Roman condemnation of the lovers is obviously inadequate. The sentimental reaction in their favor is equally mistaken. There is no so-called "love-romanticism" in the play. The flesh has its glory and passion, its witchery. Love in *Antony and Cleopatra* is both these. The love of Antony and Cleopatra, however, is not asserted as a "final value." The whole tenor of the play, in fact, moves in an opposite direction. Egypt is the Egypt of the biblical glosses: exile from the spirit, thralldom to the fleshpots, diminution of human kindness. To go further still in sentimentality and claim that there is a "redemption" motif in Antony and Cleopatra's love is an even more violent error. To the Shakespeare who wrote *King Lear* it would surely smack of blasphemy. The fourth and fifth acts of *Antony and Cleopatra* are not epiphanies. They are the ends moved to by that process whereby things rot themselves with motion—unhappy and bedizened and sordid, streaked with the mean, the ignoble, the contemptible. Shakespeare may have his plays in which "redemption" is a theme (and I think he has), but *Antony and Cleopatra* is not one of them.

Antony and Cleopatra is an account of things in terms of the World and the Flesh, Rome and Egypt, the two great contraries that maintain and destroy each other, considered apart from any third sphere which might stand over against them. How is it related to the plays of the "great period," the period which comes to an end with *King Lear*?

The clue is given, I think, in the missing third term. *Antony and Cleopatra* is the deliberate construction of a world without a Cordelia, Shakespeare's symbol for a reality that transcends the political and the personal and

redeems nature from the general curse
Which twain have brought her to.
(*King Lear*, IV.vi.209–10)

One must call the construction deliberate, because after *King Lear* there can be no doubt that Shakespeare knew exactly where he was in these matters. Both *Antony and Cleopatra* and *Coriolanus* follow North's Plutarch without benefit of clergy. Both Antony and Coriolanus were cited by the sixteenth-century moralists as notable examples of heathen men who lacked patience—the one committing suicide, the other rebelling against his country. In *Antony and Cleopatra* suicide is the general fate of those who wish to die. Cleopatra gives the audience a conscious reminder of the un-Christian ethos involved:

All's but naught;
Patience is sottish, and impatience does
Become a dog that's mad; then is it sin
To rush into the secret house of death
Ere death dare come to us?

(IV.xv.77–81)

The Christian world view in Shakespeare's time turned round a number of conceptions which were covered by the Elizabethans in their examination of the meanings of "Nature." The theme of "Nature" runs through the whole of *Macbeth, King Lear,* and *Timon.* Its absence from *Antony and Cleopatra* suggests Shakespeare's satisfaction that for him the theme is exhausted. He is inwardly free now to look at a classical story, deliberately excise the Christian core of his thought, and make up his account of what then remains over.

This explains the effect, I think, of *Antony and Cleopatra.* Freedom from the compulsive theme of the Natures, the conscious security gained from having given it final expression, enabled Shakespeare to handle something new and something which was bound to be intrinsically simpler. Part of the energy absorbed in grappling with theme now bestows itself on technique. *Antony and Cleo-*

patra gives the impression of being a technical tour de force which Shakespeare enjoyed for its own sake.

The excision also explains, I think, the tone of the play—the sense of ripe-rottenness and hopelessness, the vision of self-destruction, the feeling of strenuous frustration and fevered futility, that which finds its greatest expression in Antony's speech before he gives himself his deathblow:

> . . . now
> All length is torture; since the torch is out,
> Lie down and stray no further. Now all labor
> Mars what it does; yea, very force entangles
> Itself with strength; seal then, and all is done.
> (IV.xiv.45–49)

The excision, finally, explains what might be regarded as a diminution of scope in *Antony and Cleopatra*. (We are, of course, only comparing Shakespeare with himself.) The theme of Rome and Egypt, however, is simpler than the theme of "Nature," the trick of using the contraries (again, for Shakespeare) relatively an easy way of organizing the universe. It is unusual, at any rate, for Shakespeare to rely on one trick so completely as he seems to do in *Antony and Cleopatra*. At times we are almost tempted to believe he has fallen a victim of habitual mannerism.

One last comment might be made. We referred at the beginning of this chapter to Shakespeare's surprising capacity for self-renewal. *Antony and Cleopatra* is not the aftermath of Lear in any pejorative sense. There is something in it that is new and exciting and profound. Shakespeare remained still the youngest as the greatest of his contemporaries. In *Antony and Cleopatra* he is making his own adjustments to the new Jacobean tastes. The play is Shakespeare's study of Mars and Venus—the presiding deities of Baroque society, painted for us again and again on the canvases of his time. It shows us Virtue, the root of the heroic in man, turned merely into *virtu*, the warrior's art, and both of them ensnared in the world, very force entangling itself with strength. It depicts the "man of men" soldiering for a cynical Rome or whoring on furlough in a reckless Egypt. It is the tragedy of the destruction of man, the creative spirit, in perverse war and insensate love—the two complementary and opposed halves of a discreating society.

For more obvious, if less great manifestations of the same discreating society, interested almost exclusively in love and war (and these both more narrowly conceived and more overvalued emotionally than they ever are by Shakespeare) we must turn to Beaumont.

Suggested References

The number of possible references is vast and grows alarmingly. (The *Shakespeare Quarterly* devotes a substantial part of one issue each year to a list of the previous year's work, and *Shakespeare Survey*—an annual publication—includes a substantial review of recent scholarship, as well as an occasional essay surveying a few decades of scholarship on a chosen topic.) Though no works are indispensable, those listed below have been found helpful.

1. Shakespeare's Times

Byrne, M. St. Clare. *Elizabethan Life in Town and Country*. Rev. ed. New York: Barnes & Noble, Inc., 1961. Chapters on manners, beliefs, education, etc., with illustrations.

Craig, Hardin. *The Enchanted Glass: the Elizabethan Mind in Literature*. New York and London: Oxford University Press, 1936. The Elizabethan intellectual climate.

Nicoll, Allardyce (ed.). *The Elizabethans*. London: Cambridge University Press, 1957. An anthology of Elizabethan writings, especially valuable for its illustrations from paintings, title pages, etc.

Shakespeare's England. 2 vols. Oxford: The Clarendon Press, 1916. A large collection of scholarly essays on a wide variety of topics (e.g., astrology, costume, gardening, horsemanship), with special attention to Shakespeare's references to these topics.

Tillyard, E. M. W. *The Elizabethan World Picture*. London: Chatto & Windus, 1943; New York: The Macmillan Company, 1944. A brief account of some Elizabethan ideas of the universe.

Wilson, John Dover (ed.). *Life in Shakespeare's England*. 2nd ed. New York: The Macmillan Company, 1913. An anthology of Elizabethan writings on the countryside, superstition, education, the court, etc.

2. Shakespeare

Bentley, Gerald E. *Shakespeare: A Biographical Handbook*. New Haven, Conn.: Yale University Press, 1961. The facts about Shakespeare, with virtually no conjecture intermingled.

Bradby, Anne (ed.). *Shakespeare Criticism, 1919–1935*. London: Oxford University Press, 1936. A small anthology of excellent essays on the plays.

Bush, Geoffrey Douglas. *Shakespeare and the Natural Condition*. Cambridge, Mass.: Harvard University Press; London: Oxford University Press, 1956. A short, sensitive account of Shakespeare's view of "Nature," touching most of the works.

Chambers, E. K. *William Shakespeare: A Study of Facts and Problems*. 2 vols. London: Oxford University Press, 1930. An invaluable, detailed reference work; not for the casual reader.

Chute, Marchette. *Shakespeare of London*. New York: E. P. Dutton & Co., Inc., 1949. A readable biography fused with portraits of Stratford and London life.

Clemen, Wolfgang H. *The Development of Shakespeare's Imagery*. Cambridge, Mass.: Harvard University Press, 1951. (Originally published in German, 1936.) A temperate account of a subject often abused.

Craig, Hardin. *An Interpretation of Shakespeare*. Columbia, Missouri: Lucas Brothers, 1948. A scholar's book designed for the layman. Comments on all the works.

Dean, Leonard F. (ed.). *Shakespeare: Modern Essays in Criticism*. New York: Oxford University Press, 1957. Mostly mid-twentieth-century critical studies, covering Shakespeare's artistry.

Granville-Barker, Harley. *Prefaces to Shakespeare*. 2 vols. Princeton, N.J.: Princeton University Press, 1946–47. Essays on ten plays by a scholarly man of the theater.

Harbage, Alfred. *As They Liked It*. New York: The Macmillan Company, 1947. A sensitive, long essay on Shakespeare, morality, and the audience's expectations.

Ridler, Anne Bradby (ed.). *Shakespeare Criticism, 1935–1960*. New York and London: Oxford University Press, 1963. An excellent continuation of the anthology edited earlier by Miss Bradby (see above).

Smith, D. Nichol (ed.). *Shakespeare Criticism*. New York: Oxford University Press, 1916. A selection of criticism from 1623 to 1840, ranging from Ben Jonson to Thomas Carlyle.

Spencer, Theodore. *Shakespeare and the Nature of Man*. New York: The Macmillan Company, 1942. Shakespeare's plays in relation to Elizabethan thought.

Stoll, Elmer Edgar. *Shakespeare and Other Masters*. Cambridge, Mass.: Harvard University Press; London: Oxford University Press, 1940. Essays on tragedy, comedy, and aspects of dramaturgy, with special reference to some of Shakespeare's plays.

Traversi, D. A. *An Approach to Shakespeare*. Rev. ed. New York: Doubleday & Co., Inc., 1956. An analysis of the plays, beginning with words, images, and themes, rather than with characters.

Van Doren, Mark. *Shakespeare*. New York: Henry Holt & Company, Inc., 1939. Brief, perceptive readings of all of the plays.

Whitaker, Virgil K. *Shakespeare's Use of Learning*. San Marino, Calif.: Huntington Library, 1953. A study of the relation of Shakespeare's reading to his development as a dramatist.

3. Shakespeare's Theater

Adams, John Cranford. *The Globe Playhouse*. Rev. ed. New York: Barnes & Noble, Inc., 1961. A detailed conjecture about the physical characteristics of the theater Shakespeare often wrote for.

Beckerman, Bernard. *Shakespeare at the Globe, 1599–1609*. New York: The Macmillan Company, 1962. On the playhouse and on Elizabethan dramaturgy, acting, and staging.

Chambers, E. K. *The Elizabethan Stage*. 4 vols. New York: Oxford University Press, 1923. Reprinted with corrections, 1945. An indispensable reference work on theaters, theatrical companies, and staging at court.

Harbage, Alfred. *Shakespeare's Audience*. New York: Columbia University Press; London: Oxford University Press, 1941. A study of the size and nature of the theatrical public.

Hodges, C. Walter, *The Globe Restored*. London: Ernest Benn, Ltd., 1953; New York: Coward-McCann, Inc., 1954. A well-illustrated and readable attempt to reconstruct the Globe Theatre.

Nagler, A. M. *Shakespeare's Stage*. Tr. by Ralph Manheim. New Haven, Conn.: Yale University Press, 1958. An excellent brief introduction to the physical aspect of the playhouse.

Smith, Irwin. *Shakespeare's Globe Playhouse*. New York: Charles Scribner's Sons, 1957. Chiefly indebted to J. C. Adams' controversial book, with additional material and scale drawings for model-builders.

Venezky, Alice S. *Pageantry on the Shakespearean Stage*. New York: Twayne Publishers, Inc., 1951. An examination of spectacle in Elizabethan drama.

4. Miscellaneous Reference Works

Abbott, E. A. *A Shakespearean Grammar*. New edition. New York: The Macmillan Company, 1877. An examination of differences between Elizabethan and modern grammar.

Bartlett, John. *A New and Complete Concordance . . . to . . . Shakespeare*. New York: The Macmillan Company, 1894. An index to most of Shakespeare's words.

Bullough, Geoffrey. *Narrative and Dramatic Sources of Shakespeare*. 4 vols. Vols. 5 and 6 in preparation. New York: Columbia University Press; London: Routledge & Kegan Paul, Ltd., 1957–. A collection of many of the books Shakespeare drew upon.

Greg, W. W. *The Shakespeare First Folio*. New York and London: Oxford University Press, 1955. A detailed yet readable history of the first collection (1623) of Shakespeare's plays.

Kökeritz, Helge. *Shakespeare's Names*. New Haven, Conn.: Yale University Press, 1959; London: Oxford University Press, 1960. A guide to the pronunciation of some 1,800 names appearing in Shakespeare.

————. *Shakespeare's Pronunciation*. New Haven, Conn.: Yale University Press; London: Oxford University Press, 1953. Contains much information about puns and rhymes.

Linthicum, Marie C. *Costume in the Drama of Shakespeare and His Contemporaries*. New York and London: Oxford University Press, 1936. On the fabrics and dress of the age, and references to them in the plays.

Muir, Kenneth. *Shakespeare's Sources*. London: Methuen & Co., Ltd., 1957. Vol. 2 in preparation. The first volume, on the comedies and tragedies, attempts to ascertain what books were Shakespeare's sources, and what use he made of them.

Onions, C. T. *A Shakespeare Glossary*. London: Oxford University Press, 1911; 2nd ed., rev., with enlarged addenda, 1953. Definitions of words (or senses of words) now obsolete.

Partridge, Eric. *Shakespeare's Bawdy*. Rev. ed. New York: E. P. Dutton & Co., Inc.; London: Routledge & Kegan Paul, Ltd., 1955. A glossary of bawdy words and phrases.

Shakespeare Quarterly. See headnote to Suggested References.

Shakespeare Survey. See headnote to Suggested References.

Smith, Gordon Ross. *A Classified Shakespeare Bibliography 1936–1958*. University Park, Pa.: Pennsylvania State University Press, 1963. A list of some 20,000 items on Shakespeare.

5. *Antony and Cleopatra*

Barnet, Sylvan. "Recognition and Reversal in *Antony and Cleopatra*," *Shakespeare Quarterly,* VIII (1957), 331–34.

Cecil, Lord David. *Antony and Cleopatra.* (W. P. Ker Memorial Lecture No. 4, Glasgow, 1943.) Reprinted in *Poets and Story-tellers*. London: Constable & Co., Ltd., 1949; New York: Barnes & Noble, Inc., 1961.

Coleridge, Samuel Taylor. *Shakespearean Criticism,* ed. Thomas Middleton Raysor. 2 vols. New York: E. P. Dutton & Co., Inc., 1960; London: J. M. Dent & Sons, Ltd., 1961.

Farnham, Willard. *Shakespeare's Tragic Frontier*. Berkeley, Calif.: University of California Press; London: Cambridge University Press, 1950.

Granville-Barker, Harley. *Prefaces to Shakespeare*. 2 vols. Princeton, N.J.: Princeton University Press, 1946–47. Vol. I.

Holloway, John. *The Story of the Night*. London: Routledge & Kegan Paul, Ltd., 1961; Lincoln, Nebraska: University of Nebraska Press, 1963.

Knight, G. Wilson. *The Imperial Theme*. New York: British Book Centre, Inc.; London: Methuen & Co., Ltd., 1951.

Knights, L. C. *Some Shakespearean Themes*. London: Chatto & Windus, Ltd., 1959; Stanford, Calif.: Stanford University Press, 1960.

Leavis, F. R. "*Antony and Cleopatra* and *All for Love:* A Critical Exercise," *Scrutiny,* V (1936–37), 158–69.

Lloyd, Michael. "Cleopatra as Isis," *Shakespeare Survey,* XII (1959), 88–94.

Mack, Maynard. "The Jacobean Shakespeare: Some Observations on the Construction of the Tragedies," *Stratford-upon-Avon Studies I: Jacobean Theatre.* London: Edward Arnold (Publishers), Ltd., 1960; New York: St. Martin's Press, Inc., 1961. Pp. 11–41. Reprinted in the Signet Classic edition of *Othello.*

MacCallum, M. W. *Shakespeare's Roman Plays and Their Background.* New York and London: The Macmillan Company, 1910.

Maxwell, J. C. "Shakespeare's Roman Plays: 1900–56," *Shakespeare Survey,* X (1957), 1–11.

Schanzer, Ernest. *The Problem Plays of Shakespeare.* New York: Schocken Books, Inc.; London: Routledge & Kegan Paul, Ltd., 1963.

Spencer, T. J. B. "Shakespeare and the Elizabethan Romans," *Shakespeare Survey,* X (1957), 27–38.

Stewart, J. I. M. *Character and Motive in Shakespeare.* New York and London: Longmans, Green & Co., Inc., 1949.

Traversi, Derek. *Shakespeare: The Roman Plays.* Stanford, Calif.: Stanford University Press, 1963.

THE SIGNET CLASSIC SHAKESPEARE

The works of Shakespeare in superlatively edited paper-bound volumes. Under the general editorship of Sylvan Barnet, Chairman of the English Department of Tufts University, each volume features General Introduction by Dr. Barnet, special Introduction and Notes by an eminent Shakespearean scholar, critical commentary from past and contemporary authorities, and when possible, Shakespeare's original source material.

☐ **CORIOLANUS. Edited by Reuben Brower**
(#CQ806—95¢)

☐ **CYMBELINE. Edited by Hosley**   (#CQ763—95¢)

☐ **JULIUS CAESAR. Edited by W. & B. Rosen**
(#CT529—75¢)

☐ **HAMLET. Edited by Edward Hubler**   (#CQ771—95¢)

☐ **KING LEAR. Edited by Russell Fraser**   (#CQ795—95¢)

☐ **MACBETH. Edited by Sylvan Barnet**   (#CQ829—95¢)

☐ **THE MERCHANT OF VENICE. Edited by Kenneth O. Myrick.**
(#CT564—75¢)

☐ **OTHELLO. Edited by Alvin Kernon**   (#CQ756—95¢)

☐ **THE TEMPEST. Edited by Robert Langbaum**
(#CT527—75¢)

☐ **ROMEO AND JULIET. Edited by Joseph Bryant**
(#CQ796—95¢)

☐ **TIMON OF ATHENS. Edited by Maurice Charney**
(#CD289—50¢)

☐ **TITUS ANDRONICUS. Edited by Sylvan Barnet**
(#CD197—50¢)

☐ **TROILUS AND CRESSIDA. Edited by Daniel Seltzer**
(#CT589—75¢)

THE NEW AMERICAN LIBRARY, INC.,
P.O. Box 999, Bergenfield, New Jersey 07621

Please send me the SIGNET CLASSIC BOOKS I have checked above. I am enclosing $_____(check or money order—no currency or C.O.D.'s). Please include the list price plus 25¢ a copy to cover handling and mailing costs. (Prices and numbers are subject to change without notice.)

Name_____

Address_____

City_____State_____ Zip Code_____
Allow at least 3 weeks for delivery

SIGNET CLASSICS OF BRITISH LITERATURE

MENTOR Books of Plays

Edited by Sylvan Barnet,
Morton Berman and William Burto

☐ **EIGHT GREAT TRAGEDIES.** The great dramatic literature of the ages, eight memorable tragedies by Aeschylus, Euripides, Sophocles, Shakespeare, Ibsen, Strindberg, Yeats, and O'Neill. With essays on tragedy by Aristotle, Emerson and others.　(#ME1347—$1.75)

☐ **EIGHT GREAT COMEDIES.** Complete texts of eight masterpieces of comic drama by Aristophanes, Machiavelli, Shakespeare, Mollière, John Gay, Wilde, Chekhov, and Shaw. Includes essays on comedy by four distinguished critics and scholars.　(#ME1340—$1.75)

☐ **THE GENIUS OF THE EARLY ENGLISH THEATRE.** Complete plays including three anonymous plays—"Abraham and Isaac," "The Second Shepherd's Play," and "Everyman," and Marlowe's "Doctor Faustus," Shakespeare's "Macbeth," Johnson's "Volpone," and Milton's "Samson Agonistes," with critical essays.
(#MW1106—$1.50)

☐ **THE GENIUS OF THE LATER ENGLISH THEATER.** Complete plays, including Congreve's "The Way of the World," Goldsmith's "She Stoops to Conquer," Byron's "Cain," Wilde's "Importance of Being Earnest," Shaw's "Major Barbara," and Golding's "The Brass Butterfly." With critical essays.　(#MW1010—$1.50)

THE NEW AMERICAN LIBRARY, INC.,
P.O. Box 999, Bergenfield, New Jersey 07621

Please send me the MENTOR BOOKS I have checked above. I am enclosing $_____(check or money order—no currency or C.O.D.'s). Please include the list price plus 25¢ a copy to cover handling and mailing costs. (Prices and numbers are subject to change without notice.)

Name_____

Address_____

City_____State_____Zip Code_____
Allow at least 3 weeks for delivery

The SIGNET CLASSIC Poetry Series

THE NEW AMERICAN LIBRARY, INC.,
P.O. Box 999, Bergenfield, New Jersey 07621

Please send me the SIGNET CLASSIC BOOKS I have checked above. I am enclosing $_____(check or money order—no currency or C.O.D.'s). Please include the list price plus 25¢ a copy to cover handling and mailing costs. (Prices and numbers are subject to change without notice.)

Name_____

Address_____

City_____State_____Zip Code_____
Allow at least 3 weeks for delivery